Cuisines
of the
Southwest

*An Illustrated Food History
with More Than 160 Regional Recipes*

By Dave DeWitt

Books by Dave DeWitt

The Spicy Food Lover's Bible (with Nancy Gerlach)
Da Vinci's Kitchen
The Chile Pepper Encyclopedia
Barbecue Inferno (with Nancy Gerlach)
Peppers of the World (with Paul W. Bosland)
The Whole Chile Pepper Book (with Nancy Gerlach)
A World of Curries

And more than twenty other books on chile peppers and fiery foods.

Printed in the United States of America

ISBN 13: 978-1-58581-030-7
ISBN 10: 1-58581-030-4

Golden West Publishers
4113 N. Longview Ave.
Phoenix, AZ 85014, USA
(602) 265-4392
(800) 658-5830

Editing: Elin Jeffords
Cover Design: Aaron Salts
Book Design: The Printed Page

For free sample recipes for every
Golden West cookbook, visit:
www.goldenwestpublishers.com

Dedication

This book is for the hundreds of thousands of chileheads who have supported me over the years by buying my books, attending the National Fiery Foods and Barbecue Show, subscribing to the two magazines I've edited, entering the Scovie Awards Competition, and visiting the Fiery Foods & Barbecue SuperSite. My chile-spiced, heartfelt thanks to all of you.

Acknowledgments

I had considerable assistance with the research and writing of this rather complex book project. First, Nancy Gerlach, my long-time collaborator and coauthor of ten books, developed and tested many of the recipes over twenty-five years, and I thank her profusely. My wife, Mary Jane Wilan, also assisted in recipe development, and that was fun at dinnertime. I thank the food writers who are experts on certain regions of the food lover's Southwest. Robb Walsh, author of *Legends of Texas Barbecue* and *The Texas Cowboy Cookbook,* helped with Texas food history and co-wrote the Austin section of this book. Jim Peyton, author of *The Very Best of Tex-Mex Cooking* and *El Norte: The Cuisine of Northern Mexico*, co-wrote the San Antonio section. Elaine Corn, former food editor of the *Sacramento Bee*, assisted with the El Paso section and wrote the story of the invention of the margarita. Elin Jeffords, former restaurant critic of the *Arizona Republic*, explored Phoenix and Scottsdale for me. And Colette Bancroft, former Starlight editor of the *Arizona Daily Star*, with her husband John, a food writer, researched Tucson. Gwyneth Doland, then food editor of the *Santa Fe Reporter,* assisted with the Santa Fe restaurant descriptions. Also, thanks to the talented photographers who contributed images to match the text in this fun project, and, in some cases, needed advice: Chel Beeson, Aaron Sandoval, Mike Stines and Harald Zoschke. *Muchas gracias* to everyone who assisted on this project.

Contents

Where Is the Southwest, Anyway?

Geographical Confusion.
Photographer Aaron Sandoval

The Southwest can include as few as two states or as many as eleven. There is no debate about the location of Arizona and New Mexico, but demographers have long pondered California's location (Southwest or Far West?) and that of Texas as part of the Midwest, South, or Southwest. Guidebooks often graft Utah, Nevada, Colorado and Oklahoma onto the Southwest; and, amazingly enough, a popular national travel guide once included Kansas, Missouri, and Arkansas in the region.

Such geographical quandaries fade when confronted with culinary facts because, face it, no one really associates states like Nevada with Southwestern cuisine—although local restaurants may serve their own versions of "Mexican" food. Heavily-populated Southern California deserves its own food history, and the cities in northern and eastern Texas has such diverse culinary influences that they are beyond our Southwestern focus.

So, for the purposes of this book, the Southwest is defined as southwestern Texas, New Mexico, and Arizona—those areas most influenced by Native American and northern Mexican cookery, as well as American imports and techniques. These are the traditional locations for a unique cuisine—dating to prehistory—that continues to evolve.

What Is Southwestern Cuisine?

Mexican and *Southwestern*, the two terms used most often to describe the cuisine of the region, are misnomers in a way, yet they remain as the only food descriptors that make any sense. The term "Mexican cooking" is inadequate to describe the cuisine of the Southwest and too general to characterize the incredibly diverse dishes prepared in Mexico. I avoid that term because it conjures up visions of very poor food served by national restaurant chains.

Texas food expert Robb Walsh makes a good case against the term "Southwestern cuisine," which he says is a "fad and fading fast." Walsh points out that the nomenclature was invented by California chefs who opened "Southwestern restaurants...that carefully ignored the Mexican traditional uses of ingredients, lest they be confused with Mexican restaurants."

When the Southwestern restaurant trend spread across the country, innovative chefs incorporated all sorts of non-traditional ingredients and styles, which is why Dean Fearing, then of the Mansion on Turtle Creek in Dallas, claimed that *his* version of Southwest cuisine includes elements of Plains Indian, Asian, and Cajun cooking. Walsh agrees with Stephan Pyles, who opened the Routh Street Café in Dallas that because there are at least twenty-five national and ethnic influences on Texas cookery, the correct term for the food served there should be "Texas cuisine."

The problem with that kind of thinking is that soon we will have fifty (or more) independent cuisines in the United States and the newest rage will be restaurants in Manhattan serving "South Dakota Pronghorn Cuisine." There is no doubt that the Texas, New Mexico, Arizona and California versions of Mexican cooking differ, yet the fact remains that the ingredients used are mostly the same; it is the techniques that differ.

It gets even more confusing when we realize that there are sub-cuisines within some states. For example, since the styles of cooking vary radically from south to north in New Mexico, to be perfectly accurate, we'd have to adopt descriptors such as the "Mexican- and Native American-influenced cuisine of New Mexico, Taos-Style." And since no one's going to use such a description, there simply is no better general term to describe the food of the entire area than Southwestern cuisine. I agree with Walsh, however, that the term is misused outside the region, particularly in California.

We often think of Southwestern cuisine as imported from Mexico, but we must remember that parts of the Southwest *were* a part of Mexico for more than 200 years. In fact, as recently as 1824, New Mexico was united with the states of Durango and Chihuahua. As Jim Peyton, an expert on the cuisine of northern Mexico, points out:

"The cooking of New Mexico was not brought across the border by immigrants; the border was moved south, leaving the cuisine intact. The same is true of Texas, which developed its own version of northern Mexican cooking that was heavily influenced by Native American and early Anglo settlers. The situation was different in Arizona, as we shall see.

Southwestern cooks often claim that the food of their particular state is the most "authentic," a word that is often misused. In fact, in Mexico there are many versions of authentic cooking; each is a variation on culinary themes that had their origin in a particular region of Mexico. As travelers to Mexico know, the food served in Mexico City or Puerta Vallarta is quite different from that prepared in Ciudad Juarez, yet each is authentic Mexican cooking in its own right.

When speaking of the cuisines of the Southwest, it is better to drop the word "authentic" from the vocabulary and speak of regional variations as either "traditional" or "new." After all, the term "authentic" implies that any variations from the standard dish are corrupt forms, while the word "traditional" innocently indicates that a time-honored method has developed within a certain geographical area.

Origins: The Legacy of Old Mexico

Long before Europeans arrived in the New World, Native Americans had settled the two American continents from Alaska to the Tierra del Fuego. During the long process of migration and settlement, these native peoples developed agriculture in Central and South America independent of the Old World, and based their cookery on four staple foods uniquely American in origin: corn, beans, chile peppers, and squash. These foods—unknown in Europe—were combined with native meats and spices to create a cuisine which caught the European invaders by surprise.

For example, chile peppers were eaten in recipes using every conceivable protein source—mostly venison, fish, and fowl. But when times got tough, the resourceful and iron-stomached Indians would consume "frog with green chiles, newt with yellow chiles, tadpoles with small chiles, and lobster with red chiles," as historian Bernardino de Sahagun observed in 1569. Another observer, Francisco Hernandez, noted in 1615 that the Indians consumed at least seven different kinds of chile peppers.

The arrival of the Spanish in Mexico had a profound effect on the cuisine of the country. They brought with them pigs, cows, sheep, goats, wheat, and vegetables like onions, to name just a few of the foodstuffs which soon transformed the eating habits of the Indians. The Aztecs, however, did not give up their beloved staple foods; they combined them with the new imports and created the basis for the Mexican cuisines of today.

Throughout the centuries, an astonishing variety of Mexican cooking developed as a result of geography. From the Yucatan Peninsula, Mexico stretches over 2,000 miles to the deserts of the north, so the length and size of Mexico, combined with the fact that mountain ranges separate the various regions, led to the development of isolated pockets of regional cuisines. This is why the cooking of tropical Yucatan differs significantly from that of the deserts of Chihuahua and Sonora.

One common factor, though, in Mexican cookery is the prevalence of chile peppers. They are grown all over Mexico, from the Pacific and Gulf Coasts to mountainous regions with an altitude above 8,000 feet. Approximately 200,000 acres of cultivated land produce 500,000 tons of fresh pods and 30,000 tons of dry pods each year. Although dozens of different varieties are grown or collected in Mexico, *poblanos, serranos, mirasols, and jalapeños* account for seventy-five percent of the crop.

While chiles are grown and consumed all over Mexico, they are particularly evident in the cooking of northern Mexico, which is termed "Norteño-style" Mexican food, or the food of *La Frontera*, the frontier. In fact, in Mexico City, the fiery cooking of the states of Chihuahua and Sonora is termed *platillos nortenses*, or "northern plates." The lore of Mexican cuisine holds that Norteño-style cooking is the hottest of them, and that heat is what ended up just north of the border.

There are several ways to distinguish one cuisine from another, but the most important is probably the use of different varieties of chile peppers in the dishes. Since chiles are a common ingredient all over the Southwest, their selection and use is often a clue to the origin of a certain recipe. Another method is to observe the ways a single popular dish such as *huevos rancheros* is prepared in the various states of the Southwest. Southwestern food expert Anne Lindsay Greer adds, "Defining regional differences is like matching food and wine—significant amounts of tasting will educate the palate."

A Note on the Methodology for Retail and Restaurant Listings

My recommended establishments must have been in business for at least ten years—and in most cases, much longer. My rationale for this is simply that success for a restaurant or retail shop is measured by longevity. If you're not good at what you do, you will not survive in business. Still, some companies will simply go out of business, so I conducted a Web search for every single establishment listed here to confirm its existence. I have only included street addresses for these places, but no phone numbers or websites because that would make the listings too cumbersome. Besides, if you know the name and location of an establishment, it's very easy to search for it online.

That said, readers and travelers should remember that life goes on during the lengthy process of research, writing, production, and publishing. Although it's unlikely that the mountains will move or the borders will change position, new shops and restaurants will open, others will go out of business, and addresses will change. I apologize in advance for any discrepancies and suggest that it's always a good idea to phone ahead before risking a long journey to visit a particular attraction or establishment.

1. The Native Southwest

"Ussen [God] told Child-of-the-Water and White-Painted Woman: 'You must live on yucca fruit, piñon nuts, and all other wild plants.'"

—Chiricahua Apache Legend

Zuni "waffle" gardens, 1925.

Photographer Edward S. Curtis

When the first Spanish explorers ventured north from Mexico City in the sixteenth century and wandered into what is now the Southwest, they discovered that the indigenous Native Americans made excellent use of nearly every edible animal and plant substance imaginable. For protein, the Native Americans hunted and trapped deer, rabbits, quail, pronghorn, bison, and many other mammals and birds. However, some tribes such as the Apaches had taboos against eating certain animals that they regarded as repulsive: snakes, fish, and owls, for example. Later on, after the appearance of European food animals, game was viewed as "poor man's meat." Today, of course, game has made a comeback because of its exotic nature and appeal to an adventurous audience.

The food plants eaten by the Native Americans are divided into two categories: those harvested in the wild, and those cultivated plants that had managed to adapt to the dry desert climate or were irrigated.

Wild Ones

Harvested wild plants included acorns, berries such as chokecherry and juniper, yucca fruit, various herbs such as wild mint, mushrooms, mesquite seeds (sometimes called beans), and agave hearts (*mescal*), which were roasted in pits by the Mescalero Apaches and other tribes. Three other uncultivated crops that were very important in Native American cooking (and are most commonly used today) are cacti, *piñon* nuts, and *chiltepíns* (wild, berry-like chile peppers).

Various species of cactus were collected and eaten, including the fruit from the huge saguaros, but the most commonly used cacti were the varieties of the genus *Opuntia*, the prickly pears. The pads of the prickly pear were stripped of spines and then boiled or fried. The fruit of these cacti (called *tunas*) were picked when they were ripe and were eaten raw as a snack or dessert. Today, prickly pear pads (called *nopales*) can be found canned or fresh in some local markets, and there are many brands of cactus jellies and jams made from the tasty fruits.

The *tunas*, or fruit of the prickly pear cactus.

Photographer Dave DeWitt

Another wild plant, the *piñon* tree, was utilized to its fullest extent. The tough *piñon* tree (*Pinus edulis*), the New Mexico state tree, was nearly as important to native Americans of the Southwest as the bison was to the tribes of the Great Plains. The Ramah Navajo, for example, utilized all parts of the tree in their daily lives and gave credit in legend to the squirrel for planting the first *piñon* tree. The nuts were a food staple to be collected, traded, and sold at market, but that was just the beginning. The Ramahs utilized the wood for fuel, the logs for building hogans, fences, and corrals. Saddle horns were fashioned from the roots, and *piñon* resin was chewed as gum and used as a binder and dye in pottery making and basket making. The branches and needles of the tree were important in tribal rituals, and the dried buds were used as medicines to ease suffering from burns, earaches, coughs, and fever.

The only problem with the nuts of the *piñon* is that they are relatively scarce. The crop is dependent on the amount of moisture received each year, and insufficient rainfall in the years preceeding flowering means a scant supply of nuts from a given tree. The cones containing the nuts mature during the second year after flowering, and this fact, combined with weather variations, results in a good crop of nuts in the same region only every four or five years.

Piñon trees are evergreen survivalists because of their drought resistance and slow growth. But this toughness causes a skimpy and undependable supply of nuts. And once ripe, the tasty nuts are devoured in great quantities by deer, turkeys, javelinas, bears, birds, squirrels, and other rodents. In fact, an old trick used by Native Americans is to wait for a snowfall and follow the tracks of ground squirrels to their burrows, where sometimes as much as a twenty-pound cache of *piñons* can be found, stored by the hoarding little squirrel. But probably the most voracious consumer of *piñons* is mankind, cracking some three to five million pounds of the nuts a year collected in the Southwest and Mexico.

A *piñon* tree in the snow.
Photographer Dave DeWitt

The ripe *piñon* is contained within a pitchy cone and is usually collected by spreading blankets beneath the trees and then shaking the branches until the nuts separate from the cones. The shells can be cracked with the teeth or stronger implements, and the nuts are roasted by spreading them in a single layer on a shallow tray and baking them in a 350 F. oven for eight to ten minutes. An alternate method is to bake them in the shells, which makes the shells brittle and easier to crack, and prevents frequent trips to the dentist.

Gastronomically speaking, *piñon* nuts are usually eaten raw or roasted, and are also used in butters, candies, soups, and stuffings. The roasted nuts are high in unsaturated fats, and it is a simple matter to mash them into a butter. They also contain significant amounts of vitamins A and B, protein, calcium, and phosphorus. There are about 200 calories per ounce of nuts.

The third important wild crop is the wild chile peppers called *chiltepíns* (*Capsicum annuum* var. *aviculare*), which are the closest surviving species to the earliest forms of chiles which developed in Bolivia and southern Brazil long before mankind arrived in the New World. The small size of the fruits were perfect for dissemination by birds, and the wild chiles spread all over South and Central America and up to what is now the United States border millennia before the domesticated varieties arrived.

There is a wide variation in pod shapes, from tiny ones the size and shape of BBs to elongated pods a half-inch long. By contrast, domesticated *piquins* have much longer pods, up to three inches. The *chiltepíns* that are the most prized in Mexico are spherical and measure five to eight millimeters in diameter. They are among the hottest chiles on earth, measuring up to 100,000 Scoville Heat Units (A scale developed by Wilbur Scoville in 1912 to rate the level of pungency in peppers).

In Sonora and southern Arizona, *chiltepíns* grow in microhabitats in the transition zone between mountain and desert, which receive as little as ten inches of rain per year. They grow beneath "nurse" trees such as mesquite, oak, and palmetto, which provide shelter from direct sunlight, heat, and frost. In the summer, there is higher humidity beneath the nurse trees, and legumes such as mesquite fix nitrogen in the soil—a perfect fertilizer for the *chiltepíns.* They also protect the plant from grazing by cattle, sheep, goats, and deer. *Chiltepíns* planted in the open, without nurse trees, usually die from the effects of direct solar radiation.

Although the *chiltepín* plant's average height is about four feet, there are reports of individual bushes growing ten feet tall, living twenty-five to thirty years, and having stems as big around as a man's wrist. *Chiltepíns* are resistant to frost but lose their leaves in cold winter weather. New growth will sprout from the base of the plant if it is frozen back.

There is quite a bit of legend and lore associated with the fiery little pods. In earlier times, the Papago Indians of Arizona traditionally made

The mother of all chiles, the *chiltepín*.
Photographer Dave DeWitt

In 1794, Padre Ignaz Pfeffercorn, a German Jesuit living in Sonora, described the wild chile pepper: "A kind of wild pepper which the inhabitants call *chiltepín* is found on many hills. It is placed unpulverized on the table in a salt cellar and each fancier takes as much of it as he believes he can eat. He pulverizes it with his fingers and mixes it with his food. The *chiltepín* is the best spice for soup, boiled peas, lentils, beans and the like. The Americans swear that it is exceedingly healthful and very good as an aid to the digestion." In fact, even today, *chiltepíns* are used—amazingly enough—as a treatment for acid indigestion.

Padre Pfeffercorn realized that *chiltepíns* are one of the few crops left in the world that are harvested in the wild rather than cultivated. (Others are *piñon* nuts, Brazil nuts, and some wild rice.) This fact has led to concern for the preservation of the *chiltepín* bushes because the harvesters often pull up entire plants or break off branches. Dr. Nabhan believes that the *chiltepín* population is diminishing because of overharvesting and overgrazing. In Arizona, a *chiltepín* reserve has been established near Tumacacori at Rock Corral Canyon in the Coronado National Forest. Native Seeds/SEARCH, based in Tucson, has been granted a special use permit from the National Forest Service to manage the permanent marking and mapping of plants, and to conduct ecological studies.

annual pilgrimages into the Sierra Madre range of Mexico to gather *chiltepíns*. Dr. Gary Nabhan, former director of Native Seeds/SEARCH, discovered that the Tarahumara Indians of Chihuahua value the *chiltepíns* so much that they build stone walls around the bushes to protect them from being devoured by goats. In addition to spicing up food, various Native tribes in the Southwest use *chiltepíns* for antilactation, the technique whereby nursing mothers put *chiltepín* powder on their nipples to wean babies. *Chiltepíns* are also an aid in childbirth because when they are powdered and inhaled they cause sneezing.

Domesticated Plants

Even though wild crops were important, the ancient Anasazi culture of the Southwest—and later the Pueblo Indians—depended on some important domesticated crops: corn, beans, and squash. It is not a coincidence that these foods are the foundation of Southwestern cuisine. Although domesticated in Mexico and Central America, these crops had moved north to what is now New Mexico long before the Spanish arrived.

Maize, what we now call corn, is of Mexican origin and was first domesticated about 5,000 years ago. Early man must have had to grow tons of it, for the first cobs were about the size of pencil erasers. Maize moved north as the size of the cobs increased. In 1948, primitive ears of corn one to two inches long were discovered in the Bat Cave archaeological site in New Mexico and were dated to 3,500 years ago. By selectively breeding for larger ears, prehistoric farmers had developed two to three hundred varieties by the time Columbus arrived in the New World.

As the size of the cobs increased, maize became an increasingly important food plant in Native American culture and acquired religious as well as culinary usage. Its pollen was used in numerous ceremonies and various colors of corn were aligned with the four directions: blue with the west, red with the south, white with the east, and yellow to the north. It was grown in both dry fields and irrigated plots and was much hardier than the hybrids of today.

Recently, there has been a resurgence of interest in non-hybridized varieties of corn, especially blue corn. Blue corn tortillas and chips are everywhere these days, and home gardeners are experimenting with an astounding variety of strains that have been rescued from hybridization. These include Isleta Blue, Santo Domingo Blue, Hispanic Pueblo Red, and Rainbow.

However, most of the corn grown in the Southwest today is hybridized. It still forms the basis for what is called the "corn cuisine" of the Southwest, for the kernels are ground into corn meal and corn flour, which are then used in breads and tortillas. And, tortillas, of course, are the foundation of a number of Southwestern recipes, such as enchiladas.

Domesticated beans predate corn and were tamed about 10,000 years ago in Peru and apparently moved north into Mexico and eventually the Southwest and then to the rest of the country. When the Europeans arrived, the common bean, *Phaseolus vulgaris*, was being grown everywhere in what is now the United States. In the Southwest, another species, *P. acutifolius*, or the tepary bean, was more popular because it was a rapid grower and was resistant to drought and alkalinity. Black varieties of tepary beans, such as the Mitla Black Bean, are used in the famous black bean soups.

A *metate* for grinding corn.
Photographer Dave DeWitt

Pinto beans are most commonly used in Southwestern cuisine, and farmers grow three or four different varieties, mostly in the Estancia Valley and the Four Corners area of New Mexico. One interesting fact about pinto beans is that they must be cooked at the same altitude where they were grown. Beans grown at a lower altitude will not cook at higher altitudes and will simply rattle around in the pot no matter how long they are boiled. Pinto beans are generally boiled, mashed, and then refried in oil or lard and spiced with red chile—but traditionally are not used as an ingredient in chile con carne but instead are served on the side.

In addition to beans, another early vegetable was squash, which was first domesticated in Central

America about nine thousand years ago and eventually spread over all the Americas. It was was a staple of the Anasazi and Hohokam cultures and was passed down to the Navajos and Pueblo Indians, who loved them so much they incorporated the shape of the squash flowers into artwork and silver necklaces which are called "squash blossoms." Several ancient squash varieties are still grown today, including the blue-fruited Acoma Pumpkin, the green-striped Santo Domingo Squash and the Calabaza Mexicana, or the long-neck pumpkin. Southwestern farmers and home gardeners grow squash in profusion—but mostly zucchini, a late arrival to this cuisine.

Early Native American recipes show that squash was a common ingredient of soups and stews. In addition to the squash fruits, the blossoms were also eaten. They were added soups and stews or were boiled and mashed with corn kernels. Today, squash is sauteed with green chile and corn, baked whole, or added to casseroles.

Pumpkins are a common ingredient of stews, and early New Mexican recipes also show how to make pumpkin candies. Incidentally, an early preservation method is to bake winter varieties and then slice them thin and dry them in the sun. The slices can be put in soups and stew or rehydrated with hot water.

During the last decade, a conservation movement has been growing in the Southwest and its goal is to preserve and promote the use of the traditional native crops that are thousands of years old. Experts are urging home gardeners to forego hybridized and genetically altered commercial varieties of corn, beans, squash, and chiles, and to plant, instead, the ancient American types. As Margaret Visser points out in her 1985 book *Much Depends on Dinner*, "Worst of all, varieties of corn are disappearing by the dozen even as these words are being written. A corn not being planted is a corn which ceases to exist."

Leading the movement to preserve ancient food plants is Native Seeds/SEARCH. They provide seeds for an astounding number of varieties of traditional crops and publish a quarterly newsletter, *The Seedhead News*. (The organization is listed on page 223.) "The food crops of this region," notes their catalog, "are not only delicious and nutritious but better adapted to the harsh environments of the low hot deserts and dry rocky uplands than most modern vegetables."

Traditional Foods Combat Diabetes

After World War II, the Pima Indians of Arizona developed the highest incidence of Type II diabetes in the world. At first, the doctors were baffled, but they soon realized that the cause was quite obvious. The Pimas had stopped eating native plants and had switched to a non-traditional diet loaded with sugary and fatty fast food, and the result was that their metabolism could not handle the change.

Studies by Native Seeds/SEARCH indicate that native desert food plants control blood sugar levels because they are "slow-release" carbohydrates that are converted to glucose at a much slower rate than other foods. In fact, mesquite pods and acorns rank among the top ten percent of all foods ever analyzed for their effectiveness in controlling blood sugar.

Now, all that's needed to reduce diabetes among the Pimas is to switch them back to native foods—and that's no easy task. Native Seeds/SEARCH representatives speak at conferences, health fairs, and schools and have even produced a video entitled *Desert Food is Healthy Food*. They have also designed recipes for such "new" delicacies as prickly pear juice, mesquite tea, and a cool bean salad with cholla buds.

Exhibits and Demonstration Gardens

More that 10,000 desert plants representing 2,500 different species are growing at the Desert Botanical Garden (1201 N. Galvin Parkway, Phoenix), a fascinating collection of cacti and succulents. Of note to food lovers is the exhibit, People and Plants of the Sonoran Desert Trail, and its hands-on demonstrations of the ways the early desert people collected and grew their food. On display are native food plants, demonstration gardens, *mescal*-roasting pits, corn-grinding *metates*, *mescal* pod pounders, and more. The gift shop offers books on food, cooking, and native plants.

The food highlight at the Tucson Botanical Gardens (2150 North Alvernon Way) is the Native Seeds/SEARCH Garden, which is planted with traditional crop seeds gathered from the Southwest. Native American gardening techniques are re-created here in miniature. The gift shop is a celebration of chiles, featuring books, tee-shirts, and food products. The Gardens is the sponsor of the annual Fiesta de los Chiles, held the third weekend in October.

The Pima County Cooperative Extension Garden Center (4210 North Campbell Avenue, Tucson) has a garden center that is affiliated with the University of Arizona and has a demonstration garden of Arizona crop plants, particularly chiles (14 varieties). They also carry a useful collection of Southwestern gardening pamphlets.

A Cultural Center and a Restaurant

The central focus at the Indian Pueblo Cultural Center (2401 12th Street, Albuquerque) is a 10,000 square foot museum of the authentic history and artifacts of traditional Pueblo cultures as well as their contemporary art. The permanent exhibit highlights the creativity and adaptation which made possible the survival, diversity and achievements of each of the nineteen Pueblos.

The Tigua Restaurant, Tigua Indian Reservation (9430 Socorro Road, El Paso) has a very long tradition of serving native foods. The original restaurant, located at Ysleta del Sur Pueblo, first started serving food to Pueblo people in 1860 and finally opened to the general public 108 years later. The Indian bread served in the restaurant is made in adjacent *hornos* (outdoor ovens) and the aroma of fresh bread wafts through the restaurant. There is a red tile floor, corner fireplaces, and interesting murals painted on the walls. The food ranges from traditional (their red chile stew was named best in the world by *People* magazine) to exotic shark *fajitas* (the shark comes from Corpus Christi).

Other Native Food Plants of the Desert

Yucca. About thirty species of this relative of the lily grow in the Southwest, and virtually every part of the plant was utilized by Native Americans. The fruits, seeds, and petals were used as food, medicine, and dye. Baskets, rope, cloth, and mats were made from the fibers and leaves, and the roots were pounded into pulp for soap.

Jojoba. Early desert dwellers were roasting and eating jojoba nuts for millennia before the Spanish arrived. After the frontier was settled, the plant was called the "coffee bush" because it seeds look just like coffee beans—and indeed, it was often used as coffee substitute by Anglo pioneers in Arizona. It has recently enjoyed commercial production, but not for food. The fruits are about fifty percent oil, which is a substitute for sperm whale oil, and it is also used in the manufacture of shampoos and body oils.

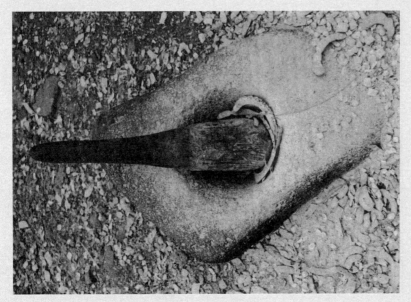

Grinding mesquite pods.
Photographer Dave DeWitt

Mesquite. The beans of this plant were more important than even corn to the Native Americans of the Sonoran desert. The ripe beans were dried on rooftops, then stored. Later, the beans were ground into flour for use in drinks, breads, gruel, and cakes. Mesquite wood and charcoal is a favorite for grilling meats and poultry in the Southwest.

2: Lone Star Cuisine: Southwestern Texas

"So many requests came in for the recipe [her Pedernales River Chili] that it was easier to give the recipe a name, have it printed on a card and make it available. It has been almost as popular as the government pamphlet on the care and feeding of children."

—Lady Bird Johnson

"Chili concocted outside of Texas is usually a weak, apologetic imitation of the real thing. One of the first things I do when I get home to Texas is have a bowl of red. There is simply nothing better."

—President Lyndon B. Johnson

Chuck Wagon—The Cowboy's Kitchen, c. 1920, Beaumont, Texas.

Photographer Thomas K. Todsen

President Johnson didn't have to come back to Texas for his favorite bowl o' red—he always carried a supply of Lady Bird's Pedernales River Chili aboard Air Force One. Such is the devotion to just one of the famous foods that originated in the Lone Star State.

Since Texas is a state larger than many countries, it is not surprising that its food should be varied and influenced by many different ethnic sources. But even as diverse as the cooking is in the state, few people would suspect that the culinary history of Texas began with wine.

From Grapes to Heifers

In the rugged land the Spanish called *El Norte*, the only route to the territories of Nuevo Mexico and Tejas was the Camino Real—the rough trail romantically called the "Royal Road"—that ran from Mexico City to Chihuahua to El Paso del Norte to Santa Fe. At El Paso in 1622, Franciscan monks planted vineyards at Ysleta Mission, and this event was the beginning of the post-Columbian culinary history of Texas.

Winemaking moved north into New Mexico (see Chapter 3), but it also spread through Texas as the Spanish attempted a spiritual conquest of Texas through the founding of missions. Trade routes were established from El Paso into the center of the state, resulting in the founding of San Antonio in 1718. The first wines that were made were sacramental in nature, and it wasn't until the mid-1800s that commercial vineyards were planted.

Meanwhile, the major symbol of Texas, the longhorn steer, was becoming entrenched on the land and in the stomachs of Texans. The first known cattle to enter Texas were 500 head brought by Coronado in 1541 as he searched for the mythical city of Quivira. Many cows escaped from that herd and formed the nucleus of the wild herds that later roamed the state. Both the explorers and the settlers brought cattle to Texas, and by 1757, the town of Reynosa had a human population of 269

Longhorn steers, 1909.

Photographer Thomas K. Todsen

and a cattle population of 18,000. Cows were worth a mere four pesos in those days, yet the cattle ranches flourished.

Modern cattle growing evolved mostly in east Texas, and by 1860, the cattle population of the state exceeded three million head. The introduction of Brahma cattle from India proved to be a momentous event because these cows were immune to tick fever. In 1874, the first the Brahmas were crossed with the native stock, resulting in a much hardier breed. But by that time, because the Civil War had prevented cattle from being shipped, Texas was overrun with longhorns, and their value had dropped considerably.

The establishment of huge ranches and cattle drives to other states soon changed that situation, and, suddenly, it seemed that everyone was flocking to Texas to buy ranches, and even English earls became cattle barons. About this same time, the buffalo were being slaughtered for their hides, and, in addition, their tongues were in demand by restaurants, which paid nine dollars a dozen for them.

It wasn't only the new types of cattle that thrived in Texas; the wine industry succeeded as well. Beginning in 1876, the wine industry was assisted by Thomas Munson, who settled near Dennison and developed more than three hundred new grape varieties. When the French vineyards were decimated by the plant louse in the 1880s, Munson sent carloads of Texas grape rootstock to France. The French grafted their vines onto the American rootstock, and the resulting plants were resistant to the louse. Munson thus saved the French wine industry, and, along with his colleague, Hermann Jaeger, became the only Americans to receive membership in the French Legion of Honor.

Munson was also instrumental in the development of the Texas wine industry. Because of his work, twenty-six wineries were in operation at the turn of the century, and nearly thirty Texas wineries were in operation when Prohibition began in 1920. When Prohibition was repealed thirteen years later, only one winery—Val Verde of Del Rio—had survived, and, as if recalling the origins of Texas wines, it owed its existence to the sale of sacramental wine and the sale of grapes to home winemakers.

The wine industry was re-established in Texas in 1975 when the Schlaraffenland Winery (now Guadalupe Valley Winery) began operation. The industry growth has been phenomenal since then. Now, Texas is the country's fifth largest producer of grapes and wine, according to a 2007 industry report. Texas has more than 220 family-owned vineyards covering 3,700 acres, and about 100 wineries. It is interesting to note that Texas Cabernet Sauvignons are commonly served with fine, aged Texas beef these days.

That Leguminous Tree with the Great Smoke

You either love mesquite or hate it, depending on whether or not you're a farmer, hunter, cook, rancher, or woodworker. Farmers and ranchers hate the tree, of course, because it chokes out needed grazing grass, and, as a result of its extensive root system, is nearly impossible to remove from pastures. The ranchers, however, were at least partially responsible for the spread of mesquite over fifty-five million acres in Texas because their cattle passed the mesquite seeds through their digestive systems unharmed, and deposited them in a perfect natural fertilizer!

Yes, mesquite is tenacious, and its thorns can puncture tires. That's the bad side. The good side is that the tree prevents erosion, and it forms a microhabitat for birds and animals in an otherwise harsh environment. A clump of mesquite trees provides shade, humidity, and food for such animals as doves, deer, javelina, and rabbits, which is why hunters like the tree. The tree, which produces a legume like peanuts, is nitrogen-fixing, so it serves as a host tree for other wild plants such as chiltepíns.

The mesquite beans, which are sugar-rich, provide food for both animals and man, and once provided up to forty percent of the food in the diet of Native Americans in Texas. The wood of the tree is variously shaded, which is why woodworkers love it for making sculptures, gunstocks, parquet floors, and other hardwood products.

Cooks love mesquite wood because it produces a sweet smoke that imparts a great flavor to grilled meats. Most mesquite trees these days are being cut down for wood chips and to make charcoal, but there's such an abundance of trees that there is no threat to mesquite.

Throughout Texas and the Southwest, travelers will have little trouble finding mesquite-grilled foods. But a hint to the home cook—the wood is used for grilling but is considered to be too acrid for the lengthy smoking or barbecuing of meats. For that, pecan or hickory wood is suggested. And if you're grilling with mesquite, be sure to use aged wood because the green wood is too oily.

Barbecues and Fajitas

Given the preponderance of beef in Texas, it's no wonder that Texans have perfected many different ways of cooking it. Perhaps their crowning achievement is Texas barbecue, which has been influenced by the style from Southern states in the U.S., by German immigrants, and by Mexican-style barbecue. In Zavala County, between San Antonio and the border, there is a norteño-style barbecue known as *barbacoa*. A whole cow's head is wrapped in soaked burlap bags, set on top of the coals of a mesquite fire in a pit, and the pit is filled with dirt.

Twelve to eighteen hours later, the head is dug up and eaten. The tongue, brains, cheeks are served with *jalapeños*, refried beans, and *guacamole*. Some sources say this dish was introduced by Spanish soldiers when Texas was part of Mexico. This method is still commonly used in northern Mexico, and in some *norteño* restaurants. If you ask for *barbacoa*, don't expect a pork sandwich. You will probably get parts of *cabeza de vaca* (head of the cow), which is delicious.

Beef is not the only meat barbecued in Texas. German immigrants have perfected the slow cooking of pork. *Cabrito*, or barbecued kid, is popular during the spring in Mexican-American communities, and lamb is also barbecued. Texas ranch barbecues are legendary for their huge size, with whole goats and pigs and sides of beef being cooked for days over low heat.

The difference between grilling and barbecuing is important to remember: grilling utilizes high heat and quick cooking, while barbecuing is "cooking meat with hot smoke," in the words of Red Caldwell, author of *Pit, Pot & Skillet*. He says, "Closed pit barbecue involves building a fire at one end of an enclosed pit and forcing the smoke to travel the length of the pit to an exit. Somewhere in between, barbecue happens."

To be more precise, the USDA has a catchy little definition: "Meat that shall be cooked by the direct action of heat resulting from the burning of hard wood or the hot coals there form for a sufficient period to assume the usual characteristics…which include the formation of a brown crust"

The earliest barbecues (the Virginia Burgesses mentioned them in 1610, and George Washington went to one in 1769) were undoubtedly events where whole hogs were slow-cooked in pits in the ground. Pits like that can still be used, but they tend to mess up the lawn. The pits most commonly used today are specially constructed smokers that separate the meat from the direct heat of the fire.

As Red Caldwell observes, "There are countless designs running from huge brick units to various large-diameter pipe fabrications to the ubiquitous 55-gallon drum, various commercial configurations designed for urban dwellers, even the odd converted refrigerator (not a bad cooker, actually)."

Fajitas.
Photographer Aaron Sandoval

Another important distinction of barbecue from grilling is that barbecue sauces are used to baste barbecued or smoked meats but are generally not placed on grilled meats because their sugar content causes them to burn easily. In Texas, the sauces tend to be tomato and chile-based, rather than the vinegar-based sauces of the Deep South.

A fairly recent innovation in Texas cooking are *fajitas*, which are prepared with skirt steak, a pretty fancy term for beef diaphragm muscle. *Fajitas* have their roots in the dish *carne asada*, thin steaks that are roasted or grilled until well done. But *fajita* skirt steak is marinated first in *jalapeño* juice and port wine, or various other concoctions prepared by innovative cooks. The name means "little belts," an allusion to the fact that after grilling, the steak is cut across the grain into thin strips. These strips are placed on flour tortillas and are topped with fresh salsa, cheese, tomatoes, and sometimes *guacamole*.

I think that *fajitas* originated on the vast *ranchos* surrounding Monterrey, Mexico, and gradually worked their way north. In the late 1960s, Sonny

Falcon learned the butcher's trade in the Lower Rio Grande Valley before he moved to Austin. While most Texas butchers threw the beef skirt steak section in with the ground meat, Mexican butchers from the valley put them aside for clients who liked to grill them for "*fajita* tacos." While working in Austin, Falcon experimented with many methods of tenderizing the *fajita* meat and finally arrived at his butterfly slicing technique. He began selling his grilled *fajita* tacos on weekends, beginning at an outdoor festival in Kyle, Texas, in 1969. Falcon's *fajitas* became a favorite at fairs and outdoor events all over Texas and he became known as Sonny "*Fajita* King" Falcon.

Soon, restaurants began making their own versions of *fajitas*. Pharr's Roundup Restaurant in Matamoros began serving them in 1977, and five years later, the Austin Hyatt-Regency was serving 13,000 orders of *fajitas* a month. But the chef at the Hyatt had no luck with skirt steak, so he substituted sirloin. Sonny Falcon would argue that a "steak taco" was not a "*fajita* taco," but no one paid much attention to the fine points of Spanish translation. As a result, anything served with fillings and tortillas came to be called "*fajitas*," including: "chicken *fajitas*," "shrimp *fajitas*," "fish *fajitas*," and "*fajita* pitas." Whether such phrases are translated as "fish skirt steaks" or "little chicken belts," all of these phrases are completely meaningless to Spanish speakers and to Mexican butchers who use the word *fajita* only to describe beef skirt steak. In other words, "chicken *fajitas*" is a contradiction in terms.

The "National Dish" of Texas

Perhaps the most famous Tex-Mex creation is that bowl o' red, *chili con carne*, a dish which most writers on the subject say did *not* originate in Mexico. Even Mexico disclaims chili; the *Diccionario de Mejicanismos*, a Mexican dictionary published in 1959, defines it as: "A detestable food passing itself off as Mexican and sold from Texas to New York City."

Despite such protestations, the combination of meat and chile peppers in stew-like concoctions is not uncommon in Mexican cooking. Mexican *caldillos* (thick soups or stews) and *adobos* (thick sauces) often resemble *chili con carne* in both appearance and taste because they all use similar ingredients: various types of chiles combined with meat (usually beef), onions, garlic, cumin, and occasionally tomatoes.

E. De Grolyer, a scholar and chili aficionado, believed that Texas *chili con carne* had its origins as the "pemmican of the Southwest" in the late 1840s. According to De Grolyer, Texans pounded together dried beef, beef fat, chile peppers, and salt to make trail food for the long ride out to San Francisco and the gold fields. The concentrated, dried mixture was then boiled in pots along the trail as sort of an "instant chili."

The New Age Version of the Origin of Chili

Some *chili con carne* fanatics are not satisfied with mundane explanations—such as cattle drive cooking—for the origin of chili. In his book, *Bull Cook and Authentic Historical Recipes and Practices*, George Herter weaves a strange tale indeed about the possible origin of chili.

The story of the "Lady in Blue" tells of Sister Mary of Agreda, a Spanish nun in the early 1600s who never left her convent in Spain but nonetheless had out-of-body experiences during which her spirit was transported across the Atlantic to preach Christianity to the peoples of the New World.

After one of the return trips, her spirit wrote down the first primitive recipe for *chili con carne*, which the now-converted Indians had given her out of gratitude: chile peppers, venison, onions, and tomatoes. Believe that one and I have a deal for you on some swampland in New Mexico.

A variation on this theory holds that cowboys invented chili while driving cattle along the lengthy and lonely trails. Supposedly, range cooks planted oregano, chiles, and onions among patches of mesquite to protect them from foraging cattle. The next time they passed along the same trail, they would collect the spices, combine them with beef (what else?) and make a dish called "trail drive chili." Undoubtedly, the chiles used with the earliest incarnations of *chili con carne* were the *chiltepíns*, called *"chilipiquíns"* in Texas, which grow wild on bushes—particularly in the southern part of the state.

Probably the most likely explanation for the origin of *chili con carne* in Texas comes from the heritage of Mexican food combined with the rigors of life on the Texas frontier. Most historians agree that the earliest written description of chili came from J. C. Clopper, who lived near Houston. He wrote of visiting San Antonio in 1828: "When they (poor families of San Antonio) have to pay for their meat in the market, a very little is made to suffice for the family; it is generally cut into a kind of hash with nearly as many peppers as there are pieces of meat—this is all stewed together."

Except for this one quote, which does not mention the dish by name, historians of heat can find no documented evidence of chili in Texas before 1880. Around that time in San Antonio, a municipal market—El Mercado—was operating in Military Plaza. Historian Charles Ramsdell noted that "the first rickety chili stands were set up in this marketplace, with the bowls of red sold by women who were called 'chili queens.'"

The fame of *chili con carne* began to spread, and the dish soon became a major tourist attraction, making its appearance in Mexican restaurants all over Texas—and elsewhere. The first known recipe appeared in 1880 in *Mrs. Owen's Cook Book*. She got it all wrong, of course, referring to the bowl o' red as "the national dish of Mexico," and added ham, carrots, celery, and cloves to it.

At the World's Fair in Chicago in 1893, a bowl o' red was available at the "San Antonio Chili Stand," and in 1896, the first U.S. Army recipe appeared in *The Manual for Army Cooks*. Incidentally, Army chili contained both rice and onions. Given the popularity of the dish, some commercialization of it was inevitable. In 1898, William Gebhardt of New Braunfels, Texas, produced the first chili powder and began canning his *chili con carne*, Gebhardt Eagle. By 1918, Walker Austex was producing 45,000 cans a day of Walker's Red Hot Chile Con Carne and 15,000 cans a day of Mexene Chili Powder.

The chili queens were banned from San Antonio in 1937 for health reasons—public officials objected to flies and poorly washed dishes. They were reinstated by Mayor Maury Maverick (a real name) in 1939, but their stands were closed again shortly after the start of World War II. But Texans have never forgotten their culinary heritage, and in 1977 the Texas Legislature proclaimed *chili con carne* to be the "Official Texas State Dish."

Ormly Gumfudgin, historian of the International Chili Society, stirs a large pot of chili.

Photographer Chel Beeson

Today there is a movement afoot by the International Chili Society (in California, of all places!) to have Congress name chili as the official national dish, but the idea isn't new. In the mid-1970s, noted food writer Craig Claiborne observed, "We thought for years that if there's such a thing as a national American dish, it isn't apple pie, it's *chili con carne*.... In one form or another, chili in America knows no regional boundaries. North, South, East, and West, almost every man, woman, and child has a favorite recipe."

Chili con carne is still enormously popular in Texas and other states, and huge chili cookoffs are held regularly. Teams of cooks use highly guarded secret recipes to compete for thousands of dollars in prizes while having a good ol' time partying. Some traditionalists, however, scorn the cookoff-style *chili con carne* as too elaborate and are promoting a return to the classic, "keep it simple, stupid" cafe-style chili.

Sam Pendergrast of Abilene is such a purist, and in his landmark article, "Requiem for Texas Chili," which appeared in *Chile Pepper* magazine in 1989, he noted: "I have a theory that real chili is such a basic, functional dish that anyone can make it from the basic ingredients—rough meat, chile peppers, and a few common spices available to hungry individuals—and they'll come up with pretty much the same kind of recipe that was for most of a century a staple of Texas tables. So all we have to do to get back to real chili is to get rid of the elitist nonsense." See his recipe for Zen Chili in Chapter 7.

Incidentally, chili lovers will rejoice to learn that since the eighties, San Antonio has been staging "historic re-enactments" of the Chili Queens' heyday. Called the "Return of the Chili Queens Festival," the event is held every Memorial Day weekend in late May in old San Antonio. The fiesta re-creates the era of the chili queens and celebrates the dish that no matter what its origin, will live forever in the hearts, minds, and stomachs of Texans everywhere.

The Advent of Tex-Mex

Throughout the Southwest, each state has its own version of what is called "Mexican" cooking. With a few exceptions, the same basic dishes—enchiladas, tacos, and the like—have become very popular, but do not truly represent the cooking of Mexico. Rather, they have become Mexican-American versions of cooking from the northern states of

Mexico, which developed when our states were a part of Mexico and evolved in their own directions, based on regional ingredients and cooking styles.

The first Mexican restaurant to open in Texas was the Old Borunda Cafe in Marfa in 1887, closely followed by the Original Mexican Restaurant in

A little Texas food humor. Feeding Time—Texas Brag, 1909.

Photographer unknown.

The chile peppers most commonly used in homemade Tex-Mex cuisine are the *poblanos* from Mexico (and their dried version, *anchos*), which are tasty and mild and the fresh ones are usually served *relleno*-style; the *serranos* for fresh salsas; the *chilipiquín* (*chiltepín*) for soups and stews; and, of course, the ubiquitous *jalapeño*. This fat and fiery pepper is popular everywhere and is served raw, pickled, stuffed, chopped up in salsas, and is even utilized in cooked sauces for topping enchiladas and *huevos rancheros*, which are served with fried eggs and salsa *ranchera* over corn or wheat tortillas. New Mexican chiles are now making an appearance in Tex-Mex cooking, especially in the dried red form. For example, Chuy's restaurants in Austin now brings in more than 10,000 pounds of fresh green New Mexican chiles from Hatch, New Mexico, and has a roasting and peeling fiesta.

San Antonio in 1900. Restaurants had a great influence on the development of Tex-Mex cooking. As Texas food writer Richard West explains, "The standard Tex-Mex foods (tacos, enchiladas, rice, refried beans, and tamales)—and newer editions, like *chiles rellenos, burritos, flautas,* and *chalupas*—existed in Mexico before they came here. What Texas restaurant cooks did was to throw them together and label them Combination Dinner, Señorita Dinner, and the hallowed Number One. In so doing, they took a few ethnic liberties and time-saving short cuts. For example: Tex-Mex tacos as we know them contain ground, instead of shredded, meat. And chile gravy is most often out of the can, instead of being made fresh with *chiles anchos* and special spices."

In addition to the standard food items of Tex-Mex, a few others deserve mention. *Menudo*, a bowl of tripe and hominy soup flavored with *anchos* or *chilipiquíns* and a calf's or pig's foot, is especially popular with Mexican-Americans, who regard it as a hangover cure. They call it "the breakfast of champions," and kid Anglos about their aversion to eating "variety meats." I've tried it numerous times and it just doesn't meet the standard for recipes in this book. Contrary to popular belief, *menudo* is not cow's intestines, but rather the lining of the second stomach chamber, which is called "honeycomb tripe." It is definitely an acquired taste.

Posole, a hominy and chile stew, is also a popular dish, as are tamale pie, *guacamole*, fried *jalapeños*, *quesadillas*, *cabrito asado* (braised kid), and desserts such as *flan*, *capirotada* (bread pudding), and *buñelos*, which are a kind of sweetened fry bread.

There are also some newer inventions such as nachos (cheese and *jalapeño*-topped tostada chips), which seem to have originated sometime during World War II at the Victory Club in Piedras Negras, although another source credits the invention to a restaurant in Villa Acuna, Mexico. The snack was served at the Texas State Fair in Dallas in 1966, and Arlington Stadium, home of the Texas Rangers, introduced the dish to baseball fans in 1975. From there, nachos spread to stadiums all over the country, but some customers complained that the *jalapeños* were too hot. "No problem," said Dr. Ben Villalon at the Texas Agricultural Experiment Station at Weslaco, and he proceeded to develop a non-pungent *jalapeño* specifically for the nacho market.

No discussion of Texas food would be complete without mentioning beans. They are cooked in many different ways and are served with all the major Texas food groups: barbecue, chili, and Tex-Mex. One of the greatest celebrators of Texas beans was the famous author, professor, and naturalist, J. Frank Dobie. "A lot of people want chili with their beans," he wrote in the 1949 Niemann-Marcus cookbook, *A Taste of Texas*. "Chili disguises the bean just as too much barbecue sauce destroys the delectability of good meat. For me, chili simply ruins good beans, although I do like a few *chilipiquíns* cooked with them. I believe, however, that the *chilipiquíns* make a better addition after the beans are cooked. I add about three to a plate of beans and mash them up in the plate along with a suitable amount of fresh onion. A meat eater could live on beans and never miss meat. When a Mexican laborer is unable to lift a heavy weight, his companions say he 'lacks *frijoles*.' As you may deduce, I am a kind of *frijole* man. On the old-time ranches of the border country, where I grew up, *frijoles* were about as regular as bread and in some households they still are."

Today, Texas cuisine is somewhat of a melting-pot, a tossed salad kind of cooking, with many different influences vying for top honors. In addition to the cooking styles covered above, Texas is influenced greatly by Gulf Coast and Louisiana cooking, Southern cooking (particularly in eastern Texas), Midwestern styles, and even New Mexican cuisine in West Texas. One of the great things about traveling through Texas is the opportunity to sample a wide variety of Southwestern cooking.

Great Eating in Austin

In 1841, the king of France's charge de affaires, "Count" Jean Peter Isidore Alphonse de Saligny, arrived in Austin to discuss business with the politicians of the newly founded Texas Republic. He brought with him a servant, a driver, and Austin's first French chef de cuisine. The house Saligny built, the French Legation, is today a fascinating museum that is located just east of I-35 at 802 San Marcos Street, off 8th Street.

The French Legation's kitchen was equipped in 1966 with a collection of antique, French-made kitchen equipment brought to the New World by French-American families and their chefs. This museum reproduction of Count Saligny's original fully-equipped kitchen is the finest example anywhere of a French Creole kitchen. Saligny stayed in Texas until 1845, wining and dining the new republic's politicians and talking them into signing a "friendship treaty" with France. In the process, Saligny and his chef began the tradition of fine dining in Austin and in the Republic of Texas.

In 1866, Austin's oldest existing restaurant, Scholz Garten, opened not far from the State Capitol building. It's a German beer garden that is still popular with state legislators, and it's listed on the National Register of Historic Places.

Tiled bullfighting scene
in an Austin restaurant.
Photographer Dave DeWitt

Wining and dining Texas politicians has always been a big part of the Austin restaurant scene. But the lobbyists have always complained that it's hard to spend enough money to impress anybody in Austin. While there is a sprinkling of fine dining experiences available, most Austin restaurants are in the lower price ranges. Mexican food, barbecue, and Southern cooking are particularly well represented. Of particular interest in Austin and the surrounding rural towns of central Texas are the funky old joints, places that seem like time capsules from another era.

Kreuz Market in Lockhart, a meat market that became a barbecue joint, is a good example of this kind of historic eatery. Opened in 1900 just off the Lockhart town square, Kreuz became famous for its smoked meats and sausage. Ask for a tour; the owners will gladly take you to the basement to see the old ammonia-powered refrigeration units, or out to the wood-pile to explain the aging system for the post oak used in the open fire pits.

Louis Mueller's Barbecue in downtown Taylor is another fabled joint with great food. Built in the 1930s, Mueller's is still owned by the family of the original owner. Try the pork ribs if you can get there early enough—Mueller's sells barbecue until they run out, and they often run out early!

Kreuz and Mueller were descendants of the many German immigrants who arrived in south and central Texas in the early 1800s, a wave of immigration encouraged by Mexico. Mexico attempted to settle the sparsely populated state of Texas by giving away

land. At the same time that Stephan F. Austin brought large groups of Southerners to Texas with their traditions of farming and southern cookery, many Germans and Czechs also arrived, bringing with them their traditions of brewing beer and smoking meats. Thus beer and barbecue have as long a history in central Texas as southern fried chicken, chicken-fried steak, and black-eyed peas.

By the early 1900s, the success of the ranching business in Texas had provided a cheap, plentiful supply of beef. But unlike the tender corn-fed beef that made the New York strip steak famous, Texas beef was as tough as it was flavorful. It was best when cooked for a long time, as in barbecue brisket, or cut up into tiny chunks for chili. Dr. Salisbury of England, who invented his famous Salisbury steak as an aid to digestion, helped increase the popularity of ground meat around the turn of the century. In Texas, where tough beef was so plentiful, the hamburger soon became ubiquitous. During the Depression, hamburgers sold for a nickel.

The Twenties and Thirties were the golden age of hamburger joints in Austin. One such place was Dirty's, also know as Martin's Kum-Back Burgers, opened on Guadalupe near the University of Texas campus in 1926. It's still a favorite of many Austin old-timers, and it was one of the most popular drive-ins in town during the drive-in craze. But the best example of the hamburger joints of that era is Hut's Hamburgers on West 6th Street—it has been described by *Texas Monthly* magazine as "a living museum." Hut's walls feature newspaper advertisements from the building's grand opening as Sammy's Drive-in in 1939.

Homer Hudson, who would eventually move Hut's into the Sammy's building in 1964, opened his original Hut's Hamburgers on Congress Avenue in 1939. Hamburger joints are still one of Austin's most popular eating institutions—as one might expect in a city dominated by college students.

Austin's oldest existing Tex-Mex joints were built in the Fifties. The Tex-Mex style has undergone major changes since these eateries opened. While we used to order the Number Two dinner, today we opt for *fajitas* or green *enchiladas*; choices that didn't exist in mid-century Tex-Mex restaurants. Lady Bird Johnson's favorite Mexican restaurant, El Patio on Guadalupe at 30th Street, hasn't changed much since it opened in 1954. If you are interested in tasting the old-fashioned Tex-Mex food that defines this much-maligned style, you can still get it here. The Señorita Platter is the most asked for item and pralines are still 10 cents. Located close to campus, the building was originally famous for its co-ed carhops when it opened as the Toonerville Drive-in in 1935. Matt's El Rancho, the king of Austin Tex-Mex restaurants, which once dominated the downtown restaurant scene, has moved to a quieter spot at 2613 South Lamar, where the formerly funky environs and food have given way to modern decor and a somewhat more contemporary style of Mexican food.

Austin's oldest existing fine dining establishment is Green Pastures (811 West Live Oak) which opened in 1946. Ken Koock, one of the current owners, is the son of the restaurant's founder, Mary Faulk Koock. Ken grew up in the Southern mansion that houses the restaurant, and, for many years, the family lived on the upper floor. Green Pastures was named one of the 100 Best Restaurants in America by the late James Beard in 1978. Beard had a long association with the restaurant through his cookbook projects. Green Pastures remains one of Austin's best restaurants, and its Sunday brunch has been called the best in Texas. Its history and fine food, as well as the landscaped grounds, complete with strutting peacocks, make it a one-of-a-kind place to dine.

In recent history, Austin claims to be the place that made *fajitas* famous. Sonny Falcon, "The *Fajita* King," opened a restaurant of the same name in Kyle, Texas, where it all began. Austin has also added its own twist to the new Southwestern cuisine, mainly by making it affordable and available in more casual surroundings. In fact, eating out anywhere in Austin is extremely casual—there isn't a restaurant in the entire city that requires men to wear ties. Austin is also well known for hot sauce and tortilla chips. Several tortilla factories are located here including Guiltless Gourmet, the company that manufactures fat-free corn chips.

The Austin Country Flea Market (9500 Highway 290E) is a great place to find food of all kinds. Known as *La Pulga*, ("The Flea") it resembles a Mexican *mercado* with 550 covered stalls. In the beginning it was just another American flea market where people sold garage sale items on the weekends. But the huge

Hispanic population in the area preferred shopping in this style of market more than in the American supermarket environment, so the flea market acquired more and more Mexican grocery items. Tiny booths selling Mexican brand name hot sauces, canned chiles, candied papaya, caramel and brown sugar, and other hard-to-find Mexican items started to take over. Today, La Pulga has several merchants who import Mexican produce items direct to their stands. They include ingredients that can be found nowhere else, including loose *chipotle* peppers, bulk spices and medicinal herbs, three varieties of prickly pear fruit and five or six kinds of bananas. There is a huge selection of dried and processed chile peppers, including African bird peppers, ground *ancho* and New Mexican chiles.

The Travis County Farmer's Market (6701 Burnet Road) has been recognized as one of the Ten Best Farmer's Markets in the Country by Judith Olney's *Farmer's Market Cookbook*. The market is the best place to buy fresh Texas produce in Austin. Saturday mornings during peak growing seasons, the market is full of unusual herbs and vegetables, local honey, jams and jellies, gift baskets of *jalapeños*, salsas, relishes and mustards, and other great things to eat like heads-on Gulf shrimp. Visitors to Texas will also be interested to note this is a good place to buy Hill Country peaches, citrus from the Rio Grande Valley, Texas onions, and several varieties of native pecans to ship home.

Central Market (4001 North Lamar) is foodie heaven in Austin. When we videotaped there, as part of the documentary I wrote and co-produced,

Heat Up Your Life, I counted 26 varieties of fresh and dried chiles. Their salsa selection numbered more that 100, and other products include hot sauce, spicy jerky, canned *chili con carne*, and tons of mustards. Plus, they carry so many Texas food products that you can get a lesson on the food of the Lone Star State just by shopping there. A good restaurant is on the premises and Central Market offers many cooking demonstrations in their test kitchen upstairs.

There are some excellent breweries and wineries in Austin, including Celis Brewery, 2431 Forbes Drive. In 1966, Pierre Celis opened his De Kluis Brewery in the Belgian village of Hoegaarden with a first year production of 350 barrels. When Celis sold the brewery in 1990, they were making 300,000 barrels a year. In 1992, the Celis Brewery in Austin began production with 12,000 barrels of three new premium American beers: Celis White, Celis Pale Bock and Celis Golden. Founded in 1909, Spoetzl Brewery (603 E. Brewery, in Shiner, southwest of Austin on U.S. 90A), brews some of the best beer made in Texas, Shiner Bock. There is a hospitality room with tastings and two tours daily but no retail sales at the brewery.

Hill Country Cellars is both a vineyard and winery. It's just north of Austin on Route 183 in the town of Cedar Park. Tours and tastings are free. This is a pleasant lunchtime diversion; you can take a tour and eat lunch on the picnic tables outside with a bottle of their fine Riesling or a wine spritzer.

As might be expected, Austin has a terrific collection of Mexican and Tex-Mex restaurants. El Azteca (2600 E. 7th Street) features original velvet paintings, Aztec maiden calendars for sale, the city's best stand of banana trees, and some of Austin's most outstanding Mexican food. A relative newcomer, El Azteca opened in 1963, in the heart of the Mexican barrio. All food is cooked to order, and it's worth the wait. Inexpensive, funky and fun, El Azteca is everybody's favorite—and the only restaurant in town where *cabrito* is served all the time.

A favorite of University of Texas students, Chuy's (1728 Barton Spring's Road, and 10520 North Lamar) is an eccentric Mexican restaurant with consistent food. The original Barton Springs location near Zilker Park features an Elvis shrine and post-serious art. The north location is home to the world's largest collection of lava lamps. Favorite dishes include "*burritos* as big as your face," Chuy's special blue corn *enchiladas,* and excellent crunchy style chicken-stuffed *chile rellenos.* Hatch green chiles are roasted at the restaurant, New Mexico-style, during the annual September Green Chile Festival.

Perhaps the finest purely Mexican restaurant in Austin is Fonda San Miguel, 2330 North Loop Boulevard. This lovely restaurant graciously serves fine interior Mexican cuisine in a magnificent setting. Sample the *ceviche,* calamari, and other *antojitos* among the tropical plants in the solarium. Admire the Fonda's Mexican art collection in the main dining room while you savor pork in *achiote* cooked in banana leaves. Tortillas are made before

How Do You Spell "BBQ"?

A fierce debate rages not only in Texas, but all over the United States, about the spelling of the word symbolized by the acronym "BBQ."

Hundreds of establishments proclaim themselves as "barbeque" restaurants. But are they really? According to all major dictionaries, the word is properly spelled "barbecue," with the "c" correct and the "q" a weird aberration.

So, what gives? Are the "ques" taking over from the "cues"? And, if so, should this trend be reversed? Should we start a campaign to rename all these restaurants?

Forget it. Etymologists (as opposed to entomologists, who only work on "b"s), tell us that the evolution of the English language is a natural occurrence, and that we should not worry about such trivial changes.

But what we do worry about is Rudy's BBQ that started in Leon Springs, Texas, and now has locations all over the Southwest, and sells its own "Bar-B-Q *Sause.*"

your eyes. Don't miss the *cajeta* dessert, a rich goat milk caramel sauce with ice cream. Finish off the evening with an espresso at the copper-covered bar. The highly recommended Sunday brunch features nearly every item on the menu in a huge buffet.

Texas is barbecue country as well, and Louie Mueller Barbecue (206 W. 2nd Street in Taylor which is north of Austin on U.S. 79), is a great example of it. Going to Mueller's barbecue restaurant in downtown Taylor is a trip to a bygone era. The walls can't possibly have been painted since the place opened in 1939. Don't come if you're in a rush. The pace of life in Taylor is positively glacial, although the people are warm and friendly. Relax, sit back, enjoy the smoky atmosphere and the overheard conversations, and pretend you're doing yoga—pork rib yoga.

A truly unique experience awaits the Southwest diner at Hudson's On-The-Bend, 3509 Ranch Road (620 North). Hudson's is a charming stone house in the Lake Travis area that serves outstanding Hill Country game dishes including venison, quail, wild boar, pheasant, and rabbit. Chef Jeff Blank is well known for imaginative creations like smoked steak and *poblano* roulade and his beautiful swordfish vegetable terrine. Excellent sauces and relishes complement the exotic meats and fish. An extensive wine list offers a variety of Zinfandels, Pinot Noirs, and some selections off the beaten track. Sauces, condiments and vinegars are also available for sale. My dinner there was memorable.

The Hill Country

No one seems to know exactly what its boundaries are, but one of the great attractions of the Austin area is the vast Hill Country. Some sources include the plains east of Austin in the Hill Country, which seems odd because the land is as flat as the proverbial pancake. The true Hill Country is west and south of Austin, and is truly a fascinating region for food lovers.

But before we get to food, a brief description of the region is in order. Geologically speaking, the hills are there because of the Balcones Escarpment, a fault zone that separates the flat coastal plains to the east from the Edwards Plateau to the west. The Hill Country is a land of artesian wells, caverns, rock formations, forests, rivers, lakes, ranches, and small towns.

Historically, the region was settled by German emigrants in the 1830s and '40s, which is why there is such a German flavor to towns like New Braunfels and Fredericksburg. In some areas, German is spoken as commonly as English, and there are the inevitably combined words such as "der *jalapeño*."

For travel lovers, the Hill Country has much to offer. There are wildflower festivals, rodeos, bed and breakfast inns, exotic animals on game farms, hunting and fishing, golf, horse racing, guest

Game was very popular in the Hill Country, as we can tell from this photo. Interior of the Buckhorn Saloon, D'Hanis, c. 1914.

Photographer Congdon.

ranches, scenic caverns, cowboy art galleries, resorts, shopping in towns like Fredericksburg—and food, lots of food.

First and foremost are the meats. The German tradition of smoked meats and sausages is very strong in the Hill Country, and it fits in well with Texans' love of barbecue. Although the two cooking techniques are technically different because the Germans do not use tomato-based sauces, in reality smoked meat is just that, and sauces can always be added by the diner. There are quite a few meat markets in the region (some nearly a century old), and one or two of them literally sell *tons* of smoked meat every week. Also in the German tradition is a love of baking, and bakeries abound, especially in Fredericksburg.

The Hill Country is also a land of fruits, with grapes and peaches taking top billing. There are numerous vineyards and wineries in the region, and some of the wine produced is award-winning. Many of the wineries are within an hour's drive of Austin or San Antonio. Most of the wineries offer tours and tastings, and vintners predict that tours of Hill Country wineries could eventually become as popular as those of the Napa Valley, which draws more tourists than Disneyland. Peaches are commonly grown in the Hill Country, especially around Stonewall, so it follows that peach preserves and jellies are found everywhere in retail shops. In fact, several shops in Fredericksburg specialize in fruit jams or in Texas products.

Interesting Hill Country wineries include Fall Creek Vineyards (1820 County Road 222) in Tow, on the shores of Lake Buchanan. It features 55 acres of vinifera vines and produces Sauvignon Blanc, Chenin Blanc, Emerald Riesling, Cabernet Sauvignon, and Zinfandel. Grape Creek Vineyard (U.S. Highway 290, 4 miles west of Stonewall) produces Chardonnay, Fume Blanc, and Cabernet, and the wines are aged in oak barrels in the cellar. There is also an orchard with peaches and other fruits and a gift shop on the premises. Sister Creek, off I-10 at the Boerne exit, is located in the heart of the Hill Country in tiny Sisterdale (population 25); this winery produces Chardonnay, Pinot Noir, Cabernet Sauvignon, and Merlot. The vineyards are located between East and West Sister Creeks, and a century-old cotton gin has been restored to house the winery.

It is interesting to experience the collision of culinary cultures in the Hill Country, with influences from Germany, Mexico, and the Deep South all mixing together. Yes, at some times during the year the Hill Country resembles a Germanland theme park because of the huge influx of tourists for such events as Oktoberfest, but if you're visiting Austin or San Antonio, don't miss a drive through one of the most fascinating regions in the country.

The San Antonio Food Scene

If there is such a thing as a "normal" Southwestern city, San Antonio is certainly not it—particularly concerning food. San Antonians, like most Texans, have a strong individualistic bent, and this characteristic has traditionally been reflected in the offbeat nature of the city's eating establishments. This tendency toward quirkiness was enhanced by several facts: first, incomes in San Antonio have always been moderate-to-low, and second, until the early 1970s, sale of liquor was forbidden in Texas restaurants.

Lacking the profits from mixed drinks, restaurateurs could not afford much in the way of decor. Depending solely on food sales also meant that the menu items had to be both delicious and inexpensive. From this background grew a profusion of unusual eateries that reflected the idiosyncracies of their owners rather than market research. The situation has made San Antonio one of the most enjoyable and fun places to eat out in the Southwest—particularly for the adventurous and unpretentious diner.

In recent years, San Antonio has grown tremendously and, at least on its north side, is much like any other U.S. city with its complement of franchise fast-food outlets and neon-lit restaurants. However, it is the old-style, eclectic restaurants that are dear to old San Antonians.

San Antonio's first and possibly most colorful food purveyors were the chili queens. First noted around 1880, these women set up carts at dusk in Military Plaza, where they cooked *chili con carne* in iron pots over mesquite coals. Their flirtatiousness and

San Antonio Riverwalk, location of many fine restaurants.

Photographer Dave DeWitt

the aroma of chili were their sales tools. Frank X. Tolbert, writing in his famous paen to chili, *A Bowl of Red*, described them: "The chili queens dressed gaily and, according to one account, pinned bunches of roses, in season, to their bosoms. Street musicians serenaded the chili eaters."

Unfortunately, health regulations drove the chili queens away in the late 1930s, though they do make a comeback in the guise of latter-day impersonators every year during the Return of the Chili Queens celebration over the Memorial Day weekend. Unfortunately, most San Antonio restaurants have not carried on the tradition of Texas-style chili, preferring instead to serve a chile-based *enchilada* sauce.

One typical San Antonio haunt that still does serve *chili con carne* is the Original Donut Shop. While it prepares fine donuts, its main attractions are the *gorditas*, flour tortillas, tacos, and *barbacoa*. Other spots that deliver fun and a nostalgic slice of San Antonio's past (and interesting food, to boot) include Little Hipp's Gimmedraw Parlour, Henry's Puffy Taco, Bob's Smokehouse, the Tip Top Cafe, and the Esquire Tavern. There is nothing fancy (indeed, quite the opposite) about these eateries, but they provide a lot of fun for visitors who like offbeat spots and good food.

As far as San Antonio markets are concerned, HEB Marketplace (5601 Bandera Road and other locations) is, to food lovers, one of San Antonio's main attractions. Customers enter through a produce section that contains items from all around the world. At last count the store carried twenty-two different kinds of fresh and dried chiles. From the produce section, customers wander into the Italian deli section, which boasts a wood-burning oven for cooking fresh pizza. The Mexican section of the Marketplace has a small tortilla factory which continuously produces both corn and flour tortillas. The bakery features more than thirty kinds of ethnic breads that are baked daily. The meat department features sausages from around the world, hormone-and additive-free meats, and hard-to-find specialty meats such as *cabrito*. The cheese department offers an international cheese selection with a particularly fine representation from Italy. The fresh seafood section carries a huge offering of fish flown in daily. There are also a fresh- roasted coffee department, a sushi department, food stalls, fresh herbs by the ounce, and much more.

Market Square (514 West Commerce) is the largest Mexican market in San Antonio with more than 50 shopping opportunities including Rivera's Chile Shop. Not only are all the pods here, but just about every other chile-related product you can imagine, including clothing, jewelry, posters, salsas, jams, jellies, candies, and many other food items.

Additionally, Rivera's has a fine collection of Mexican and Southwestern cookbooks. The Farmer's Market section of Market Square consists of shops and food courts selling Southwestern and Mexican foods. Located here is Mi Tierra Cafe and Bakery, 218 Produce Row. The restaurant has been in the same location, originally a red light district, for more than sixty years. Although it was located in a rough neighborhood, people from all walks of life and all parts of town found their way to Mi Tierra. In 1974 the area was developed into a tourist-oriented marketplace with a Mexican atmosphere, and Mi Tierra expanded to its current large size. There is also an adjacent bakery here. Specialties include *cabrito*, *chilaquiles*, beef *chiles rellenos*, and the ubiquitous Tex-Mex favorites. Also at Market Square is Pico de Gallo, 111 South Leona. Under the same ownership as Mi Tierra, this restaurant features *Norteño* cooking such as char-broiled chicken, beef *fajitas*, sausage, grilled onions and penchiladaotatoes, *frijoles a la charra*, tortillas, and, of course, *pico de gallo* salsa. The restaurant is decorated with stone sculptures and a hand-carved bar.

As food lovers might expect, there are many other great restaurants in San Antonio. Los Barrios Mexican Restaurant (4223 Blanco Road), in business since 1979, serves, in addition to their Tex-Mex specialties, signature items like their "*mofofo*" grill, *churrasco* steak, *cabrito* dinner, and *milaneza papas*. Biga on the Banks (203 South St. Mary's Street) on the Riverwalk, is owner/chef Bruce Auden's showplace for innovative dining. The starters include Asian spring rolls filled with minced venison, buffalo, ostrich, and pheasant accompanied by two spicy dipping sauces. A specialty entrée is the bone-in tenderloin steak with beer-battered onion rings and *habanero* ketchup.

La Calesa (2103 East Hildebrand) features interior Mexican dishes from as far south as Merida in Yucatán and the specialities of the house include *cochinita pibil* (pork stew), *enchiladas potosinas* (with potatoes and *chorizo),* and *rajas poblanas* (*poblano* chile strips) in cream sauce. El Chaparral Mexican Restaurant (15103 Bandera Road, in picturesque Helotes just north of San Antonio) has been serving fine Tex-Mex food for more than thirty years. The most popular items are the basic Tex-Mex *enchiladas*, green *enchiladas*, and the unusual Creole tacos. Ernesto's (2559 Jackson-Keller Road) is one of those collision-of-cultures restaurants that dazzles with a combination of Mexican traditions, fresh seafood, and French influences. Signature dishes include snapper with salsa Veracruzana, *enchiladas* a la Ernesto, *ceviche*, green chicken *enchiladas*, and fish with garlic sauce. Ernesto's has a fanatically loyal clientele.

Once an abandoned filling station, La Fogata ("The Flame") (2427 Vance Jackson) is now regarded as San Antonio's premier Mexican restaurant with a complex of spreading terraces. The food, in the style of North Central Mexico, includes such temptations as *queso flameado* (flaming cheese), *guayaba* s (with guava), and the *carne adobada*, with rich chiles and a hint of cinnamon. Be prepared for a wait at this very popular restaurant. La Fonda on Main (2415 North Main) has been serving Tex-Mex favorites since 1932 and is considered to have mastered the style. It is probably the oldest continually operated Mexican restaurant in San Antonio and one of the oldest in the country. Recommended dishes are chiles *rellenos* stuffed with meat and raisins, chicken tortilla soup, and chilled avocado soup.

Over a reasonable amount of time, you will see just about anybody who counts in San Antonio at El Mirador (722 South St. Mary's Street). It's been serving innovative Mexican and Tex-Mex dishes for nearly forty years. The best time to arrive at this cafe is Saturday after 11 a.m., when the restaurant serves the soups for which it is justly famous. Recommended are the *caldo xocitil, huevos rancheros*, the *enchiladas*, and the mind-boggling *caldo azteca*, which contains chunks of chicken, fresh spinach, strips of corn tortilla, chiles, sliced avocado, melted cheese, zucchini, carrots, and potatoes! Rosario's Restaurant y Cantina is one of the only restaurants in San Antonio that makes its own corn tortillas by hand. The food served here comes from all states of Mexico and favorites are *rajas con queso blanco*, black bean soup, and tortilla soup.

And let's not forget barbecue. Rudy's Country Store and Barbecue (downtown in Leon Springs, north of San Antonio off IH 10 W) bills itself as serving "the worst barbecue in Texas" in its advertising.

The reverse psychology seems to work because the place is jammed. In addition to the usual brisket, spare ribs, and sausage, Rudy's serves barbecued prime rib, rainbow trout, baby-back ribs, and pork loin. All of these items are served on butcher paper, the old fashioned way. A unique aspect of Rudy's is the pit, which is designed in such a way that the burning oak logs heat the outside dining area while providing heat and smoke for cooking.

San Antonio's largest ethnic heritage is Spanish, followed by German, and both cultures are known for injecting heavy doses of food and merriment into their celebrations. The biggest of all the festivals in San Antonio is the Fiesta of San Jacinto (also called Fiesta San Antonio), which officially commemorates Texas' independence from Mexico (April 21). The highlight is A Night in San Antonio, or NIOSA as it is now called, which combines the joyousness of a Mexican fiesta with the raucous bonhomie of Oktoberfest. For a full week, San Antonio reverts to its colorful past, including food stalls that serve everything from Peruvian *anticuchos* to sausages from the nearby German towns in the Hill Country.

So, if you're coming to San Antonio, be prepared to party!

El Paso and Ciudad Juárez

Culturally, scenically, economically, and gastronomically, El Paso belongs more to New Mexico than to Texas. El Pasoans, who despite living in the fourth-largest city in the state, often feel isolated from and slighted by the rest of Texas, love New Mexico, and visit the state frequently. Thus, the trade between the city and the region to the north that began with treks up and down the Camino Real ("The Royal Road") continues today along Interstates 10 and 25.

The modern history of the region began in 1659, when Fray Garcia de San Francisco y Zuniga constructed a small sanctuary and named the location the mission of Our Lady of Guadalupe of Paso del Norte, which later became the Mission of Guadalupe. The settlement that slowly grew around the mission was named El Paso del Norte—the Pass of the North. El Paso became a major stop on the Camino Real, that connected Mexico City with Santa Fe. From El Paso, travelers and explorers had the option of moving further north to Santa Fe or heading east to San Antonio.

During the Pueblo Revolt of 1680 in New Mexico, El Paso del Norte gave asylum to the Governor of the Province of New Mexico, Don Antonio de Otermín, who improved the city and organized an army to defend it. Along with Otermín, came friendly Indians from Isleta Pueblo, who did not participate in the revolt. They founded a new pueblo, spelled it "Ysleta," and have survived to this day.

In 1847, Susan Magoffin, visiting El Paso del Norte, noted: "Our dishes are all Mexican, but

Taking Care of Your Ristra

Should you have an opportunity to purchase a *ristra* (string of chile pods) in El Paso or New Mexico, here are some tips for their care and preservation:

◆ Once the freshly strung chiles are completely dried and you have decided to use them for decoration instead of cooking, dip them in Johnson's Wax or spray them with polyurethane to seal in the moisture. They should last several years.

◆ Never ship fresh *ristras* in plastic. The *ristra* may rot or arrive infested with insects. And, they will stink!

Chile *ristras* for sale in El Paso.

Photographer Dave DeWitt

◆ Allow the *ristra* to dry in El Paso before shipping it (this may take weeks) because it will weigh less.

good ones, some are delightful; one great importance, they are well cooked; their meats are all boiled, the healthiest way of preparing them, and are in most instances cooked with vegetables, which are onions, cabbage, and tomatoes; with the addition of apples and grapes."

During Prohibition, Cuidad Juárez became a mecca for Americans eager to enjoy the pleasures that were illegal in the United States, especially drinking. Distilleries were constructed which supplied bootlegged liquor to cities as far north as St. Louis, and Avenida Juárez had more saloons that any other street in the world, a bar every twenty feet for six blocks!

"Juárez is the most immoral, degenerate, and utterly wicked place I have ever seen or heard of in my travels," raged American Consul John Dye in 1921. "Murder and robbery are everyday occurrences and gambling, dope selling and using, drinking to excess and sexual vices are continuous."

An American evangelist of the time added: "I would rather shoot my son and throw his body in the river than have him spend one hour in the raging inferno of Juárez."

Juárez has mellowed out considerably since then. I have visited the city perhaps fifty times since 1965 and have never experienced any problems at all—except for the long wait at customs to return to the States. On the contrary, the people there—as in all of Mexico—are gracious and helpful. Juárez has also boomed positively since the days of vice and bootlegging. Over 1.3 million people live there now, in addition to the 700,000 across the river in El Paso. Passports are now needed to return to the U.S., but visas are required if you venture further into the interior of Mexico; you can bring back $400 worth of merchandise per person without being charged duty.

El Paso and Juárez offer a lot of food and fun, and some interesting sightseeing as well. There are some off-beat museums here, like the the Border Patrol Museum (4315 Transmountain Road), which is devoted to smuggling interception history. The Wilderness Park Museum (4301 Transmountain Road) features displays of early man and Native Americans before the arrival of Europeans, while the El Paso Museum of History (510 North Santa Fe Street) tells the story of the region from the coming of the Spaniards to the present day. In Juárez, the Juárez Museum of History and Art in the Plaza de las Americas exhibits ancient artifacts from Mexico's earliest inhabitants as well as striking works from modern Mexican artists.

Also telling the history of the region are the Spanish missions, which still stand today. The Socorro Mission (Socorro Road, lower valley) is the oldest continuously occupied active parish in the U.S., built in 1681. Even older is the Guadalupe Mission (two blocks west of Avenida Juárez in downtown Juárez), which was built between 1658 and 1668. The Ysleta Mission (Zaragosa Drive in the lower valley) is adjacent to the Tigua Indian Reservation.

Margarita Man

The 50th anniversary of the *margarita* was the Fourth of July, 1992, according to Francisco "Pancho" Morales' calculations. Morales should know. He invented the drink—no matter what anyone else says. Claims to the origin of the margarita are as common as Elvis sightings. Some stories say that the margarita was created by a bartender at the Tail o' the Cock in Los Angeles in the early Fifties. That *margarita* was named for a customer (a Margaret Whatsherface, of course). The bartender used the macho-man tequila José Cuervo, and when the word spread, the drink became Heublein's financial equivalent of an endless night on the town. Anyway, that's how the advertising copywriters tell it.

Neon sign for Tequila Sauza.
Photographer Dave DeWitt

America in Mexico. During those days, just over the bridge in Juárez's busiest commercial district, you could celebrate anything you wanted.

Morales was tending bar at Tommy's Place, a favorite hangout for GIs from Fort Bliss. A lady walked in, sat at the bar, and ordered a magnolia. The only thing Morales knew about a magnolia was that it had lemon or lime in it and some kind of liquor. So he did what any good bartender would do—he winged it and used the most popular liquor served in Juárez: *tequila.*

With a single taste, the woman, who knew a magnolia was made of gin, cream, lemon juice, and grenadine, realized that the drink was an imposter, but liked it anyway because Morales had loaded it up with enough tequila to make anyone smile. When she asked what the new drink was called, Morale's brain was thinking flowers and "m"s, and had leaped from magnolia to *margarita*—Spanish for daisy.

And so mixology history was made, and Morales later immortalized the drink when he taught at the bartender's school in Juárez before immigrating to El Paso in 1974. In the 1990s, Morales, then a retired milk truck driver, still received calls from reporters all over the country asking him questions about the invention of the *margarita*. What about the bartender in Los Angeles?

"A kook," replied Morales.

How about that Margarita in San Antonio?

"I don't even want to know her."

Another yarn holds that a San Antonio socialite named Mrs. William Sames devised the drink in 1948 when she hastily combined tequila and Cointreau to serve to her wealthy friends. Her family called it "the drink" until her husband gave it his wife's first name—you got it —Margarita. Wrong again.

A lot of people probably think that singer/songwriter Jimmy Buffet first concocted the *margarita* because of all the publicity he gave the drink while wasting away in his fictional Margaritaville. But Jimmy was merely the musical pitchman for a lively libation that was created because of miscommunication and bartender hustle. And it was all Pancho Morales' fault.

It was American Independence Day, 1942. The heat was sweltering, and the scene was Juárez, Mexico. Not that you couldn't celebrate the independence of

What about the claims of the management of La Florida, another popular Juárez bar, that they created the drink?

"They're kooks, too."

Morales used to say that today's *margaritas* are breaches of trust: "All these guys, they put bananas in the *margaritas*. They put in cactus, onions, and pink color and serve it in champagne glasses. And they use too much salt. Kooks, all of them."

His recipe is simple and given in the language of a true barkeep. Here it is.

Juice of 1/2 lime
2 parts white tequila
1 part Cointreau

Now, here's the translation. Squeeze about an ounce of lime juice from a Mexican *limón* (not a Persian lime) into a shaker glass filled with chunks (not cubes) of ice (never shaved). Take the squeezed *limón* and run it around the rim of a cocktail glass. Put the glass on a towel, sprinkle it lightly with salt, and then shake off *all* the excess salt. Now, allowing for the juice already in the glass, and any ice that may have melted to contribute to the 4-ounce final tally of liquid, the remainder of the formula requires enough tequila (please, a great tequila like Herradura) and Cointreau (never Triple Sec), two parts to one, to equal exactly 4 ounces of drink to be shaken, strained, and poured off into a 4-ounce cocktail glass. This takes some skill, but it's not brain surgery.

"The two parts doesn't mean jiggers and it doesn't mean bottles," warns Morales. "I've seen this all mixed up."

The El Paso and Juárez Food Experience

Begin with a winery and a couple of specialty shops and you'll get an idea of the variety of the foods in this region. Bieganowski Cellars (5923 Gateway West) is a winery that produces thousands of cases annually from Texas-grown grapes, including an award-winning Merlot, a Blanc de Noir champagne from Pinot Noir grapes, and a white Zin. The facility has a tasting room and a large room for parties. Azar Nut Factory (1800 Northwestern. I-25 West, exit Transmountain, right on Northwestern) sells both locally grown (pecans and pistachios) and imported nuts such as cashews. There is sampling on premises to educate the palate and learn more about the exciting world of nuts. Products include gift baskets, *jalapeño* snack mix, perfect pecans for show-off baking, and deluxe almonds. El Paso Chile Shop (909 Texas Avenue) carries the full line of El Paso Chile Company Products, plus wreaths and Indian folk art, an extensive supply of chiles, chile topiaries, and chile products. Some of their products include Snakebite Salsa, Cowboy Catsup, Coyote Nuts, plus pastas and vinegars.

The restaurant scene in El Paso/Juárez is lively. Cafe Centrál (109 Oregon Street) is where El Pasoans "play society," with appearances by politicians, designers, photographers, and travel guide writers. "It's like a Thirties movie," says food writer Elaine Corn. Some of their eclectic specialties include *asadero quesadillas* with Hatch green chiles, red chile pasta, steak *Tampiqueña* with chiles and jack cheese, and pepper steak with extremely spicy Moroccan *harissa* with seven peppers. Since 1976, The Canutillo Tortilla Factory and Little Diner (7209 Seventh Street in Canutillo, east on I-10) has served great chicken tamales with cheese, and huge, fat *gorditas* in browned tortillas. Elaine Corn observes: "This food is without a doubt the classiest ode to an ancient cuisine, with sparkling fresh ingredients and profound flavor. Okay, so what if the place looks like a bus depot?"

Casa Jurado (226 Cincinnati and 4772 Doniphan Drive) has been open since 1972. Henry Jurado credits his mother, Estela, with the recipes for his restaurants. Some of her favorites include chicken *mole* (made from scratch from pecans, chile *ancho*, almonds, and chocolate), *salpicón*, filet Casa Jurado with *asadero* roasted tomatoes, and green chiles. Their to-die-for smooth salsa contains three different kinds of chiles, plus *tomatillos*. Loaded with history, La Hacienda (729 W. Paisano) was built in 1851 and is now a National Historic Site. It was part of the original Fort Bliss, and the Rio Grande still flows just behind the building. Specialties

More Texas food humor.
Photographer Dave DeWitt

include green chile chicken *enchiladas* with an egg on top, steak *Tampiqueña*, *chile colorado con carne*, and "Charlie Brown" beans, which are more of a soup topped with chopped onions.

Named for the tree out front, Forti's Mexican Elder (321 Chelsea) features tacos *al carbón*, *salpicón*, fish Veracruzano, Mexican shrimp, a searing table salsa full of texture, and magically greaseless *flautas*. "Forti's combines border food with the food of the interior of Mexico," notes Elaine Corn, "and its heat level is a few notches above average." Another

Original sign for Julio's.

Photographer Dave DeWitt

restaurant of historic note is Grigg's Restaurant, 9007 Montana. Since 1939, El Pasoans have feasted on Grigg's generous New Mexico-style dishes. Try their green chile chicken *enchiladas,* the red *enchiladas* with an egg cracked on top just before they remove them from the oven, or the *guacamole* tacos. The stuffed *sopaipillas* look like they're covered with red chile sauce, but the sauce is really green-based, with the addition of tomatoes.

I would be remiss if I didn't mention The State Line Barbecue, 1222 Sunland Park Drive. It's a large restaurant (with a long wait) decorated in a Wild West/Gay Nineties saloon style. They serve enormous prime beef ribs that are slowly cooked in a pit, as well as an 18-hour smoked prime rib roast. Other south Texas specialties include tons of slaw,

potato salad, beans, and BBQ brisket. Elaine Corn comments: "The best BBQ I've ever had."

Since its founding in Juárez in 1944, Julio's Café Corona (8050 Gateway East) has been a major force in border cookery. They are justly famous for their *salpicón* (see recipe, Chapter 8), and their green *mole* made from sunflower seeds, peanuts, chiles, radish leaves, and three pounds of bananas. Also great is their *cochinta pibíl,* the "state dish" of Yucatán—pork shredded in orange juice and *achiote.*

In Juárez, undoubtedly the most famous restaurant is Martino's (Nuevo Restaurante Martino), 417 Avenida Juárez. Martino's is the most "Continental" restaurant in Juárez, featuring a huge menu that offers many variations on classic dishes. Regional specialties include Boquilla black bass, *caldillo*, and *entrecote* Mexican-style. On the bulletin board is a Polaroid snapshot of me and wife-to-be Mary Jane cuddling in Martino's on one of our first dates. The service—provided by jacketed waiters who've been there since the Jurassic Period—is impeccable. Another excellent Juárez restaurant serving seafood is Villa del Mar, 1400 Avenida de las Americas. Some must-try suggestions include the *pulpo* and shrimp Villa del Mar.

Texas Food Celebrations

◆ *The Texas Hill Country Wine and Food Festival* is held in Austin in late March. It is the premier food and wine event in the state and includes the induction ceremony for the "Who's Who in Food and Wine in Texas" awards. www.texaswineandfood.org

◆ *Fiesta San Antonio* takes place along the Riverwalk in April. San Antonio's 10 day city-wide multi-cultural celebration features over 100 different events that include music, art, food, dance, parades and fun of all kinds. www.sanantonioriverwalk.com

◆ *Cinco de Mayo* celebrates the expulsion of the French from Mexico with food and fun, May 5, San Antonio Market Square. http://san.antonio.eventguide.com

◆ *Return of the Chili Queens*, a chili celebration on Memorial Day Weekend in Market Square in San Antonio. http://san.antonio.eventguide.com

◆ *St. Anthony's Day at Tigua Indian Reservation*, June 13th in El Paso offers traditional Native American fare. www.travel.state.tx.us

◆ *Republic of Texas Chilympiad*, third weekend in September, in San Marcos is the largest chili cookoff in the world. www.sanmarcos.net/chilympiad

◆ *Oktoberfest*, first Weekend in October in Fredericksburg, features a German Bier Tent, an Oktoberfest Vineyard area, plus delicious food and drink. www.oktoberfestinfbg.com/

◆ *Wurstfest*, actually the bestfest for sausage, happens in New Braunfels the first week in November. www.wurstfeStreetcom

◆ *World Championship BBQ Goat Cookoff* has been held every Labor Day Weekend since 1973 in Brady. These days, the event attracts upwards of 15,000 curious folks. www.bradytx.com/goat_cookoff_web/index.html

3. An Enchanted Feast: New Mexico

"The extravagant use of red pepper among the [New] Mexicans has become truly proverbial. It enters into nearly every dish at every meal, and often so predominates as entirely to conceal the character of the viands."

—Josiah Gregg,
The Commerce of the Prairies, 1844.

We can only hope that Josiah Gregg eventually built up a tolerance to spicy food and learned that rather than concealing the character of a meal, chile greatly enhances it—eliminating blandness while adding flavor. His opinion illustrates the typical collision of cultures that resulted from exploration and settlement of the Southwest by Spanish and Anglo cultures.

Peppers drying in the backyard of a grocery store, San Juan, New Mexico, 1928.

Photographer Irving Galloway

The Early Invasion of Old World Foods

Imagine Southwestern cuisine without beef, lamb, pork, chicken, cilantro, cumin, limes, onions, wheat bread, rice, beer, and wine. That's where New World cooking would be without the Old World, and it is particularly true of New Mexico.

The first and most obvious Old World influences on the cooking of the New were meats and grains. "Wherever Spaniards went, they took their livestock with them," notes John C. Super, an expert on colonial Latin American history. "Pigs, sheep, and cattle were as much a part of the conquest as Toledo steel and fighting mastiffs."

Herding sheep north of Santa Fe, c. 1979.

Photographer Dave DeWitt

Indeed they were. In fact, the introduction of live-stock was so successful that the animals thrived even when they escaped into the wild. Within a century after the arrival of Columbus, the estimated New World population of cattle was 800,000 and sheep an astonishing 4.6 million. With all that additional meat available, no wonder the cuisines of the Americas changed radically.

Wheat was also instrumental in changing the ways the Americas cooked. It was planted in such abundance throughout Mexico that by the middle of the fifteenth century, it was more common in the New World than in Spain, where wheat supplies had dropped and the people were eating rye bread. The same patterns repeated in New Mexico. Sheep were introduced by Juan de Oñate in 1598, and by the 1880s there were millions of sheep in New Mexico and about 500,000 a year were exported. Today, the number of sheep produced remains at about half a million.

The Columbus Exchange

Here is a basic list of Old World and New World foodstuffs. Some foods, such as coconuts, mushrooms, venison, fish, shellfish, crustaceans, ducks, rabbits, horseradish, and various beans and berries, are native to both worlds.

Old World Foods

Apples, bananas, barley, basil, beef, beer, beet, black pepper, cabbage, capers, celery, cheese, cherries, chicken, cilantro, cinnamon, citrus fruits, cucumber, cumin, eggplant, garlic, ginger, grapes, olives, onions, lamb, lettuce, melons, mint, mustard seed, nutmeg, parsley, peaches, peas, pistachios, plums, pork, rice, soybeans, spinach, turnips, wheat, wine.

New World Foods

Allspice, amaranth, avocados, bayleaf, brazil nuts, butternuts, cactus, cashews, cassava, cherimoyas, chile peppers, corn, culantro, guava, hickory nuts, lima beans, papayas, passionfruits, peanuts, pecans, pineapple, pinto beans, potatoes, pulque, pumpkins, quinoa, squash, strawberries, sweet potato, tamarillos, *tomatillos,* tomatoes, turkey, vanilla, walnuts.

It is not generally known that New Mexico, along with El Paso, are the two oldest wine-producing regions in the United States. A Franciscan friar, Augustín Rodríguez, is credited with bringing grape vines to southern New Mexico in 1580, about a hundred years before the friars in California planted their vineyards. By 1662, priests in the Mesilla Valley were regularly producing sacramental wine for Mass.

Winemaking gradually spread north, and grapes, wine, and brandy were common subjects in the reports of explorers and travelers to New Mexico. In 1846, a traveler and author (*El Gringo, or New Mexico and Her People*), W. H. H. Davis

commented about the Mesilla Valley to El Paso: "The most important production of the valley is grapes, from which are annually manufactured not less than two hundred thousand gallons of perhaps the richest and best wine in the world. This wine is worth two dollars per gallon, and constitutes the principal revenue of the city. Also, a great quantity of grapes of this valley are dried in clusters and preserved for use through the winter…. I regard them far superior to the best raisins that are imported the United States…."

But grapes were not the most important New Mexican crop. That honor goes to one of New Mexico's state "vegetables."

The Ubiquitous Chile

According to many accounts, chile peppers were introduced into what is now the U.S. by Capitan General Juan de Oñate, the founder of Santa Fe in 1598. However, they may have been introduced to the Pueblo Indians of New Mexico by the Antonio Espejo expedition of 1582-83. According to one of the members of the expedition, Baltasar Obregón, "They have no chile, but the natives were given some seed to plant." By 1601, chiles were not on the list of Indian crops, according to colonist Francisco de Valverde, who also complained that mice ate chile pods off the plants in the field.

After the Spanish began settlement, the cultivation of chile peppers exploded, and they were grown all over New Mexico. It is likely that many different

Chile pods on the plant.
Photographer Dave DeWitt

Not Everyone Liked Chile at First

Susan Magoffin, the teenaged bride of American trader and agent, Samuel Magoffin, wrote in her diary in 1846 about her first taste of New Mexican green chile stew: "Oh how my heart sickened to say nothing of my stomach…(from) a mixture of meat, chilly verde & onions boiled together completing course No. 1…. There were a few mouthfuls taken, for I could not eat a dish so strong, and unaccustomed to my palate."

However, Susan did become accustomed to spicy food and even wrote a "cookery book" so that her friends in the States (New Mexico was a territory, of course) could experience New Mexican cuisine.

varieties were cultivated, including early forms of *jalapeño*s, *serranos*, *anchos*, and *pasillas*. But one variety that adapted particularly well to New Mexico was a long green chile that turned red in the fall. Formerly called "Anaheim" because of its transfer to California around 1900, the New Mexican chiles were cultivated for hundreds of years in the region with such dedication that several land races developed. (Land Races are chile varieties grown in the same region for hundreds of years that acquire specialized flavor profiles.) These land races, called "*Chimayo*" and "*Española*," are varieties that adapted to particular environments and are still planted today in the same fields they were grown in centuries ago; they constitute a small but distinct part of tons of pods produced each year in New Mexico.

In 1846, William Emory, Chief Engineer of the Army's Topographic Unit, was surveying the New Mexico landscape and its customs. He described a meal eaten by people in Bernalillo, just north of Albuquerque: "Roast chicken, stuffed with onions; then mutton, boiled with onions; then followed various other dishes, all dressed with the everlasting onion; and the whole terminated by chile, the glory of New Mexico."

Emory went on to relate his experience with chiles: "Chile the Mexicans consider the chef-d'oeuvre of the cuisine, and seem really to revel in it; but the first mouthful brought the tears trickling down my cheeks, very much to the amusement of the spectators with their leather-lined throats. It was red pepper, stuffed with minced meat."

The earliest cultivated chiles in New Mexico were smaller than those of today; indeed, they were (and still are, in some cases) considered a spice. But as the land races developed and the size of the pods increased, the food value of chiles became evident. There was just one problem—the bewildering sizes and shapes of the chile peppers made it very difficult for farmers to determine which variety of chile they were growing from year to year. And, there was no way to tell how large the pods might be, or how hot. But modern horticultural techniques finally produced fairly standardized chiles.

Today, New Mexico is by far the largest commercial producer of chile peppers in the United States, with about 20,000 acres under cultivation that produce about 36,000 dry tons of chile peppers each year. California is in second place, Texas is third, and Arizona is fourth in chile pepper production. Also, about 10,000 metric tons of chiles are imported into the United States from major foreign producers such as Mexico, India, Pakistan, the Peoples Republic of China, South Korea, and Costa Rica.

All of the primary dishes in New Mexico cuisine contain chile peppers: sauces, stews, *carne adovada*, *enchiladas*, *posole*, *tamales*, *huevos rancheros*, and many combination vegetable dishes. The intense use of chiles as a food rather than just as a spice or condiment is what differentiates New Mexican cuisine from that of Texas or Arizona. In neighboring states, chile powders are used as a seasoning for beef or chicken broth-based "chili gravies," which are thickened with flour or cornstarch before they added to, say, *enchiladas*. In New Mexico, the

The Best Chili Debate Goes On and On

Regardless of geographical location, every cook in the Southwest has his or her own perfect recipe for chili. In 1969, *Life* magazine ran an article on Texas *chili con carne*, which prompted Arch Napier of Albuquerque to fire off a letter of protest.

"Sirs," he wrote, "you are giving this exciting food a bad name by linking it to the crude stuff served in Texas. Texas chili is a test of endurance, primarily useful for terrorizing tourists and fracturing oil wells. Last year, the Texans had a kind of chili cooking contest— conducted like a shoot-out—and it was publicized on the front page along with crimes and disasters. When New Mexico chili cuisine is discussed in our newspapers, it is usually carried on the Art and Music pages."

sauces are made from pure chiles and are thickened by reducing the crushed or pureed pods.

New Mexico chile *sauces* are cooked and pureed, while salsas utilize fresh ingredients and are uncooked. Debates rage over whether tomatoes are used in cooked sauces such as red chile sauce for *enchiladas*. Despite the recipes in numerous cookbooks (presumably none of whose authors live in New Mexico), traditional cooked red sauces do *not* contain tomatoes, though uncooked salsas do.

Carne adovada, pork marinated in red chiles and then baked, is one of the most popular New Mexican entrees. Another is *enchiladas*; in fact, there are so many variations on *enchiladas* that cooks soon determine their favorites through experimentation.

New Mexicans love chile peppers so much that they have become the *de facto* state symbol. Houses are adorned with strings of dried red chiles, called *ristras*. Images of the pods are emblazoned on signs, tee-shirts, coffee mugs, posters, windsocks, and even underwear. In the late summer and early fall, the aroma of roasting chiles fills the air all over the state and produces a state of bliss for chileheads.

"*A la primera cocinera se le va un chile entero*," goes one old Spanish adage: "To the best lady cook goes the whole chile."

Chile is recognized as a New Mexico State Vegetable, but in reality it is a fruit. The other State Vegetable, the pinto bean, is a legume, not a vegetable!

The Two State "Vegetables"

In 1965, the New Mexico State Legislature was locked in a bitter struggle, with the pinto bean growers on one side and the chile pepper producers on the other. Each group was lobbying fiercely for their crop to be named the official state vegetable. New Mexico politics being what they are, there was only one real solution: name them both as state co-vegetables.

The only problem, agronomists and horticulturists point out, is that neither beans nor chiles are vegetables. Beans are legumes, like the peanut (which is not a nut), and chiles are fruits.

The politicians didn't care. If it's eaten like a vegetable, a vegetable it must be, they reasoned. Well, beans are beans, but chiles are a bit more complicated. Botanically, they're berries. Horticulturally, they're fruits. When used in their green form, the produce industry calls them vegetables. When dried in their red form, they're a spice. No wonder the politicians got confused.

The Later Invasion of Old World Foods

Unlike livestock, imported grains such as wheat were not immediately successful in New Mexico. Corn was still raised in small plots by both Hispanics and Native Americans, but wheat and other crops did not flourish until the arrival of the railroads. In fact, agriculture was so primitive in the region that one writer, Antonio Barreiro, noted in 1832: "Agriculture is utterly neglected, for the inhabitants of this country do not sow any amount, as they might do to great profit without any doubt. They sow barely what they consider necessary for their maintenance for part of the year, and the rest of the year they are exposed to a thousand miseries."

The situation improved shortly after the U.S. Army raised the American flag over the Palace of the Governors in Santa Fe in 1846, and New Mexico was opened up to further settlement by American pioneers. The introduction of modern tools and techniques and new crops such as apples, peas, melons, and others helped the farmers greatly. By 1900, more than five million acres were under cultivation in New Mexico. Gradually, wheat production surpassed corn in the state. In 1987, corn production was 7.6 million bushels while wheat was 10.8 million bushels. However, wheat tortillas have not totally supplanted corn tortillas.

Cattle had been introduced by Oñate but did not assume a significant role in New Mexico until after Civil War. Soon after the great cattle drives to the New Mexico gold mines, there were 1.34 million head of cattle in the state in 1890. Remarkably, the figures nearly a hundred years later (1988) were almost identical—1.32 million head.

Fabian Garcia in a cornfield with 14-foot-high stalks, southern New Mexico, c. 1914.

After the Homestead Act of 1862 and the arrival of the railroad between 1879 and 1882, settlers from the eastern U.S. flooded into the state. The railroad also led to the first railroad restaurants, the Harvey House chain. New Mexico boasted sixteen of these establishments, including five that were the grandest of the system: Montezuma and Castañeda in Las Vegas, La Fonda in Santa Fe, Alvarado in Albuquerque, and El Navajo in Gallup. Harvey hired young women between the ages of eighteen and thirty to be his hostesses and they were quite an attraction on the western frontier, where women were scarce. The humorist Will Rogers once said, "Fred Harvey kept the West in food and wives." He also commented that the Rio Grande was only river that he had ever seen that needed irrigating.

The Harvey Houses attempted to bring "civilized" food to the frontier, and early menus reveal dishes such as chicken croquettes, baron of beef, turkey stuffed with oysters, vermicelli with cheese al la Italian, and the ever-delectable calf's brains scrambled with ranch eggs. "Mexican" food was considered too "native" for travelers and rarely appeared on the hotel and restaurant menus.

The railroads brought the settlers and these pioneers brought with them new food crops. At first, vegetables such as tomatoes, asparagus, cabbage, carrots, lettuce, onions, and peas were produced in home gardens on a small scale, but after extensive irrigation facilities were constructed shortly after the turn of the 20th century, commercial vegetable production began.

In addition to these vegetables, several other notable crops appeared, namely fruits and nuts. Although the nuts were relatively new to the area, fruit growing was actually a rejuvenation of a very old enterprise—wine-making.

The European grapes that had been established in southern New Mexico in the seventeeth century did well, and, by the 1800s wine was being produced from the Mexican border to Bernalillo, which was the heart of wine production. By the middle of the nineteenth century, New Mexico was producing more wine than California and, in 1880, produced just under a million gallons. But a series of natural, economic, and political disasters ruined the wine industry.

First, there was the flood of 1897, which was followed by a severe drought. Soon after these discouraging developments, grape growers discovered that cotton was far more profitable. Finally, Prohibition completely wiped out what was left of the wine industry and New Mexico grape growing fell from 3,150 acres to a mere eight.

But during the 1970s and Eighties, the wine industry in New Mexico made a dramatic recovery. Spurred by foreign investment from the French, Italians, Germans, and Swiss, new vineyards have been planted all over the state, and the total acreage now approaches 5,000 and total wine volume produced is about 400,000 gallons. New Mexico now has about thirty-five wineries in production, numerous wine festivals, and has finally rediscovered part of its heritage.

A similar situation occurred with apples. Although they have been grown in New Mexico since the early 1600s, extensive cultivation did not really begin until after the Americans arrived. Today, apples are grown in the Mimbres and Ruidoso valleys in the southern part of the state and between Santa Fe and Taos in the northern part.

One of the most famous apple growers in New Mexico is Fred Dixon, who moved to the state in the early 1940s. He took over a former dude ranch in northern New Mexico and transformed it into very productive orchards that featured his own patented varieties, Champagne and Standard Winesap. The only problem with apples is that when an early spring frost hits the apple blossoms, the crop is ruined. For example, in 1988 the apple crop was ten million pounds, and a year later, it was only half that figure.

Other tree crops which have prospered in the state are pecans and pistachios. The largest nut industry in New Mexico is pecan growing, as evidenced by the huge pecan forests (actually groves) that stretch north and south of Las Cruces. The trees were introduced from Texas and northern Mexico and first planted at the Fabian Garcia Agricultural Science Center in Mesilla in 1915 and 1916. The original planting was just four acres, and many of those trees are still producing.

The first recorded commercial pecan production in the state was in 1920, when a mere 626 pounds were harvested. Pecans did not enjoy much popularity in New Mexico until the 1960s, when the orchards totaled 6,000 acres. It takes a lot of room to grow pecans, and that's why there are more than 25,000 acres with about 1.3 million trees in New Mexico, an average of about fifty-two trees per acre. By contrast, Texas has well over seventy million pecan trees, but most of them are wild. There is a saying that "Texans will buy anything with pecans in it," which bodes well for the New Mexico crop. In 1986, 27 million pounds of pecans were produced in New Mexico, about ten percent of total U.S. production. Twenty years later, 46 million pounds of pecans were produced in 2006, and growers in New Mexico rejoiced at the title of America's Number One pecan producer.

Also in the shell game of nut growing in New Mexico are pistachios. They thrive in the Tularosa Basin because the climate and altitude is quite similar to that of Iran and Turkey, noted pistachio growing regions. Pistachios are smaller trees than pecans, growing only about thirty feet tall, so many more trees can be planted per acre, about 120. They are hardy, tolerant of drought and alkaline soils, and can live to be hundreds of years old.

The primary pistachio grower in New Mexico is Eagle Ranch Pistachio Groves in Alamogordo, which markets the tasty nuts under the brand name "Heart of the Desert." Eagle Ranch is owned by Marianne and George Schweers, who started their groves in 1974 with 200 two-year-old trees. They

now have more than 3,000 trees and can harvest as much as 1,800 pounds an acre.

The Alamogordian pistachios are marketed in small designer burlap bags and sold by mail order and in gift shops. They are touted as "health nuts" because they are cholesterol-free, high in fiber, and low in saturated fats. They are a snack food that is also used in pates and sausages, are the greenish ingredient in pistachio ice cream, and can be substituted for other nuts in cooking. In fact, they make an excellent pesto if *piñon* nuts cannot be found.

The appearance of the newer food crops, together with experimentation by talented chefs, has led to the development of what is called "New Southwest" cuisine. Some of the tenets of this style of cooking are the use of fresh, locally-produced crops, the elimination of fattening or high cholesterol ingredients, the regular appearance of more exotic chiles (rather than just the usual New Mexican varieties), and a dedication to the beautiful presentation of the meal. Another tenet is the use of game and indigenous crops, which, of course, returns us to pre-Columbian times. In fact, there is a quite a bit of the oldest Southwest in New Southwest Cuisine.

"Southwestern cuisine today is frozen in time," says Mark Miller of Santa Fe's Coyote Cafe. "It neither looks to the past nor progresses into the future. In New Mexico, for instance, most people think the 'traditional' foods can be traced back only a few generations to the Spanish, when in reality the food tradition extends all the way back to the ancient Anasazi culture."

Although disconcerting to some, the innovations of the New Southwest chefs are fully in keeping with historical tradition—the interaction of various cultures with different ideas of what constitutes Southwestern cookery. In New Mexico, the traditional cuisine based upon corn, beans, squash, and chile will probably be cooked for centuries to come with little or no change. But that fact doesn't mean that all the cooking of New Mexico will remain static.

Traditional New Mexican cuisine today enjoys a rich heritage that has evolved from Native American, Mexican, and European sources. Despite its uniqueness, it's only during the past 25 years that it has achieved the fame it justly deserves—perhaps due to tourism and a resurgent interest in ethnic cuisines. In addition to its traditional elements, the cuisine of the state will continue to evolve as long as innovative chefs create new combinations of the foods being produced around them.

Las Cruces, Home of the Chiles

New Mexico's second largest city is current undergoing a transition from farming community to metropolitan area, which is reflected in the fact that Las Cruces has been in the top ten fastest-growing regions of the country for several years now. Although there are still chile, onion, and cotton fields within the city limits, residents fear the loss of their rural identity.

Early Spanish settlements in the area did not begin at the Las Cruces site. The little town of Doña Ana, north of Las Cruces, was first settled in 1839. Ten years later, the first buildings were erected in Las Cruces, and Mesilla, south of Las Cruces, was founded shortly afterward because of a set of unusual circumstances.

In 1846, the United States declared war on Mexico and claimed New Mexico as its own. When American troops moved into the Mesilla Valley in 1848, half the populations of Doña Ana and Las Cruces

Seven men sacking chile peppers, Mesilla Valley, c. 1925.

Photographer unknown

founded Mesilla, which was still in Mexico because it was then across the Rio Grande. Mesilla remained in Mexico and Las Cruces in the Territory of New Mexico until 1854, when Mexico sold

30,000 square miles of land to the U.S. during the Gadsden Purchase. On July 4, 1854, the purchase was celebrated in the Plaza at Mesilla, but many of the residents missed it because they had moved even further south in order to remain Mexican citizens. It is unlikely they would do the same today.

Mesilla flourished despite the departure of many of its citizens and soon became a booming town of 5,000—larger than both Las Cruces and El Paso. In fact, for a while, Mesilla was the largest city west of San Antonio. Part of its success was due to the fact that Mesilla was chosen as a major station along the 2,800-mile-long Butterfield Stage route from St. Louis to San Francisco.

Mesilla briefly became the capital of the Confederate Territory of Arizona in 1861 and headquarters for the Rebels' military governor of the southwest, Lt. Col. John Robert Baylor. But the town was retaken by Union forces from California thirteen months later. In 1863, nature played a cruel trick on Mesilla as the Rio Grande shifted course and turned the town into an island.

During the 1870s, Mesilla was occasionally the scene of violence. In 1871 rival Democratic and Republican factions started a bloody riot on the Plaza, leaving nine dead and 50 wounded, and in 1880 Mesilla was the site of the first trial of Billy the Kid. He was found guilty of murder, sentenced to hang, but escaped and later participated in the Lincoln County War.

When the Santa Fe Railroad selected Las Cruces rather than Mesilla for its route in 1881, Mesilla declined in importance as a Territorial city. Las Cruces soon became the commercial center of the Mesilla Valley, which was a fertile agricultural region. Farmers grew pecans, onions, alfalfa, vegetables, and of course, the famous New Mexico chile peppers.

There are some interesting historical sights in the area. The Old Armijo House, on Lohman Avenue, is over 120 years old and has been restored and decorated with original furnishings. Another famous site is the Amador Hotel, one of the earliest buildings in town at Amador and Water Streets, which was built in 1850 by Don Martin Amador and has been a hotel, post office, jail, and courthouse. As a hotel, the Amador hosted such luminaries as Pat Garrett, Billy the Kid, and the Mexican president Benito Juárez. It now houses the Dona Ana County offices, but special rooms upstairs have been restored with period furniture and artifacts.

The Branigan Cultural Center, in the Downtown Mall, houses artifacts from nearby Fort Selden and produces shows by local artists and crafts persons. The center also presents lectures, concerts, and performing arts. The facility has a gallery, museum, and an auditorium. An interesting sight downtown at Water and Lohman Avenues is El Molino, a grinding wheel from an 1853 flour mill, which commemorates the work and hardships of the early settlers.

At New Mexico State University, south of University Avenue, there are several museums and galleries worth visiting. The University Museum, in Kent Hall has displays of artifacts from prehistoric and historic Native American cultures of the region, plus traveling shows and art exhibits. The University Art Gallery, in Williams Hall offers monthly exhibits of historical and contemporary art, plus a permanent collection of prints, photographs, and folk art. Visitors interested in the latest advancements in science and technology will be fascinated by the Southwest Residential Experiment Station, which has eight working solar photovoltaic prototypes on display. There's a visitor center and guided tours can be arranged.

For food lovers, the New Mexico Farm and Ranch Heritage Museum is a must-visit. It is located on Dripping Springs Road just off Interstate 25 in Las Cruces; take the University Exit (Exit 1) and go east 1.5 miles. The museum is 47 acres packed with real stories about real people. Working the land has been a key ingredient in the cultural mosaic of New Mexico for many generations, uniquely blending farming and ranching methods from Indian, Spanish and Anglo cultures. The interactive museum brings to life the 3,000-year history of farming and ranching in New Mexico. The museum's main building—named for former governor Bruce King—contains more than 24,000 square feet of exhibit space, along with the Museum Grill, Eagle Ranch Gift Shoppe and a theater. Fun and learning go hand-in-hand as visitors can watch a cow being milked, stroll along corrals filled with livestock, enjoy several gardens and orchards or drop by the blacksmith shop or another venue to watch one of the growing number of demonstrations.

Mesilla, also called La Mesilla and Old Mesilla, is a charming village that retains much of the feel of Spanish colonial days. A major tourism center much like Albuquerque's Old Town, Mesilla (located southwest of Las Cruces on Avenida de Mesilla) has restaurants, shops, galleries, and a museum. The Plaza, site of celebrations and riots, has been well preserved over the years and serves as the center of town. The San Albino Mission, with its twin towers, adjoins the Plaza. It was founded in 1851 by Fray Ramon Ortiz. The Gadsden Museum on Barker Road has displays of artifacts and relics relating to the turbulent history of Mesilla.

Redesigning Chile Peppers

In 1888, the founding of the New Mexico College of Agriculture and Mechanical Arts ushered in a new era for the Las Cruces area. The college, which later became New Mexico State University with the world's largest campus (6,250 acres), assisted in bringing Las Cruces into the modern age by educating the youth of New Mexico; researchers assisted local growers with the latest techniques in horticultural science.

The most immediate problem was chile peppers — there was no control at all over what seeds were planted, so farmers could never predict how large the pods would be—or how hot. The demand for chiles was increasing as the population of the state did, so it was time for modern horticulture to take over.

In 1907, Fabian Garcia, a horticulturist at the Agricultural Experiment Station at the College of Agriculture and Mechanical Arts, began his first experiments in breeding more standardized chile varieties, and, in 1908, published "Chile Culture," the first chile bulletin from the Agricultural Experiment Station. In 1913, Garcia became director of the Experiment Station and expanded his breeding program.

Finally, in 1917, after ten years of experiments with various strains of *pasilla* chiles, Garcia released New

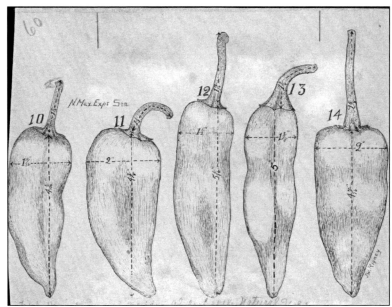

Drawings of variations of chile pods,
New Mexico Experimental Station, 1914.

Fabian Garcia.

Mexico No. 9, the first attempt to grow chiles with a dependable pod size and heat level. The No. 9 variety became the chile standard in New Mexico until 1950, when Roy Harper, another horticulturist, released New Mexico No. 6, a variety which matured earlier, produced higher yields, was wilt resistant, and less pungent than No. 9.

The New Mexico No. 6 variety was by far the biggest breakthrough in the chile-breeding program. According to the late Dr. Roy Nakayama, who succeeded Harper as director of the New Mexico Agricultural Experiment Station, "The No. 6 variety changed the image of chile from a ball of fire that sent consumers rushing to the water jug to that of a multi-purpose vegetable with a pleasing flavor. Photovoltaic production and marketing, especially of green chiles and sauces, have been growing steadily since people around the world have discovered the delicious taste of chile without the overpowering pungency."

In 1957, the New Mexico No. 6 variety was modified, made even less pungent, and the new variety was called New Mexico No. 6-4. The No. 6-4 variety became the chile industry standard in New Mexico and over fifty years later is still the most popular chile commercially grown in the state. Other chile varieties, such as *Nu Mex Big Jim* and *NuMex R-Naky*, have been developed but became popular mostly with home gardeners.

Today, Dr. Paul Bosland, who took over the chile-breeding program from Dr. Nakayama, is developing new varieties that are resistant to chile wilt, a fungal disease that can devastate fields. He has also created varieties to produce brown, orange, and yellow *ristras* for the home decoration market. The breeding and development of new chile varieties—in addition to research into wild species, post-harvest packaging, and genetics—is an on-going, major project at New Mexico State.

Visitors to the region are often eager to visit the chile fields and watch harvesting in progress. Such excursions are possible, but don't be disappointed to find that, for the most part, the only thing happening is chiles growing—except, of course, during the Whole *Enchilada* Fiesta in Las Cruces or the Hatch Chile Festival.

The best way to tour the chile fields is to take a drive north from Las Cruces on Highway 185 (the back way) to Hatch, and then proceed further north on Highway 187 through the chile-growing towns of Salem, Garfield, Derry, and Arrey. Signs will point the way to chile farms on the side roads. During the winter, of course, you will see only fallow fields (except for some onions or lettuce), but in the summer months there are thousands of acres planted in chile and cotton. During chile harvesting (late July-September for green, October-December for red), you will see teams of pickers roaming through the fields carrying buckets full of green chiles or *jalapeños*, which are then dumped into large, wooden-sided carts. Photography is permitted from a distance, but do not trespass, interfere with the pickers, or take any chiles yourself. The pungent pods are available by the bushel from roadside stands.

Chile sign in the Mesilla Valley.
Photographer Dave DeWitt

The Department of Plant and Environmental Sciences at NMSU will, on occasion, conduct tours of their greenhouses, laboratories, and acres of exotic chile plants by appointment only—and usually only for people who have some professional connection to botany, horticulture, or food manufacturing. The Chile Pepper Institute grows a chile demonstration garden each year with hundreds of varieties from all over the world. Contact them at hotchile@nmsu.edu for more information.

Wining and Dining in the Lower Rio Grande Valley

My favorite winery in the area is St. Clair Winery & Bistro, 1800 Avenida de Mesilla in Mesilla. I usually drink their St. Clair Cab-Zin when having their spicy Pasta Danielle. The best beer I've had in Las Cruces is at the High Desert Brewing Company, 1201 W. Hadley Avenue. They specialize in ales, like Wheat Ale, Peach Wheat, India Pale Ale, Anniversary Ale, Irish Red Ale and Amber Ale.

Without question, the most famous restaurant in the area is La Posta ("The Mail Station"), just off the Plaza in Mesilla. Built as a stage station along the Butterfield Overland Mail Route, this building is over 175 years old and has been a restaurant since 1939. In fact, it is one of two way stations on the entire stage route still serving visitors—the rest were burned to the ground by Apaches. Several dining rooms in the sprawling complex feature authentic New Mexican foods (try the *tostada compuesta*) amidst plants, tropical birds, and stage-coach artifacts. Because it serves so many tourists, its chile specialties tend to be milder than usual, so chileheads should request their sauces extra-spicy.

Chope's Bar and Café, sixteen miles south of Las Cruces on Highway 28 in La Mesa, has been in business for more than 75 years. Chope's is legendary in southern New Mexico as the watering hole for politicians, university professors, and chileheads who appreciate the hot chile that is grown nearby.

Historic La Posta Restaurant in La Mesilla.
Photographer Dave DeWitt

Everything is excellent, but especially try the *chiles rellenos* and the *enchiladas*.

Stahmann's Country Store (Highway 28 South of Mesilla), in the middle of a vast pecan orchard, sells the Del Cerro brand of pecans grown by the Stahmann orchard plus twenty-five different kinds of candy—most of which, naturally, features pecans. As might be expected, there are chile-flavored pecans and pecan brittle. The store also carries gift items.

The legendary Owl Bar, nine miles south of Socorro on U.S. Hwy. 380 in San Antonio, open since 1945, is a compulsory stop on the trip from Albuquerque to Las Cruces or El Paso. In the parking lot, a BMW will be parked between a Harley and a pickup—a sure sign of the diversity of the clientele. Sure, you can order a variety of New Mexican foods, but the specialty of the house is a green chile cheeseburger, so have one of those with green chile cheese fries and a Dos Equis. Heaven. You might run into anyone at The Owl, from Sen. Pete Domenici to beauty pageant hopefuls to the local basketball team to bird watchers from nearby Bosque del Apache Wildlife Refuge to tourists from the Peoples' Republic of China, Germany, or Israel.

Peppers Café, on the Plaza in Mesilla, is set in an old adobe house that's on the National Register of Historic Places. It is atypical of the area in that New Mexican specialties take a back seat to innovative hot and spicy dishes using *poblano* and *chipotle* chiles. Its unique entrees include *chile molido*

spit-roasted chicken, shark *fajitas* (occasionally), Mexican wontons, spicy baby back ribs, and banana *enchiladas* for dessert. There is a small retail store in the front of the restaurant. The indoor patio is intimate and warm.

Roberto's Mexican Food (908 East Amador) has been selling tortillas since 1968 and opened as a full-fledged restaurant in 1987. They serve the usual New Mexican dishes and specialize in tamales, *burritos*, and *gorditas*, which they make by stuffing fresh corn dough with either beans or a combination of beef, lettuce, and tomato, and then frying them. The owner of Roberto's, Robert Estrada, is the maker of The World's Largest *Enchilada* annually at the Whole *Enchilada* Festival. He designed the special equipment used in the making the *enchilada*, including the press, the carrying plate, the cooking vat, and the serving plate. The ingredients are:

❖ 750 pounds of stone-ground corn to make the tortillas

❖ 175 gallons of vegetable oil, heated, to cook the tortillas

❖ 75 gallons of red chile sauce

❖ 175 pounds of grated cheese

❖ 50 pounds chopped onions

It takes fourteen men and two hours to prepare The World's Largest *Enchilada*, which is served free to the festival crowd.

Duke City Dinners

As a metropolis of more than a half million people in the center of a vast state with a small rural population, Albuquerque, the "Duke City," has often been forgotten by tourists and criticized by other cities in New Mexico for its size and its supposed emphasis on sprawling growth, freeways, and commerce rather than history or the arts. But the real Albuquerque is a city that cares about all aspects of its culinary, historical, cultural, and natural environments.

The city was named in honor of Don Francisco Fernandez de la Cueva Enriquez, Eighth Duke of Alburquerque (the extra "r" was later dropped) and Viceroy of New Spain. The name Albuquerque is said to be a corruption of *albus quercus*, or "white

oak" in Latin. The Dukedom of Alburquerque still exists, and visits by the current Spanish Duke are always the height of the social season in this city.

Albuquerque was founded in 1706 on the spot where Old Town Plaza is today by families from nearby Bernalillo. One of the first buildings was the San Felipe de Neri Church (rebuilt in 1793), which is an interesting blend of Spanish colonial, gothic, and Pueblo revival architectural styles. It is open to the public for visits and prayers. Albuquerque soon became a major trade center along the Camino Real de Tierra Adentro ("Royal Road of the Interior"), the main road from Mexico City to El Paso del Norte to Santa Fe, also called the Chihuahua Trail.

In her 1947 book, *Albuquerque*, Erna Fergusson discussed the long tradition of New Mexican cooking, which stretched back to the early days of the settlement of the town. "The larder was limited. Beef, mutton, pork and fowl were varied by game and dried buffalo meat from the plains. Vegetables grew but were used in sauces and gravies rather than alone. Fruit was eaten fresh in its short season, and dried on wide trays for storing. Corn was used in every way, from soup to desserts, and the lowly brown bean appeared at every meal. Chile grew in every man's garden

Second Street looking south from Central Avenue, Albuquerque, c. 1910.

Photographer Thomas K. Todsen

and was the only condiment. A limited diet, but good cooks invented many a savory combination and the modern epicure rates New Mexican cookery—when properly done—with the best."

During the Indian wars and Civil War in New Mexico, Albuquerque became a principal supply center for the forts being built all over the Southwest, and warehousing became an important business. In the early to mid-1800s, the area around Albuquerque was the largest sheep-growing district in the state, which meant that mutton was a large part of the diet. Subsistence farming was common on small parcels of land in the north and south valleys and extra fruit and vegetables were peddled to the nearby pueblos. There was a cattle boom after the Civil War and particularly during the 1880s, and beef replaced mutton as the most common meat served in Albuquerque.

The railroad arrived in Albuquerque in 1881, transforming it into the trade center of the entire state. Another settlement two miles east of the Old Town Plaza was dubbed "New Town" and now serves as the downtown area. Principal industries at the turn of the century were wool, livestock, alfalfa, and lumber.

The hot spot in town soon became the Alvarado Hotel. This magnificent structure, which opened in 1902 at a cost of $200,000—a huge amount

Dining Room, Alvarado Hotel, 1904.
Photographer Louis Charles McClure

then— was considered to be the "finest railroad hotel on earth" and was hotel magnate Fred Harvey's ultimate lodging creation. Located along the railroad tracks facing First Street, the Spanish Mission-style Alvarado featured eighty-eight guest rooms, a gigantic dining room, Spanish-tiled roofs, swimming pools, many patios with cascading fountains, and the beautiful "Harvey Girls," who were the hostesses and served "all you could eat" New Mexican food for one dollar.

The hotel was named after Hernando de Alvarado, Commander of Artillery in Coronado's great

Southwest expedition. Charles F. Whittlesey designed the hotel and Mary Elizabeth Colter decorated the Indian building, a museum and store located next to the hotel.

Many celebrities stayed at the Alvarado: Rudolph Valentino, Albert Einstein, Charles Lindbergh, Joan Crawford, Katherine Hepburn, and Jack Benny, to name just a few. U.S. Presidents selecting the Alvarado included William H. Taft (who got stuck in the bathtub), Herbert Hoover, Woodrow Wilson, Franklin D. Roosevelt, and Theodore Roosevelt.

The Alvarado fell on hard times when serious competition—like the first Hilton Hotel—opened up. Eventually, the Alvarado was abandoned and despite efforts to preserve this historic site, it could not be saved and one of Albuquerque's architectural masterpieces—as well as a significant part of the city's history—was torn down in 1970. A train station, built in a similar style, has now replaced the original hotel.

Sightseeing and Food

There's much to do and see in Albuquerque. The Albuquerque Museum (2000 Mountain Road in Old Town) has assembled the largest collection of Spanish colonial artifacts in the U.S. and utilizes it as a centerpiece for a permanent exhibit entitled "Four Centuries: a History of Albuquerque." The New Mexico Museum of Natural History (1801 Mountain Road NW) is a two-minute walk from Old Town and traces the 4.6 billion-year geology, paleontology, botany, and zoology of the region. The Maxwell Museum of Anthropology, off University, two blocks north of Central, has great displays of Indian artifacts and explains the human habitation of the area.

The Sandia Mountains rise five thousand feet above Albuquerque and remain preserved as Cibola National Forest and the Sandia Wilderness Area, so within fifteen miles of downtown are golden eagles, black bears, and mountain sheep. It's fun to take the Sandia Peak Tramway, the world's longest tram, up to the top of the mountain, where you'll find a ski area, wildlife, great views, and a bar and restaurant.

The Rio Grande Nature Center (2901 Candelaria NW) has interesting exhibits and walking tours of the *bosque*, the twenty-mile cottonwood tree forest that lines both sides of the Rio Grande. The Rio Grande Zoological Park (903 10th Street SW) is one of the finest zoos in the country and offers such interesting exhibits as Cat Walk with its cheetah run, Jungle Habitat with exotic birds, and Ape Country. Recently opened Petroglyph National Monument, west of Coors Road on Unser Boulevard, protects the artistic rock carvings that are thousands of years old.

New Mexico Food Events

◆ *National Fiery Foods & Barbecue Show*, first weekend in March in Albuquerque. The most popular food show in the Southwest has been delighting chileheads for more than twenty years. www.fiery-foods.com/shows.asp

◆ *Hatch Chile Festival*, Hatch, Labor Day Weekend, is a celebration of chile in a county fair atmosphere. www.hatchchilefest.com

◆ *New Mexico Wine Festival*, Bernalillo, Labor Day Weekend, is the largest of many wine festivals in the state. www.newmexicowinefestival.com

◆ *New Mexico State Fair*, Albuquerque, early September, offers many different styles of food. Try the smoked turkey legs. www.exponm.com

◆ *Santa Fe Wine and Chile Fiesta,* late September, offers samplings of wine and food from the best restaurants in Santa Fe. www.santafewineandchile.org

◆ *Whole Enchilada Fiesta*, Las Cruces, early October, features the making of the World's Largest Enchilada. www.enchiladafiesta.com

◆ *Harvest Festival*, El Rancho de Las Golondrinas at La Cienega, early October, spotlights native foods. www.golondrinas.org

Besides the malls, two shopping areas come to mind. The first is Old Town (Central and Rio Grande), which has twenty-five galleries and about fifty shops that offer everything from chile peppers to turquoise jewelry. The other is the University-Nob Hill area from the 2000 to 4000 blocks of east Central. There are fashion shops, bookstores, record shops, cafes, restaurants, and other delights along this strip.

The food scene in Albuquerque is incredibly varied. In addition to an extraordinary number of restaurants serving New Mexican dishes, most of the other world cuisines are well represented—especially those famous for serving up hot and spicy dishes. There are many Chinese restaurants serving Sichuan and Hunan dishes, several Thai and East Indian restaurants, and several hot and spicy barbecue joints. Foodies will love the markets and shops in Albuquerque. The markets have chiles galore plus other Mexican and Southwestern ingredients. There are shops devoted just to chile peppers, and most of the specialty food stores carry Southwestern foods as well as cookbooks.

Chile Traditions (8204 Montgomery NE) is a shop that specializes is all things chile-related, and it carries an incredible collection of salsas, hot sauces, and other condiments. It ships frozen green chile *ristras*, and red chile pods year-round and also carries non-food chile items such as ceramics and clothing. Chile Patch USA (204-B San Felipe NW) has an excellent selection of New Mexico chile products and a very complete hot sauce selection. Bueno Foods is the largest food manufacturer in

Swayze's Dinner Bell, on U.S. 66 in Albuquerque, c. 1940.

Photographer Thomas K. Todsen

the state, and their Bueno Foods Factory Store (2001 Fourth Street SW) is dwarfed by their huge processing plant, but you can find red chile powders and pods, blue corn meal, packaged spices and herbs, and their frozen green chile and entrees. Ta Lin Supermarket (230 Louisiana Blvd. SE) is an Asian-oriented market but also has an astounding collection of Latin American foodstuffs, including all the unusual, hard-to-find specialty items like guava paste, mango pickles, taro, and seven different kinds of bananas. Their collection of worldwide hot sauces is not to be believed. Think you're going to escape hot and spicy food by going to an Italian market? No way. Tully's Meat Market (1425-A San Mateo NE) has a great *putanesca* sandwich and a delicious *pannino*, which combines sausage, cheese, and green chile all baked together.

Bread sculptor Pat "Hot Buns" Morales, owner of the Golden Crown Panadería (1103 Mountain Road NW) has created a bull-shaped bread for an investment firm, a B-52 bomber for a party, a castle for the Duke of Albuquerque, and a three-breasted French woman (mythological, of course) for a gift, so you can trust his chile pepper-shaped bread that he ships out by UPS. When visiting in person, try the green chile bread (you may have to call for it in advance) or any other Mexican bakery item—*bolillos*, yum.

New Mexico wines are becoming more and more popular, and Albuquerque has two notable wineries. Anderson Valley Vineyards (4920 Rio Grande NW) specializes in Chardonnay and Cabernet Sauvignon Reserve. There is a wine room here that's available for special events, plus a gift shop. Gruet Winery (8400 Pan American Freeway N.E) makes great sparkling wines, specializing in Brut and Blanc de Noirs, made by Methode Champenoise. There is a tasting room here and you can buy the wine by the bottle or case. They produce about

80,000 cases of wine every year and are distributed in 47 states.

My favorite Albuquerque brewery is the Chama River Brewing Company, 4939 Pan American Freeway NE. Their Rio Chama Amber Ale is highly recommended, and I've also enjoyed their Broken Spoke Honey Wheat Ale and Jack Rabbit IPA. For dinner, I recommend their Chama-churri steak, which is a *Chimichurri*-marinated prime rib steak, accompanied by green chile polenta and baby carrots.

I'm going to start the restaurant recommendations with the earthiest ones, like The Frontier Restaurant, 2400 Central SE. Here it is, the people zoo of Albuquerque—and it's open all night! You're likely to see everyone from the TV news anchorman to a professor of semiotics to a self-proclaimed medicine man here. Breakfast—quick and spicy but served cafeteria-style—is available all day and night long, and their Western hash browns with cheddar cheese and green chile with ranchero sauce is recommended. Grandma's K and I Diner (2500 Broadway SE) is a charmingly madcap diner and the home of "The Travis Mexican Special," Grandma Warner's own style of *burritos* smothered in red and green chile that will serve an entire family of four for under $10. Some customers have been so intimidated they have ordered a "one-eighth Travis." Grandma serves up about fifteen gallons of green chile and 400 pounds of french fries a day here, which is a testament to her popularity. The Original Garcia's Kitchen (1113 4th Street NW) is the kitsch capital of the Southwest, with the most ridiculous decorations

The Meaning of "Mexican"

Albuquerque has nearly one hundred Mexican restaurants listed in the Yellow Pages, and all but three do not serve Mexican food at all, but rather *New Mexican* meals. The locals make that distinction in order to avoid being accused of serving the kind of American Mexican food found, say, in Baltimore.

It's interesting to note that national restaurant chains that specialize in Mexican food have not fared well in Albuquerque. Both Chi Chi's and Garcia's of Scottsdale failed in the city because their versions of Mexican were too bland for local palates. The only chain which has flourished is Taco Bell, but their success is the result of fast, cheap food rather than great Mexican cuisine.

El Pinto's beautiful patio.

Photographer Josh Costanza.

imaginable, including a mechanical monkey on a tightrope. I love it, and I love their *carne adovada*, green chile stew, homemade flour tortillas, and *biscochitos*, the official New Mexico State Cookie.

There are so many New Mexican restaurants in Albuquerque that the visitor can easily become bewildered. I have limited my choices to restaurants that have been around for at least twenty years and have superior food. Cervantes Restaurant and Lounge (5801 Gibson Boulevard SE) was established in 1975 by Roberta Finley, and she still owns it. The restaurant features her original, award-winning recipes for red and green chiles sauces and three salsas. All the food there is made fresh daily, and here's an unusual note: on St. Patrick's Day, they serve the best corned beef and cabbage in town! Los Cuates (4901 Lomas NE) is named "The Twins" because of Frank Barela's own twins; this highly-regarded New Mexican

restaurant is appreciated because of the complimentary salsa and because of its excellent *carne adovada* and *chiles rellenos*. Now we have chile combined with drugs and colognes! Duran Central Pharmacy (1815 Central NW) is a 48-seat restaurant adjacent to the pharmacy and is famous for its red chile sauce, which tops great *enchiladas* and *burritos*. Locals and politicos tend to gravitate here. Monroe's Restaurants (1520 Lomas NW and 6051 Osuna NE) use over 100,000 pounds of green chile every year, and it's all chopped by hand. Their signature items are green chile cheeseburgers, taco fingers, blue corn *enchiladas*, and a simple bowl of green chile. They are good about accommodating their menu to customers' desires, so go ahead and order that blue corn *carne adovada* enchilada.

The patio is nice in the summer, at El Patio, 142 Harvard SE near the University of New Mexico. David and Gloria Sandoval have fashioned a great and quaint, understated restaurant here with modest prices. Chef Tom Baca refuses to compromise on the heat of his chile and often fends off complaints about it being too hot by shrugging and saying, "There's other restaurants around." Try the green chile chicken *enchiladas*, the blue corn red *enchiladas*, or the *chiles rellenos*.

El Pinto Restaurant (10500 4th Street NW) open since 1962, is New Mexico's largest restaurant, seating over 1,000 patrons when all the patios are open during the summer. But don't let that fact scare you off, since it's also one of the most beautiful places to eat in the state—on one of the patios beneath the towering cottonwood trees and surrounded by blooming gardens. El Pinto's commercial salsa is the best-selling salsa in New Mexico, with more than a million jars sold every year. Between the restaurant and their salsas, El Pinto goes through more than 240 *tons* of green chile every year! No wonder the New Mexico Department of Agriculture loves them so much. My favorite dish here is the chile ribs *adobada*-style, spiced up considerably with hot New Mexican red chile *caribe*.

Although greatly outnumbered by New Mexican restaurants, El Norteño (7306 Zuni SE) is a wonderful northern Mexican restaurant. The entire Nuñez family pitches in to serve up the greatest soft tacos this side of Guadalajara. You can mix and match about fifteen different fillings, including *carne al carbón*, *barbacoa*, *lengua*, *cabrito*, and *carne asada*. Top them with *pico de gallo* or the famous *El Norteño guaca-chile salsa*.

Albuquerque has some mighty fine barbecue, too. Pete Powdrell, the godfather of Duke City "Q", is retired from day-to-day smoking, but his restaurant, Powdrell's Bar-B-Que (11309 Central NE) is still hoppin'. The best BBQ here is their smoked prime ribs of beef—outstanding. Since I have eaten lunch at The Quarters (905 Yale SE, and two other locations) more than 1,500 times (once a week for thirty-two years will do it!), the restaurant has been adequately tested. The Quarters is famed for barbecue (their pork rib sandwich is outstanding), but it's also the size and quality of the their numerous sandwiches, combined with their policy of liberal pouring at the bar, that has kept hungry people coming back for at least 35 years. This is the best all-around lunch place in the city.

Santa Fe and Northern New Mexico

Santa Fe lays claim to having the "oldest house" in America, which is only the tip of the iceberg of other declarations of "ancient" status. Its lengthy history has led to many claims of antiquity for buildings, such as the "oldest mission church in the U.S." Santa Fe itself is often referred to as the

"oldest continually occupied city in the U.S.," "the oldest seat of government in the U.S.," and sometimes simply, "the oldest city."

Sorry folks, it's just not that old. Four hundred plus years is simply a tick of a clock when compared to,

A chile wreath, a popular
Santa Fe door decoration.

Photographer Harald Zoschke

say, the 6,000 years that have elapsed since the city of Sumer was established on the site of Babylon. Juan de Oñate established the first Spanish settlement in this region in 1598 and Santa Fe was made the capital of the frontier of New Mexico 1610, forty-five years after Street Augustine, Florida, was settled. But such facts do not qualify either city for the title of the oldest.

Since Santa Fe rests upon the ruins of an ancient pueblo, the "Oldest City in the U.S." title must go to an Indian settlement rather than a Spanish town. In reality, Santa Fe is the second-oldest city *founded by Europeans* in this country. No one knows for certain which Indian ruin is the most ancient, but the consensus seems to be that Acoma Pueblo is the oldest continually occupied settlement in the Southwest, dating to about the year 1000, or 600 years before Santa Fe.

A Food Mecca for Centuries

The Spaniards who first settled Santa Fe brought with them the necessary livestock to grow herds of cattle, sheep, and horses, and the seeds to plant the crops they needed. Since Santa Fe was the terminus of the 1,500-mile-long Camino Real, or "Royal Road" from Mexico City, it became a trading center and the both the beginning and the end of the caravans of wagons that moved back and forth along the royal road. The Plaza in Santa Fe was where the wagons unloaded, and vigorous trading was done in foodstuffs.

Another town that became a trading mecca was Taos. During the early 1700s, the village became one of the most important trade centers in New Spain by holding what became known as the "Taos Trade Fairs." And during the early 1800s, Taos became the headquarters for many of the famous mountain men who trapped beaver and other fur-bearing animals in the surrounding mountains. The town became one of the most important markets for beaver pelts in North America, and where there's trading, there's food.

Interestingly enough, most of the food was of New World origin—namely, corn, beans, and squash. Wheat adapted well to the high valleys of Taos and Peñasco, but not the lower elevations. Barley was used primarily for feeding livestock. Historian Marc Simmons commented about the early Spanish agriculture: "Other field crops included the *frijol* bean, horsebean, peas, squashes and pumpkins, melons, chile, tobacco, and cotton. Only a limited variety of garden vegetables seem to have been cultivated in the later Colonial period. Onions and garlic were regarded as staples in the diet, but other things, such as cucumbers, lettuce, beets, and the small husk-tomato, are mentioned in the documents only rarely. The potato was practically unknown."

The establishment of contact with Americans and the Santa Fe Trail from Missouri in the 1820s led to even more trading (which was prohibited by Spain, necessitating smuggling), and soon Santa Fe was the terminus of *two* major trade trade routes. After Santa Fe fell to the Americans in 1846, Santa Fe really opened up.

By that year, champagne and oysters were available, and flour for making bread sold for $2.50 per *fanega*. If that sounds expensive, consider that a *fanega* was 144 pounds. About this time, a Lt. James Abert was traveling extensively throughout New Mexico. Later, in his book, *Through the Country of the Comanche Indians*, he described the market at Santa Fe: "The markets have great quantities of chile *colorado* and *verde*, *cebollas* or onions, *sandias* or watermelons, *huevos* or eggs, *uvas* or grapes, and *pinones*, nuts of the pine tree."

Prices were relatively high. Corn was two dollars a bushel, beef and mutton eight to ten cents a pound, sugar and coffee were twenty-five cents a pound, and tea was very expensive at $1.25 a pound. About this time, W.W.H. Davis traveled to Santa Fe and sampled the native cuisine. In his book, *El Gringo*, he described his encounter: "The meal was a true Mexican dinner, and a fair sample of the style of living among the better class of people. The advance guard in the course of the dishes was boiled mutton and beans, the meat being young and tender, and well flavored. These were followed by a *sui generis* soup, different from any thing of the kind it had been my fortune to meet with before. It was filled with floating balls about the size of a musket bullet, which appeared to be a compound of flour and meat. Next came mutton stewed in chile (red peppers), the dressing of which was about the color of blood, and almost as hot as so much molten lead."

After mentioning the *albóndigas* soup and the mutton, Davis described the standard beans, tortillas, and *atole*, and then commented on chile: "Besides those already enumerated, there are other dishes, some of which have come down from the ancient inhabitants of the country. The chile they use in various ways—green, or *verde*, and in its

Wagon trains, San Francisco Street at the
Plaza, Santa Fe, c. 1879.

Photographer Nicholas Brown

dried state, the former being made into a sort of
salad, and is esteemed to be a great luxury."

Santa Fe survived the Civil War without a scratch.
Hotels and restaurants flourished with the coming
of the railroad in the early 1880s, but the citizens
had to put up with unprecedented lawlessness. As
historian Warren Beck described the situation:
"During the period following the Civil War and
lasting approximately until the turn of the century,
New Mexico experienced a wave of rampant lawlessness unparalleled in the history of the United
States. It was an era when stealing, killing, and

lynching were so common as to be hardly worth of
mention in the press.... Other parts of the nation
had experienced a breakdown in law and order, but
in few areas had it lasted or been as complete as it
was in the territory of New Mexico."

Reasons for the wave of lawlessness include New
Mexico's reputation for being a land of great trea-
sures and it's remoteness, which tended to attract
criminals on the run. The federal government back
in Washington also regarded the territory as an out-
post in a wilderness and virtually ignored the needs
of the citizens there. During the years immediately
following the Civil War, Santa Fe witnessed a dazzling diversity of crime—the death of a judge in a
gunfight, the theft of government fortune, the mass
murder of nine innocent travelers, and a colossal
diamond hoax.

During the years following World War I, Santa Fe
began to emerge from obscurity as the city—and
the rest of the state—was discovered by artists such
as Peter Hurd and Georgia O'Keefe, authors such
as Willa Cather and D.H. Lawrence, as well as
other prominent sculptors, poets, photographers,
and musicians. The high concentration of artists in
the city combined with Santa Fe's tradition as an
Indian trading center, produced one of the top art
sales markets in the world. Over 150 art galleries,
concentrated principally around the Plaza and
along Canyon Road, now feature local as well as international artists, and special events such as Indian
Market in mid-August ensure that the ancient
artistic traditions are kept alive.

Historic Sightseeing

Within walking distance of the Plaza, there's a lot of history to see. Don't miss the Loretto Chapel, with its supposedly miraculous staircase, located at 219 Old Santa Fe Trail. Santa Fe's most famous church is Street Francis Cathedral, at San Francisco Street and Cathedral Place. It was begun by Santa Fe's first archbishop, Frenchman Jean-Baptiste Lamy in 1869, who is buried beneath the altar. Santuario de Guadalupe (located at Guadalupe and Agua Fria streets) features displays of Spanish colonial art and religious artifacts, including a large painting of Our Lady of Guadalupe, patron saint of Mexico.

One of the oldest mission churches in the U.S., San Miguel Chapel (Old Santa Fe Trail and De Vargas Street) was totally rebuilt (including new foundations and walls) after it was burned to the ground during the Pueblo Revolt, so to say that this building is the oldest church is a fallacy akin to claiming one has Abe Lincoln's original axe, except for three new handles and four new heads.

Called "The Roundhouse" by locals, the State Capitol (Paseo de Peralta and Old Santa Fe Trail) was built in 1966 in the shape of the Zia symbol, now the New Mexico state insignia. Built in 1610,

The Road to Santa Fe via La Bajada Hill, c. 1910.
Photographer unknown

the Palace of the Governors on the Plaza was originally part of the royal presidio of Don Pedro de Peralta, the first colonial governor of New Mexico, and served as the residence and offices of succeeding Spanish, Mexican, and American governors.

Located just off the Plaza at Palace Avenue and Lincoln Street, the Museum of Fine Arts houses a permanent collection of over 8,000 works of regional art. Other great collections are housed at the Laboratory of Anthropology and the Museum of Indian Arts and Culture, located in the Camino Lejo museum complex, south of town off Old Santa Fe Trail, which also includes the Museum of International Folk Art and the Wheelwright Museum. The Museum of International Folk Art has collected over 120,000 objects from 100 countries.

structure was built in 1912 and has been enlarged and remodeled several times since then.

As part of the renowned Harvey House chain of hotels for forty years, La Fonda became the premiere hotel in the state and the starting point for the famed Indian Detours, which allowed train passengers to explore the wonders of the state by automobile for the first time. Since that time, La Fonda has retained its reputation as a first-class destination. Early hotel registers from La Fonda reveal hundreds of celebrity guests: Kit Carson, General William T. Sherman, Ulysses S. Grant, President Rutherford B. Hayes, Billy the Kid and Sheriff Pat Garrett (but not at the same time). More recent celebrities include James Stewart, Errol Flynn, John Travolta and Diane Keaton—the list is seemingly endless.

Without a doubt, La Fonda (100 East San Francisco Street) is the most famous and historic hotel in New Mexico. A brochure entitled "The History of La Fonda," published by the hotel, claims that the hotel has been in existence since 1610, the founding date of Santa Fe. That date is a bit misleading because although there might have been a *fonda* (inn) near the Plaza then, it certainly was not the same building that sits there now. The present

La Fonda Hotel, c. 1928.
Photographer T. Harmon Parkhurst

The Restaurant Scene

People used to joke that Santa Fe was the only city in the United States with more art galleries than gas stations. Well, there are now more restaurants than galleries! The tradition of great restaurants in Santa Fe was born more than fifty years ago when Rosalea Murphy opened The Pink Adobe. As Rosalea recalled, when The Pink first opened, Santa Fe was not the tourist mecca it is today, but rather a "lazy, sleepy town." She served twenty-five cent Pink Dobeburgers, then imported chicken enchiladas from Mexico, and eventually became the first chef in Santa Fe to serve seafood. Rosalea never bothered to obtain a liquor license until 1972, when she realized that visitors expected fine restaurants to serve mixed drinks.

Today the restaurant is located in a former barracks for Spanish soldiers, Barrio de Analco, one of the oldest parts of Santa Fe at 300 years plus. Despite its name, The Pink Adobe is no longer pink but rather a shade of sandstone. Santa Fe's Historical Design Review Board has refused to allow the restaurant to be painted its original color because, according to the board, pink is not an earth tone. During a hearing on the issue, Rosalea presented several samples of pink rocks collected in the desert and mountains around Santa Fe, but the board still refused permission for her to paint The Pink Adobe pink.

The Dragon Room bar of The Pink was named one of the nineteen best bars in the world by *Newsweek International* in 1986, perhaps because The Pink is *the* hangout for visiting celebrities. Such notables as John Erlichman, Robert Redford, Cher and Vincent Price often frequented The Pink. In 1981, Paul Newman wandered into the Pink but, according to Rosalea, "No one recognized him, and I think he was upset because we didn't make a fuss over him. One thing you get here is privacy, and besides, we didn't really know him." Such indifference to celebrities is one aspect of an attitude called "Santa Fe blasé." The owner of a gallery close to The Pink Adobe once sold a work of art to *Star Trek* actor Leonard Nimoy, and, after examining the name and address on the check, remarked: "Nimoy, huh? I knew some Nimoys back in Cleveland." Now, the Dragon Room has been remodeled into a wine bar. The most popular dish ordered at The Pink is steak Dunigan, a New York cut sirloin smothered in mushrooms and green chile sauce. A recent addition to the menu is clams Lucifer, Manila clams and tequila in a red chile broth.

There are more fine restaurants per capita in Santa Fe than probably anywhere else in the U.S. As is true of New Mexico in general, people living in and visiting The City Different love their food spicy hot. In fact, a study done by *Chile Pepper* magazine in the mid-Nineties determined that Santa Fe was the fiery food capital of the country, on the basis of the number of "Mexican" restaurants compared to the population. (Incidentally, Las Cruces was second, Austin third, San Antonio fifth, El Paso sixth, Albuquerque tenth, and Tucson twelfth; of the cities in this book, only Phoenix didn't place in the top fifteen.)

An Alternative Guide to the City Different

Santa Fe too tame for you? Well, Pancho Epstein's *Santa Fe Ole!* is subtitled "A Guide to the Real Santa Fe," but actually is a droll, fantasy-induced tour guide to the City *Weird*. Included in his listings are the following imaginary foodie haunts:

◆ *Anasazi Brewery.* Established in A.D. 1275, it is the oldest continually operating brewery in the world. According to Pancho, "These created-in-Santa Fe beers contain the highest alcoholic content of any brew in the world and produce an hallucinogenic effect."

◆ *Dyed Blue Corn Meal Manufacturing Company.* Developed by the same people who brought you the atomic bomb, Los Alamos National Laboratories, this blue corn meal "has the exact formula of color, texture, and taste to deceive out-of-state visitors, and the blue corn tortilla has its normal moldy look that so appeals to travelers."

◆ *Anglo Herb Store and Food Market.* "The owners sell only the highest quality artificially produced and preserved health products manufactured in America. The pharmacy's catchy motto is, "If you've got a symptom, we've got a drug."

◆ *Armida's Vegetarian Bountiful Barbecue.* "This is the only vegetarian restaurant in the world that barbecues all its food. From all vegetable *fajitas* to *flan*, everything has that wonderful mesquite flavor at Armida's. This is one of the real 'in' places for Santa Fe's holistic new-age crowd."

The book is out of print but available from online used book sellers.

Despite the heat of the Santa Fe food, visitors should note that there are a wide variety of cuisines available to sample because Santa Fe attracts great culinary artists as well as great visual artists. Since Santa Fe restaurants usually are crowded, especially during the summer, calling in advance for hours and reservations is suggested.

Within a few of blocks of the Plaza in Santa Fe, foodies can indulge every gastronomic whim imaginable. Want to buy the hottest salsa known to man? Like some to-die-for blue corn *enchiladas* with killer red chile? Care to taste some New Mexican wines? Need a *ristra* for your front porch? How 'bout some cast bronze chile pulls for your kitchen cabinets? It's all here in Santa Fe, and here are the foodie haunts that I like best in northern New Mexico.

Beginning with beverages, I recommend two wineries and two breweries. Santa Fe Vineyards, Highway 285 in Española, is located 20 miles north of Santa Fe on the highway to Taos. It has the winemaking facility, gift shop, picnic area, and tasting room. Founded in 1982 by Len Rosingana, it is one of the oldest modern wineries in New Mexico and well-known not only for excellent wines but also for their distinctive labels. A selection of 10 wines is offered including Chardonnay, Cabernet Sauvignon, White Zinfandel, and Indian Market White. La Chiripada Winery is in Dixon, on Highway 76, off Highway 68 between Santa Fe and Taos. This "Lucky Break" winery produces about 3,000 cases a year of their Primavera white and Rio Embudo Red brands of wine. There is a

tasting room here, and sales by the case. A good time to visit is during the Artist's Studio Tour, the first weekend in November. It's beautiful mountain country up here.

Blue Corn Café and Brewery (133 Water Street and 4056 Cerrillos Road) brews up Atomic Blonde Ale, Roadrunner IPA, End of the Trail Brown Ale, and Sleeping Dog Stout. The café specializes in *fajitas,* including sliced marinated steak *fajitas*, surf & turf *fajitas*, marinated portobello *fajitas*, and spicy shrimp *fajitas*. Apparently they haven't heard that the only true *fajitas* are made with skirt steak. Santa Fe Brewing (35 Fire Place) is New Mexico's oldest microbrewery, brewing Santa Fe Pale Ale, Santa Fe Wheat, Santa Fe Nut Brown, State Pen Porter, Chicken Killer Barley Wine, Fiesta IPA, Viszolay Belgian Ale and Maxwell's Silver Stout.

There are many great shops offering foods of the region. The Chile Shop (109 E. Water Street) was founded in 1985 and was the first shop in the country devoted entirely to products made from the peerless pods. It's a small shop, to be sure, but it's crammed with the very best chile pepper food and non-food items, with an emphasis on unique salsas and cookware. There is a good selection of books and cloth goods emblazoned with chiles as well. The Fruit Basket, Highway 68 in Velarde, between Santa Fe and Taos, is a roadside market that's been serving travelers since the early 1940s when the Velarde family established it to sell locally grown fruits and produce. During the chile season, the Fruit Basket sells land races of chiles grown only in northern New Mexico—and if you ask nicely they'll give you a tour of their orchards and chile fields, but call the day before. *Ristras* are available all year long, garlic ropes in October, and apples and other fruits in season.

There are two cooking shops in Taos that sell local food products. Monet's Kitchen (124 M Bent Street) has a strong collection of cookbooks, kitchenware, and gadgets and offers a fine selection of hot and spicy foods, much of it produced in New Mexico. It is one of the few places where you can find locally-harvested mushrooms. Taos Cookery (113 Bent Street) has an extensive collection of Southwestern foods, including salsas, chile pastas, cookies, jams, and candy. There are general cooking supplies also, as well as Steve Kilborn's exquisite pottery with chile motifs.

At the Salman Ranch Store (Highway 518 in La Cueva) north of Las Vegas, they specialize in raspberries because they grow them. There are twenty acres of 'em here in the late summer and fall on a ranch so scenic it's a national Historic Site. The Salman family make their own raspberry jams and vinegars, which they sell at the store along with other New Mexican food products. If you'd like to picnic, feel free to use the tables inside the livestock corrals. They like hot and spicy—their "Nathan" gift basket is composed of Fiery Raspberry Salsa, Salman Ranch Raspberry Jam, Bronco Bob's Roasted Raspberry Chipotle Sauce, and Coyote Cocina New Mexico Green Chile Salsa.

A great place to shop for locally-produced foods is the Santa Fe Farmers Market. In the summer, it's located in the parking lot of De Vargas Center on Paseo de Peralta. In the winter, it moves indoors to 519 Cerrillos Road at the intersection of Cerrillos, Sandoval, and Manhattan Streets. Both growers and food manufacturers come out in full force during the summer and fall. Virtually every Northern New Mexico product is available for sale, which is a boon for tourists and locals alike. Although visitors are unlikely to take home fifteen pounds of purple cabbage, they will enjoy the salsas, jams, jellies, and chiles. In 2008, the farmers market is scheduled to be relocated to a permanent, new structure at the Railyard year 'round.

Here are my recommended restaurants, focusing on those that serve Southwestern cuisines. The venerable La Casa Sena (125 E. Palace Avenue in Sena Plaza) was built by Major Jose Sena in the late 1860s in the classic adobe style and is now on the National Historic Register. While it was the residence of Major Sena, the hacienda hosted such notable guests as L. Bradford Prince, Governor of the Territory from 1889 to 1893, and Colonel Kit Carson of Taos. The historic architecture, combined with its extensive collections of Southwest, Indian, and Taos art combine to give the restaurant an elegant yet warm ambience. The restaurant serves "New Southwest" cuisine. Its patio is the most beautiful in Santa Fe, and the restaurant has the largest wine selection in the city.

The Coyote Café (132 West Water Street) offers a truly special dining experience because anthropologist-turned-executive chef Mark Miller re-creates Southwestern and Latin American dishes which

Original sign for the Coyote Café, c. 1988.
Photographer Dave DeWitt

pre-date the arrival of Europeans. It is difficult to suggest any one particular item because the menu changes so much, but here are some samples from past menus: *chipotle guacamole* made to order; barbecued duck *crepas (*layered corn crepes with roast duck, barbecue sauce, and corn chile relish), red chile quail (fresh Texas bobwhite quail marinated in dried chiles and wild mushrooms), and grilled prime ribeye (a pecan-grilled ribeye steak with roasted garlic and orange-*chipotle* butter). The Rooftop Cantina, open April to October, serves *tortas*, duck *quesadillas*, and *Ensenada*-style tacos.

The elegant Inn of the Anasazi (113 Washington Avenue) is decorated in ancient Indian motifs. The food is eclectic and past menu items include venison chili with an aged cheddar *quesadilla*, Navajo flatbread with fire-roasted sweet peppers, and vegetable *empanadas* with yellow *mole*. Over 75 selections of wine are available by the glass. The Pink Adobe, described in detail earlier, is located at 406 Old Santa Fe Trail. The popular dinner menu,

which rarely changes except for specials, offers an eclectic selection of complementing cuisines: French, Creole, Spanish, and, of course, New Mexican. Santacafe (231 Washington Avenue) began in 1983 as a Southwest-meets-Asia restaurant and soon became one of Santa Fe's toniest spots. Now, their wesite says that they are "serving unique American cuisine with a Southwestern flair." The menu changes seasonally, but here were some recent menu choices: smoked pheasant spring rolls with four-chile dipping sauce, grilled filet mignon with *mole verde* sauce, and Oriental duck breast with sweet and sour sauce. The beautiful inner courtyard is a popular spot for lunch when the weather is nice.

Moving to the more traditional restaurants, a great choice for New Mexican cuisine is Tomasita's, 500 S. Guadalupe Street. Lodged in a former train station, this restaurant sells *margaritas* by the liter and hot red chile sauce by the gallon. Specialties are the *chiles rellenos* and the *carne adovada,* but the blue corn, red chile cheese *enchiladas*—the key comparison dish for New Mexican restaurants—are nothing short of superb. At Maria's New Mexican Kitchen (555 W. Cordova Road), tequila and *margaritas* are the specialties. Owner Al Lucero, author of *The Great Margarita Book*, offers an astounding number of "real" *margaritas*—more than 100 of them! The food is classic New Mexican—since 1952. Café Pasqual's (121 Don Gaspar) has traditional New Mexican food but also offers authentic Mexican entrees like *cochinita pibil*, Yucatan-style tacos with Niman Ranch pork, slow cooked in *achiote* and orange sauce, and innovative *enchiladas* like the ones made with sautéed chard, grilled zucchini and jack cheese, served with a *guajillo, ancho* and *chile de arbol* sauce accompanied by cilantro rice and grilled banana. The food here is almost entirely organic. It is very popular for breakfast on weekends. The Shed (113 1/2 E. Palace Avenue) has been around since 1953 but the building housing it is part of a hacienda dating back to 1692. All the traditional New Mexican specialties are served here, but there are some innovations like *pollo adobo* (chicken chunks roasted in the Shed's red *adobo* marinade) and Shed chowder, with roasted chicken, green chile, corn, and carrots topped with blue corn tortilla strips, that's a winter specialty.

Here are some specialty restaurant recommendations. Tecolote, "The Owl" (1203 Cerrillos Road), is *the* place for breakfast in Santa Fe since 1980. There is a comfortable, diner-like atmosphere here in this 82-seat restaurant. Try the *atole-piñon* pancakes, or a breakfast *burrito* in the morning or a traditional northern New Mexican enchilada plate with *posole* in the afternoon. The pork chops *verde* are smothered in green chile and cheese and are highly recommended. "Good meals at reasonable prices" is the motto here. Works for me. The Plaza Café (54 Lincoln Avenue) is the oldest, continuously operated restaurant in Santa Fe, established in 1918. Conveniently located on the Plaza, it has a very casual atmosphere. The cafe serves up an eclectic mix of American, New Mexican, and Greek specialties, including roast beef soft tacos, blue corn enchiladas, *moussaka*, and *gyros* sandwiches. Try the homemade fruit pies for dessert. Great barbecue is served at The Cowgirl Bar & Grill (319 S. Guadalupe Street) and one reviewer has called it "Santa Fe's social center." There are billiards room, a Kiddie Corral, a shady patio for summer dining, and, of course, a bar for serious celebrating. Mesquite-smoked ribs, chicken, and brisket are featured at The Cowgirl.

It's worth a 20-mile trip out of town to dine at Rancho de Chimayó, Highway 520 in Chimayó. There is nothing *nouveau* on the menu at Rancho de Chimayó, just the classic cuisine of northern New Mexico. The favorites are *carne adovada*, pork marinated in red chile and served with *posole*, and *fajitas al Estilo Chimayó*, beef marinated in chiles and wine, then grilled, sliced, and served with a spicy *pico de gallo* salsa. According to Florence Jaramillo, more and more of her customers are requesting vegetarian entrees, so she has removed the traditional lard from all her recipes and replaced it with high-quality vegetable oil. During the summer, dining outdoors here on the huge patio is a delightful experience.

Rancho de Chimayó

When Florence Jaramillo first opened Rancho de Chimayó in 1965, everyone told her she was crazy to attempt to operate a fine restaurant twenty miles from Santa Fe and off the established tourist track. But she had a hunch that the combination of traditional Hispanic New Mexican cuisine, the beautiful Chimayó valley, and the sprawling Jaramillo hacienda, which had belonged to her husband's grandparents, would make her restaurant unique.

She was right, but the struggle took over five years of hard work. In addition to limited financing, none of her food suppliers would deliver out of town, so Jaramillo was forced to drive into Santa Fe to buy everything necessary for a restaurant to prepare and serve fine food. On one trip back to the Rancho, she recalls, she was stopped for speeding by a state police officer who asked the usual question about "What's the hurry?" she got out of the car, opened the trunk, and showed the officer 300 pounds of fresh meat which would spoil if she didn't speed back to Chimayó. She got off with a warning, and the pork for the *carne adovada* made it safely into the kitchen.

In the early days, visitors from other parts of the country would ask, "Is it safe to drink the water" and "Should we pay in pesos?" Jaramillo would then patiently explain that New Mexico became a State of the Union in 1912 and readily accepts dollars. The most frequently asked question still is, "Why is this chile so hot?" The answer to that one was easy. Rancho de Chimayó uses locally grown Chimayó chiles, which are more fiery than most New Mexico chiles, as is indicated by its smaller pods. Hatch Valley chile from the southern part of the state serves as a backup because local growers alone cannot meet the demand of the restaurant, which serves an astounding two to three *tons* of green chile a year and about a half-ton of red chile, which weighs considerably less than the green because it is dried.

During the summer, Rancho de Chimayó opens its multi-terraced patio, increasing the number of tables to 200 in order to accommodate the flood of diners. The restaurant serves an incredible *1,000* meals a day during its peak summer business, which usually revolves around a holiday such as Father's Day or the Fourth of July. Such a volume requires a staff of 130, recruited mostly from Chimayó and nearby towns. Jaramillo believes that working at Rancho de Chimayó has helped to educate the young people of the area to the cosmopolitan ways of the outside world. Indeed, many of her employees paid their college expenses with salaries and tips earned at the restaurant.

A Living Museum

El Rancho de las Golondrinas (Ranch of the Swallows) was the last stopping place before Santa Fe along the Camino Real from Mexico City. Imagine a small colonial village which has been restored to the way it was during the 17th and 18th centuries—with chapel, shepherd's kitchen, *torreon* (defensive tower), weaving rooms, and village store. Then imagine this village as a living museum, complete with volunteers dressed in authentic costumes who demonstrate weaving, spinning, threshing, farming, and blacksmithing.

The museum features special Spring, Summer and Harvest Festivals during the first weekends of June, August, and October, where Spanish folk dances with traditional music are performed. Open houses are held the first Sundays in July, August, and September, when visitors may take self-guided tours. The museum is closed from November through March.

El Rancho de las Golondrinas is 15 miles south of Santa Fe off I-25 at exit 271. www.golondrinas.org

4. Desert Dining: Arizona

"The spread was excellent in variety and style…. The sight of the little roasted porkers, chickens, and other fixings caused our bosom to swell and our heart to beat with emotion."

—Newspaperman John Marion, describing one of the first Thanksgiving Day dinners at Territorial Governor A.P.K. Safford's residence in Prescott, 1869.

Interior of American grocery, Tucson, 1880.

Photographer unknown.

Today, Arizona is a vibrant state with millions of residents in addition to the tourists who revel in the luxury of its resorts. But such growth was slow in coming. Arizona remained sparsely settled (as compared to New Mexico and Texas) until the arrival of cattlemen and miners during the mid-1800s. There was no Camino Real connecting the region with Mexico City and the rest of the interior, so settlement and trade from the south was slow in developing.

The first trickle of Spanish pioneers faced many hardships in what is now southern Arizona: the heat, lack of water, hostile Apaches, and a scarcity of what they considered to be proper food. But they didn't let a lack of larder bother them—they brought their own.

Domesticating the Desert

Covered wagons, c. 1890.

Photographer unknown

settlers who followed after his death in 1711—introduced cattle, sheep, goats, horses, mules, and chickens into Arizona. Additionally, the Spanish planted wheat, barley, grapes, onions, garlic, cabbage, lettuce, carrots, peaches, apricots, pomegranates, figs, pears, peaches, quinces, and mulberries.

Chile peppers were probably introduced about this time as well, though any records about them appear to be lost. We do know that in 1776, as the eastern colonies were fighting for their independence from England, Fray Pedro Font was describing the agriculture and food of the Spanish settlers of the desert in his diary: "They plant with a stick and grow maize, beans, squash, and chiles. With their fingers, they eat tortillas and beans, chiles, and tomatoes. They begin their day hours before breakfast, stopping about 10 a.m. for maize cereal, sweet with honey or hot with red pepper. The main meal is in the early afternoon, usually tortillas, beans, and salsa. On special occasions, bits of meat in cornmeal are steamed in husks."

The Spanish had already been settled in New Mexico for a century before they undertook the taming of the Sonoran desert near what is now Tucson. It wasn't until 1700 that the Jesuit priest Padre Eusebio Francisco Kino founded the San Xavier del Bac Mission, said to be the finest example of mission architecture in the United States. Kino spent the last twenty-four years of his life on a missionary tour of Sonora and Arizona that covered 75,000 miles and resulted in the founding of seventy-three *vistas* (local churches) and twenty-nine missions. In addition to converting the Native Americans to Christianity, Kino—and the Spanish

Font's description of tamales is still accurate today, and despite the introduction of European foods into Arizona, the Spanish *padres* were quite aware of the native plants growing around them. In 1794, an improbably named missionary, Ignatz Pfeffercorn, described his encounter with the wild chile, the chiltepín: "After the first mouthful the tears started to come. I could not say a word and believed I had hell-fire in my mouth. However, one does become accustomed to it after frequent bold victories, so that with time the dish becomes tolerable and finally very agreeable."

In the late eighteenth and early nineteenth centuries, there was little development of Arizona crops and food because of cultural and political turmoil. First, the Spanish battled the Yumas and the Apaches. Then, during the Mexican wars of independence from Spain (1811-22), the northern settlements such as Arizona were neglected and thousands of lives were lost as the Indians destroyed ranchos, haciendas, and mining camps. In 1824, Mexico became a republic and established the Territory of Nuevo Mexico, which included the present states of New Mexico and Arizona. Santa Fe was the capital and had about 4,500 inhabitants. New Mexico had about 20,000 non-Indians, while Arizona had been almost totally abandoned and there were only two tiny settlements, Tucson and Tubac, each protected by a small garrison of Mexican soldiers.

The U.S. war with Mexico that began in 1846 was soon concluded to America's advantage with virtually no fighting in the Territory of Nuevo Mexico, and by the early 1850s, American pioneers began

Followers of Euell Gibbons, Take Note

The early settlers of Arizona—like their Native American predecessors—occasionally had to eat every imaginable plant and animal substance. In addition to the native plants mentioned in Chapter 1, here are some other edible oddities.

Acorns. The nuts of oak trees were usually ground into flour and cakes made from the flour were baked on hot rocks or allowed to dry in the sun.

Creosote bush. The leaves and bark of this pungent bush were used to make medicinal teas and poultices for the relief of arthritis, but the flower buds were also a substitute for capers.

Wild grapes. "The fruit is quite acid and occasionally is used to make vinegar and even wine," wrote Juan Nentvig in 1764.

Diamondback rattlesnakes. The snakes were carefully caught, killed, skinned, and the meat was cut off, rolled in flour and cracker crumbs, and deep-fried.

Bears, squirrels, and more. Bear steaks were fried and squirrel carcasses were baked. The journals of the early explorers and settlers record the consumption of other questionable delicacies, such as skunk, dog, shelf fungus, and sumac berries.

trickling into Arizona, attracted by the high prices paid by military posts for hay, corn, and beef. Their attraction soon turned to aversion, however, because settlers and soldiers alike complained of the heat and dryness. One soldier's journal of the time reported: "Everything dries. There is no juice left in any living thing. Bacon is eaten with a spoon and chickens hatched come out of the shell cooked."

Food on the Frontier

But the arid conditions of the Arizona deserts were actually a boon for some foods. The ancient Indian method of preserving meat—drying it in the sun—was reborn as jerky for the Americans and *carne seca* for the Mexicans. In 1844, Josiah Gregg described in his book, *Commerce of the Prairies*, how the pioneers in their caravans moving west treated meat—mostly buffalo: "They find no difficulty in curing their meats even in mid-summer, by slicing it thin and spreading or suspending it in the sun; or if in haste, it is slightly barbecued. This is done without salt, and yet it rarely putrifies. The flesh (can be) 'jerked' or slightly barbecued, by placing it upon a scaffold over a fire. The same method is resorted to by Mexicans when the weather is too damp or cloudy for the meat to dry in the open air."

The meats used to make jerky were, in addition to buffalo, venison, beef, and even pork. The Americans apparently did not season the jerky, except for sprinkling it with a little salt. However, the Mexican version, *carne seca*, is seasoned with vinegar, black pepper, and some salt before drying and then is rubbed with garlic and sprinkled with chile powder after it has dried completely in the sun. In

Red meat drying at Ah Tso Liege,
Red Lake, Arizona, c. 1910
Photographer unkonwn

some cases, the *carne seca* was lightly smoked over mesquite wood before air-drying. The key to proper drying is to slice the meat along the grain as thinly as possible. When dry, the meat can be stored indefinitely.

Another staple of the settlers arriving in caravans of wagons was sourdough, a bread that made its own

Tohono O'odham woman grinding corn.

Photographer unknown

yeast. The "starter" was simply flour mixed with warm water that was allowed to sit in the open. Yeasts occurring naturally in the air would settle on the starter, multiply furiously, and cause the starter to ferment. This process took between three and five days and the starter was usually kept in a wooden keg or a porcelain crock, but never in a metal container. Early cookbooks suggested wrapping a blanket around the starter in cold weather, or even taking it to bed with the cook in the event of a hard freeze! The starter would last only about two weeks before being renewed.

When the cook was ready to make bread, it was a simple matter to mix the starter with more flour and water and make dough. After retaining a cup or two of the dough for more starter, the remaining dough was allowed to "proof" (or rise), and was then pushed down for a second proofing. After the dough had risen the second time, it was baked.

One of the most basic and necessary cooking tools of the frontier was precursor of the crockpot, the Dutch oven. The "spider" Dutch oven was a heavy, cast-iron pot with three legs and a thick lid. It served as a combination kettle, frying pan, and oven that could be hung above a fire or set in the coals, and sometimes coals were placed on the lid. Sourdough bisquits were commonly baked in this manner, and the method was known to Mexicans as *entre dos fuegos*, between two fires. Meats were commonly cooked with vegetables in a Dutch oven to make a pot roast. Around the turn of the century, a ranch cook described the food of the frontier: "*Frijole* beans, potatoes, and hot biscuits were served at every meal. Lick [syrup] took the place of butter. Dried fruit cooked with plenty of sugar was the usual dessert. Huge Dutch ovens were used for outside cooking."

In 1860, a census of sorts was taken in Arizona and the population of the territory was determined to be 6,482—and that only included settlers, soldiers and "tame" Native Americans. By contrast, the population of New Mexico was about 70,000. The price of imported food was outrageous—flour was fifty-five dollars a barrel; sugar, coffee, tea, and bacon were seventy-five cents a pound; butter was two dollars a pound and eggs were two dollars a dozen—a fortune in today's dollars.

But the high price of food did not prevent the opening of restaurants. In 1864, the Juniper House, a combination hotel and restaurant, opened in Prescott, the territorial capital. On the menu were fried venison and chile for breakfast, roast venison and chile for dinner, and simply chile for supper. On a sadder note, that same year Kit Carson destroyed the Navajo peach orchards during the relocation of the tribe to New Mexico. In doing so, he wiped out the peaches that had been imported by the Spanish nearly two centuries earlier.

During the Indian wars, one of General George Crook's most trusted Indian scout, Wales Arnold, ordered breakfast around 1873: "I want a can of peaches, six biscuits, a dozen eggs scrambled with green chiles, and a quart of hot coffee." The meal probably cost $4, a fortune for breakfast in those days. But prices were bound to get better as more settlers arrived in Arizona territory and modern transportation and agriculture techniques found their way into Arizona.

In 1879, Nellie Cashman opened Delmonico's Restaurant on Church Plaza in Tucson. The restaurant had a Mexican cook and meals were priced at four bits—fifty cents. The prices of food in the grocery stores that year were fluctutating; tea had doubled to a dollar fifty a pound while the price of sugar dropped to fifty cents a pound.

Finding firewood to cook the food was always a problem on the frontier, so the ingenious pioneers resorted to using "hay boxes" to save fuel. They

Helpful Cooking Hints from the Frontier

There was no lack of cooking innovation in early Arizona. Here are some helpful hints even for modern kitchens.

◆ Old bread should be dried thoroughly, ground up, and put away to make bread pudding when unexpected guests arrive.

◆ Dip fish in boiling water for a minute to make them easier to scale.

◆ A bay leaf will keep weevils out of oatmeal and cornmeal.

◆ Parsnips that are peeled, sliced, roasted, and powdered make an excellent coffee substitute.

◆ Adding a half-teaspoon of baking soda to the water used to boil beans will eliminate "repeating" and the gas caused by eating them.

◆ Soak bacon in cold water for a few minutes to reduce curling and shrinking when it is fried.

Arizona grapefruits.

Photographer Dave DeWitt

excellent fruit in the gardens of Phoenix show that climate and soil are well adapted to their culture." The first commercial orange groves were planted in 1891 at Ingleside, northeast of Phoenix, and grapefruit growing began in 1894. Severe freezes as low as twelve degrees nearly wiped out citrus in 1913, but the industry rebounded. Indeed, the Arizona 1983 citrus crop was valued at $53 million, but citrus orchards are continually threatened by development.

In 1912, dates were introduced into the Salt River Valley, and in 1920 the first pecan orchards were planted. The pecan acreage increased to 4,000 in 1932, but later declined to 500 acres because of inferior adaptability of older varieties. The Western Schley variety, introduced from New Mexico, was well-adapted and acreage zoomed to 22,000 today.

By 1920, Arizona's population had increased to 334,162, a gain of over five thousand percent in a mere sixty years. Much of that increase was the result of a change in immigration patterns. As the population of northern Mexico—particularly Sonora—increased, it was natural that immigrants would more even farther north and cross the border into Arizona. And of course, they brought their own cuisine with them.

would take a metal box or a trunk, make certain it was airtight, and pack it three-quarters full of finely cut, fresh hay. Then they made depressions in the hay large enough to hold a Dutch oven or other cook pot. The food was brought to the boiling point on the stove or over the fire, then the pot was transferred to the hay box. Pillows were placed over the pots for insulation, the top closed, and the meal would continue to cook. The method took twice as long as stove cooking, but it saved fuel and many cooks swore that the food tasted better.

Beginning in 1870, the Salt River irrigation project produced 35,000 irrigated acres near Phoenix, leading to extensive citrus production.

By 1885, Territorial governor Frank A. Tritle commented that "orange trees loaded down with

Sonoran Style

Unlike the food in New Mexico and Texas, "Mexican" cooking was not well established in Arizona until much later in time. Whatever Mexican cuisine had been established there was wiped out in the early 1800s, and did not reappear until the immigration from Mexico began later in the century. In fact, as late as 1880, the Mexican-American population of Arizona was less than 10,000 people. Thus, Arizona versions of *norteño* cookery were developed at least two centuries after New Mexicans were growing and eating their heavily-spiced versions.

Generally speaking, Arizona cuisine is not as fiery as that of New Mexico or Texas; the chiles used most are mild New Mexican types and many Sonoran recipes call for no chiles at all. Mexican *poblanos* and dried *anchos* are surprisingly uncommon except in heavily Hispanic neighborhoods. These general rules are often contradicted when the fiery *chiltepín* enters the picture. This progenitor of the modern chile pepper grows wild in Sonora and southern Arizona on perennial bushes, as in Texas. The red, berry-like pods are harvested and dried and then crushed and sprinkled over soups, stews, and salsas.

However, as is true for the entire country, *jalapeños* and the hotter New Mexican varieties are steadily invading Arizona. Growers are increasing the size of fields and more of the fiery fruits are being imported from New Mexico. *Jalapeños*, *chipotles*, and *serranos* are also being imported from Mexico, so as with the rest of the country, Arizona is starting to heat up.

Perhaps the most basic Sonoran-style dish is *machaca*, which evolved from *carne seca*. These days, the words are used interchangeably in Arizona, but they are actually two different things. In frontier times, dried beef was rehydrated, then allowed to stew with chiles and tomatoes until it fell apart. These days, since it is no longer necessary to dry meat, *machaca* is simply meat that is stewed, again with chiles and tomatoes, until it can be shredded (the Spanish verb *machacar* means "to pound). The shredded meat is then used to stuff *burros*, as *burritos* are called in Arizona.

Another basic Sonoran-style dish is *chiles rellenos*, like this recipe from the *Bazar Cook Book*, published in 1909 by the Ladies' Aid Society of Tucson's First Congregational Church: "Take green chile peppers, roast on top of the stove, roll in cloth to steam until cold, then peel (after being steamed in this way, the skins are easily removed). Cut off tops. Scoop out carefully to remove the seeds and veins and fill with mixture made of grated Mexican cheese, chopped olives, chopped onion. Dip in egg and cracker meal and fry in hot lard as you would oysters. Serve hot."

In Arizona, *huevos rancheros* are surprisingly served Texas-style, with fried eggs served over wheat or corn tortillas and then smothered in a mild *ranchero* sauce that often contains tomatoes. There are at least three different styles of "Sonoran-style" *enchiladas* served in the state. One version, prepared around Douglas (where most of the New Mexican types of chiles are grown) is similar to New Mexican enchiladas in that it uses a chile sauce rather than a gravy. Another is more like the Tex-Mex enchiladas, and a third has been moved virtually intact from Sonora.

In the westernmost part of the Southwest, wheat tortillas are more popular than corn, primarily because farmers in both Sonora and Arizona grow more wheat than corn. These tortillas are usually quite large—as much as sixteen inches across—and are stuffed with meat, beans, cheese, and called *burros*, which are more popular than *enchiladas.*

Perhaps the most famous Arizona specialty dish is the *chimichanga,* a dish whose name is translatable only as "thing-a-ma-jig." It is a *burrito* (usually stuffed with beans or ground meat, chiles, and cheese) that is deep-fat fried and served with *guacamole* and a *pico de gallo*-type salsa.

In addition to its Sonoran style establishments, Arizona has seen a steady growth in New Southwest restaurants during the past few decades. Restaurants such as Vincent Guerithault on Camelback in Phoenix, the Piñon Grill in Scottsdale, and Janos

Indian corn with Navajo blanket, c. 1955.
Photographer unknown

and Cafe Terra Cotta in Tucson have led the way in combining regional ingredients in often startling new ways.

Phoenix and Scottsdale

Phoenix and its attendant suburbs sprawl across the aptly-named Valley of the Sun, which broils in the sun during the fierce summer yet remains warm and pleasant during the winter. November through April is the time the tourists flock to the numerous resorts that offer golf, tennis, and total relaxation.

Despite the artistic and shopping attractions of Scottsdale, Phoenix remains the dominant city in the area. Besides being the state capital and financial center, it is the home of major league football team (the Cardinals), a major league baseball team (the Diamondbacks) and a pro basketball team (the Suns). Phoenix is America's fifth largest city and the largest in land area with nearly four hundred square miles.

The ancient Hohokam civilization first settled in the Valley and tamed the Salt River for irrigation around 300 B.C. By A.D. 1100, the Hohokam settlements approached 100,000 population and their culture (along with the Anasazi) was the most advanced north of Mexico City in prehistoric times. By 1450, though, the Hohokam civilization had collapsed and the people had dispersed. Their artifacts remain preserved at the Pueblo Grande Museum (4619 E. Washington Street) along with pit houses, irrigation canals, and ball courts.

Americans began arriving in the area shortly after the Civil War when the Army built Fort McDowell and settlers arrived to provide hay and crops for the troops. A former Confederate soldier named Jack Swilling was the first to dig out the Hohokam canals and to grow irrigated crops. Other farmers soon followed and a small city was laid out in 1870 and finally incorporated in 1881. It was named Phoenix by Darrell Duppa, one of the early settlers, who predicted that the city would rise from the ashes of the Hohokam civilization like the mythical bird, the phoenix. He was right.

By 1889, Phoenix was large enough to snatch the title of territorial capital from Prescott. After the turn of the century and the construction of the Theodore Roosevelt Dam, which provided sufficient water for the city, Phoenix began to boom. It really came into its own after World War II when its income base changed from farming to manufacturing and tourism.

But evidence of the early Phoenix still remains at Heritage Square (Sixth and Monroe Streets) where homes built between 1890 and 1930 comprise the last existing block of the original Phoenix town site. Anchored by the Rosson House, which is open for tours, Heritage Square is an interesting diversion in a fast-moving town. So is the Pioneer Arizona Living History Museum (Pioneer Road exit off I-17) with its reconstructed historical buildings of a pioneer town. Blacksmiths, printers, dressmakers, and other craftspeople ply their trades among the exhibits.

One of the finest museums in the world devoted to the native peoples of the Southwest is located in Phoenix. The Heard Museum (22 E. Monte Vista Road) boasts extensive and outstanding exhibits on the culture, artifact, and art of indigenous peoples. Other interesting museums in the Valley include the Pueblo Grande Museum and Cultural Park (4619 E. Washington), the Phoenix Art Museum (1625 N. Central Avenue) with more than 11,000 works of art, the Arizona Museum of Science and Technology (80 N. 2nd Street) and the Hall of Flame, a collection of antique fire-fighting equipment (6101 E. Van Buren Street).

Existing in the desert seems to be the theme of a number of Phoenix attractions. Arcosanti, futuristic architect Paolo Soleri's ecologically designed town, is *still* under construction (since 1970) at exit 262 of I-17 at Cordes Junction. There's a foundry, gift shop, bakery, and cafe there. Another architectural masterpiece, Frank Lloyd Wright's Taliesin West (Cactus Road and Frank Lloyd Wright Boulevard at approx. 114th Street in northeast Scottsdale) is available for tours. The Desert Botanical Gardens (1201 N. Galvin Parkway) has the country's largest collection of arid-land plants and also displays pre-Columbian food collecting techniques. And the Desert Center at Pinnacle Peak (8711 E. Pinnacle Peak Road) teaches ethnobotany, archaeology, and ancient Native American skills.

Lovers of the out-of-doors will enjoy the Phoenix Zoo (5810 E. Van Buren Sreet) with its special Arizona Exhibit and one of the largest herds of Arabian oryx in world. Also outdoors, and for good reason, is the world's highest fountain in the aptly-named community of Fountain Hills. Drive east of Scottsdale and look for the 560-foot-high plume of water and ponder how much of it evaporates in the Valley's 116-degree summer temperatures.

Other attractions in the Valley include Rawhide at Wildhorse Pass (5700 West North Loop Road) which is a large western theme park complete with a Wild West museum, twenty retail shops, a saloon, restaurant, and, to assist your digestion, gunfights. The Rockin' R Ranch (6136 E. Baseline Road in Mesa) is another Wild West town featuring chuck wagon suppers, gold panning, wagon rides, and entertainment. Castle lovers will enjoy Mystery Castle (800 E. Mineral Road) which was built by Boyce Gulley for his daughter in 1930. It has eighteen rooms and thirteen fireplaces, but hey, who's counting?

It wouldn't be fair to the Valley not to mention Scottsdale, with its sprawling resorts, shopping malls, art galleries, and numerous restaurants. Old Town (bordered by Brown Avenue, 2nd Street, Indian School Road, and Main Street) is a section of downtown Scottsdale with frontier-style buildings rapidly being replaced by new developments. From October to May, horse-drawn carriages and open-air trolleys carry visitors through the shops, restaurants, and galleries. Nearby is Fifth Avenue, with its collection of eclectic shops. Scottsdale rivals Santa Fe as a center for Southwestern art, although the galleries also carry many other styles of art.

Valley of the Sun Food and Dining

It is no surprise that the style of Mexican food most typical of Arizona originates from Sonora, the neighboring Mexican state. Sonora is cattle country and wheat is one of the primary crops. Flour tortillas, beef, cheese, sour cream and, of course, the ubiquitous chiles and beans are the staples the cuisine is built on.

After World War II, the widespread use of air conditioning and a flood of young veterans looking for a fresh start and a place to raise families swelled sleepy, dusty little Phoenix to city size. The newcomers learned to eat the hearty, spicy food found in dozens of unpreposessing *taquerias* and cafes—*tacos, tamales, tostadas, machaca, quesadillas* and enough smooth-textured but fiery red sauce to irrigate the desert.

Woody Johnson, the founding father of the Macayo's chain, opened what was probably the first "upscale" Mexican restaurant, El Nido, near downtown Phoenix in 1950. The atmosphere may have been fancy but the food was still straightforward.

Suddenly, in the early Seventies, things began to change. Along with the complimentary pre-meal basket of chips and familiar squeeze bottle of sauce, shallow bowls of chunky and mild tomato, onion and chile salsa appeared on tables. There are still plenty of old-timers who swear never to have sullied their lips with the wimpy stuff.

A hybrid dish called the *chimichanga* turned up on menus all over town. No one knows exactly what the name means or where it came from. It is basically an enormous *burrito* with a choice of fillings such as *machaca*, which is deep-fried and smothered in cheese, sauce, *guacamole* and sour cream. The appearance of sour cream has outraged some purists. "As for the person who slopped sour cream on a *chimichanga*, or any Mexican food," said railroader Joe Lancaster, "I use a cowboy phrase, 'Get a rope.'"

The *chimichanga* has always commanded a premium price—based no doubt on its size. An astonishing number of local restaurateurs have taken credit for originating this dish, which rivals fry bread for the Alka Seltzer Award of all time. Claims have also come in from Tucson's El Charro restaurant, La Frontera in Nogales, and other restaurants all over the state. The consensus seems to be that the *chimi*, as it is fondly known, is the creation of the Garcia family, who also gave birth to the national chain of restaurants of the same name.

Creeping California-ism has brought the taco salad and *fajitas* crept up from Texas. Blue corn and green chiles were a welcome infusion from New Mexico. Arizonans also learned in the Eighties that there were other styles of Mexican food besides Sonoran, when restaurants opened offering specialties from Central and Coastal Mexico.

Sign on a South Phoenix
restaurant.

Photographer Dave DeWitt

But ask anyone who has lived in Phoenix for any
length of time where they head upon returning home
after being out of town. Chances are they will tell you
Rosita's, La Perla, Pedro's or any other of many Mexican restaurants untouched by time or trend, where
they will order a Number 5 plate— taco, tostada and
enchilada awash in that river of hot sauce.

I'm going to start the listings with the best retail
locations for finding Phoenix foodstuffs. El Fenix, a
classic Mexican bakery, is located at 6219 S. Central
Avenue, in South Phoenix. It specializes in *bolillo*
rolls, sweetcakes, pumpkin candy, and tortillas, but
also has some hot sauces and some Mexican grocery
items. Food City (1648 S. 16th Street, and other
locations around the Valley) carries a complete line
of Mexican food ingredients (*chorizo*, beans, chiles,
dozens of sauces and salsas, tripe, etc.). Open since
1931, it has an eye-popping automated tortilla
maker that turns out the thinnest, most delicious
product in town. The Desert Botanical Garden

Gift Shop (1201 N. Galvin Parkway) is a great
place to shop after experiencing the incredible
cactus and succulent collection. Just about everything concerning the desert, including plants,
guidebooks, tee-shirts, cookbooks, and more is
available here. There is also a good collection of
Arizona foods, such as salsas, at the Pinnacle Peak
General Store (8711 E. Pinnacle Peak Road in
Scottsdale) which has a courtyard and plaza mod-
eled after the one in Alamos, Mexico, plus a lovely
cactus garden. Stephen Simonson, general manager
here since 1974, says modestly that the general
store is "even more than a legend—it's an institu-
tion." The store also has its own bakery and soda
fountain.

It's easy to find a date in the Valley—just buy one.
At the Sphinx Date Ranch (3039 N. Scottsdale
Road in Scottsdale) *medjool* dates are harvested and
packed during September and October, but they're
available year-round because of proper cold storage

techniques. Besides *medjools*, they've got dates you've never heard of (*dayri, zahidi, barhi,* and *khadrawy,* for example). Additionally, they have a huge selection of nuts, fruits, honey, Southwestern salsas, and jams and jellies. They'll ship anywhere, so call for mail order information. Sphinx has been open since 1951.

My favorite brewery in the area is Papago Brewing, (7107 East McDowell Road, Scottsdale). They have a 30-tap bar where the line-up changes daily, plus a beer engine for cask-conditioned ales. Their own line-up is excellent: Sledgehammer, a heavy brew; Hopfather, a Double India Pale Ale; El Robusto, a Baltic Porter; Orange Blossom, a Mandarin Hefeweizen; and Hop Dog, an India Pale Ale. Su Vino Winery (7035 E. Main Street, Suite 110, Scottsdale) has more than 34 medals for their wines, and are the only winery in Arizona to offer customers the opportunity to have wine made specifically for them and their palate. Many of the wines come from their operation in appropriately-named Grapevine, Texas.

I'm going to start the restaurant recommendations with upscale places, and most are located at the major resorts. La Hacienda at The Princess Resort (7575 E. Princess Drive, Scottsdale) is where Mexican goes uptown. This "Rancho Elegante" free-standing restaurant in the desert is decorated in Territorial style. The menu serves up such Mexico City temptations as roasted suckling pig, honey-almond glazed duck, crab-stuffed sea bass, roasted quail stuffed with *chorizo* and topped with *chipotle* sauce, and beef tenderloin glazed with *Chihuahua* cheese and salsa.

New Southwest cuisine is the highlight at the Palo Verde Room at The Boulders Resort, 34631 N. Tom Darlington Road in Carefree. Lamb, veal chops, off-beat vegetables and desserts highlight this restaurant. It has fresh, light-hearted decor and a charming patio. This is worth a visit just to experience a world-class resort.

The Piñon Grill (7401 N. Scottsdale Road in Scottsdale) is a fine Southwestern restaurant with attractive Indian motif designs and a view of a small lake. Some of the specialities include venison and papaya in blue corn tacos, double breast of chicken filled with *chorizo*, and yellow pepper-cilantro rice. The salads (with homemade dressing), the grilled veal chop, and the desserts are all excellent.

Windows on the Green at The Phoenician Resort (6000 E. Camelback Road, Scottsdale) is situated above the pro shop with a wonderful view of the golf course, so you might expect middle-American food instead of Southwestern inventions like lobster-corn chowder, venison chili, and bacon and *jalapeño* polenta.

For more than twenty years, Vincent Guerithault on Camelback (3930 E. Camelback Road) has been dazzling diners. With dishes such as duck *tamales*, rack of lamb with spicy pepper jelly, salmon with *jalapeño h*oney, and shrimp *quesadilla* with fresh basil, this restaurant—one of the finest in Phoenix—simply blows diners away. French-born chef Vincent seamlessly combines classic French techniques and Southwestern ingredients. The same mix of styles is evident in the sophisticated decor.

Moving on to the more traditional Sonoran-style restaurants, I'll begin with Macayo's Mexican Kitchen, 4001 N. Central Avenue, and 15 other locations in Arizona. One of the Valley's oldest Mexican food chains, Macayo's was founded in 1945. The food is standard but dependable and the restaurants always have enjoyable Cinco de Mayo celebrations and specialties. Try the tacos, *tamales*, *enchiladas*, and *chimichangas*. Ajo Al's, 9393 N. 90th Street in Scottsdale also has three other locations. This yuppie-family restaurant serves up decent Sonoran-style dishes. Try the salad *carbón* with grilled shrimp and avocado, or the shredded beef *enchiladas*. Also recommended are the steak *picado* with salsa and cheese, and the best *chile con queso* ever found in a restaurant.

Los Dos Molinos (8684 S. Central Avenue) is one of a mini-chain that originated in Springerville, a small town near the New Mexico border. The other is in the Phoenix suburb of Mesa. The newest Los Dos Molinos is located in an old adobe house rumored to have once been owned by silent film cowboy star Tom Mix. They serve a terrific hot sauce, great *adovada*, and anything with green chiles is good.

La Perla (5912 W. Glendale Avenue), aka "The Pearl," has been serving Mexican food since 1946. It's not fancy, but it is comfortable and always consistent. The expanded hours are great for folks needing a late night chile fix. Try the *albóndigas* soup, the *mole*, and the *frijoles borrachos* ("drunken beans").

Across town in Scottsdale, at Los Olivos (7328 2nd Street) meet the stars. During the warm nights in the Valley of the Sun, owner Elvaro Corral gives the order and the entire roof of "The Olives" slides back to reveal the starry Arizona sky—a perfect environment for listening to salsa music while sipping on a Mexican beer. The menu features Sonoran specialities, plus two homemade salsas each day (one made with *serranos*). For dessert under the stars there's *flan* and fried ice cream.

For students at Arizona State University, a real treat is El Pollo Supremo, 221 W. University Drive in Tempe. Here is the Valley's answer to the Mexican fast-food "pollo" shops so common in border towns. El Pollo Supremo ("the supreme chicken") offers citrus- and garlic-marinated grilled chicken served with ranch beans and chunky salsa. It's very good. While in Tempe, also visit Restaurant Mexico, 120 E. University Drive. This restaurant has mild, Central-Mexican style food served by folks who treat everyone like family. Recommended are the soft pork tacos, the bean soup, and the chunky *guacamole* with white cheese.

Poncho's Mexican Food (7202 S. Central Avenue) is a genuine community gathering place for all ages, ethnicities, and economic groups. Part of the reason is cheery *mariachi* music on weekends, and part is their excellent Sonoran-style cuisine. Recommended are the *albóndigas* soup, the *machaca,* and *guacamole*. I asked them for their recipe for green corn *tamales,* and they were nice enough to give it to me. (See Chapter 12). Rosita's Place (2310 E. McDowell Road) has only been in its present location since

Arizona Food Events

◆ *West of Western Culinary Festival*, late March in Phoenix, was founded to celebrate Arizona's Chefs and culinary culture. www.westofwestern.com

◆ *Scottsdale Culinary Festival*, the longest running festival of its kind in the United States, draws more than 40,000 visitors looking to enjoy fabulous food, fun and festivities. Early April, Scottsdale Mall. www.scottsdaleculinaryfestival.org

◆ *My Nana's Salsa Challenge* is a statewide culinary festival showcasing the prominence and popularity of our #1 condiment in the United States: salsa! Late April in Tempe and early November in Tucson. www.salsachallenge.com

◆ *Great Tucson Beer Festival*, late September, Hi Corbett Field. Also in Tempe in April. www.azbeer.com

◆ *Tucson Culinary Festival*, early October at Loews Ventana Canyon Resort, with tastings from 40 Tucson restaurants. www.tucsonculinaryfestival.com

◆ *La Fiesta de los Chiles*, late October, Tucson Botanical Gardens, is a very popular event celebrating the chile pepper. ChileFiesta@tucsonbotanical.org

On the way to Arizona food events, stay at the Wigwam Motel in Holbrook, built in 1950 and still open.

Photographer Aaron Sandoval

1989, but it has been around since the mid-Fifties. It has some killer red and green hot sauces and some excellent Sonora-style dishes. There is absolutely no ambience here but it's an in-spot for hard-core local Mexican food fans.

However, over in Cave Creek there's a ton of ambience at The Satisfied Frog, 6245 E. Cave Creek. This brew pub has a pseudo-western atmosphere that's rustic and fun. Their website describes it as "featuring bikers and babes, tee-shirts, off track betting, Chili Beer, micro-brewed beer, whiskey, BBQ, a wedding chapel, food, and entertainment." Now that's my kind of place! It was pretty quiet when Mary Jane and I had lunch there, but still fun because of the ambience. The burgers, ribs, fried chicken, and basic Mexican dishes are great, but the wonderful, made-on-the-premises beer is the keynote here. Try the chili beer with whole *serrano* chiles afloat in the bottle, a creation of the owner, "Crazy" Ed Chilleen.

Tacos in Tucson—and Way More

Tucson reminds me in many ways of Albuquerque. The cities are similar in size, and both have a major state university, an Air Force base, scenic mountain backdrops, a Spanish-Indian-Anglo heritage, wonderful food, excellent zoos, and loads of history and culture. Tucson, of course, has the striking saguaro cacti that are mostly missing from New Mexico—except in Las Cruces, where they will grow if properly protected during the coldest nights.

The often misspelled name of this city derives from a Pima Indian word, *stjuk-shon*, meaning "foot of a dark mountain," an allusion to Sentinel Peak— the mountain with the large "A" for the University of Arizona on it. The location was originally a Pima village, and the Spanish padre Eusebio Francisco Kino selected it as the site of the first San Xavier del Bac Mission in 1700. The existing mission, which was moved from its original site a couple of miles away, was constructed between 1783 and 1797 and today is a striking example of mission architecture. "The White Dove of the Desert," as

The giant saguaro has tasty fruits.
Photographer Aaron Sandoval

it's called, is located at 1-19 at San Xavier Road, and it is one of the most photographed missions in the Southwest.

El Presidio Historic District, bounded by Alameda, Church, and Franklin Streets, contains some of the oldest buildings in Tucson. The district has such attractions as the Tucson Museum of Art (140 N. Main), with its permanent collection of Western, Pre-Columbian and Spanish Colonial art; the El Charro Restaurant, one of the oldest in town; and restored private residences, mansions, galleries, and shops. South of this area, on the other side of the Convention Center, is the *Barrio Viejo*, the oldest neighborhood, which includes such sights as the Cushing Street Bar and Restaurant (343 S. Meyer Street), a former country store built over a hundred years ago, and El Tiradito (Main Street), a shrine commemorating a tragic love triangle.

Like Phoenix, there are numerous outdoor attractions in Tucson. The Tucson Botanical Gardens (2150 N. Alvernon Way) is small compared to the Desert Botanical Garden in Phoenix but still has nice displays of cacti, succulents, native plants, and herbs. Just off 1-10 (Speedway exit) are three different and fascinating outdoor fun spots: The International Wildlife Museum (4800 W. Gates Pass Road) with wild animals from six continents in 300 exhibits; Old Tucson Studios (201 S. Kinney Road), a classic movie set which features gunfights, illusion shows, shops, restaurants, and stunt demonstrations; and the Arizona-Sonora Desert Museum (Tucson Mountain Park on W. Gates Pass Road), which is an absolutely

fascinating combination zoo-museum-botanical garden with 200 animal species and 300 plant species preserved in their native Sonoran habitat.

Surrounding the Arizona-Sonora Desert Museum is the western part of Saguaro National Monument, a preserve for those huge cacti which can grow forty feet tall. The monument offers spectacular vistas and wildlife such as javelinas, coyotes, and bobcats. Wildlife can also be found at the Reid Park Zoo on E. 22nd Avenue, which is one of the finest small zoos in the country with more than 450 animals.

One park not to miss is Tohono Chul Park (7366 N. Paseo Drive), with its spectacular views—and a tea room. A reporter for the *Tucson Weekly* reported ecstatically: "While the courtyard is delightful, the patio facing a meandering path into the thirty-seven acre park is paradise. The umbrellas over the tables are hardly needed as you dine beneath a canopy of palo verdes, cottonwoods, and other non-thirsty trees. While you make your selection from a menu of inviting fare, you'll be entertained by hummingbirds darting among a wide variety of desert flowering shrubs like salvia, fuschia, and penstemmon. Birds sip from a shallow-tiled fountain. Monarchs and other butterflies inspect the potted greens. And the agaves in the distance look like they've been carefully sculpted. Lately, a white dove has been hanging around, waiting for crumbs."

Tucson has its share of fine museums. The Arizona State Museum (Park Avenue at University Boulevard) has exhibits on the natural, environmental, archaeological, and cultural history of the Southwest.

Arizona's history from the Spanish period to modern times is featured at the Arizona Historical Society Tucson Museum (949 E. 2nd Street). The Old Pueblo Museum in Foothills Mall (7401 N. La Cholla Boulevard) has a large collection of Southwestern art and artifacts, and the Amerind Foundation Museum, about sixty miles east of Tucson between Benson and Wilcox off I-10, is an archaeological and ethnographical museum with fine displays of jewelry, pottery, baskets, and other crafts.

Near Tucson are several interesting towns, including Bisbee, a mining boomtown complete with open pit, architectural wonders, and galleries. Also interesting is Tombstone, once one of the West's wildest towns but now a tourist resort, health center and National Historical Landmark. Don't miss the O.K. Corral, Boothill Cemetery, and the Bird Cage Theatre.

Tumacacori, forty miles south of Tucson, has a National Historical Park with a garden and a museum; Casa Grande National Monument, about seventy miles west of Tucson, is a prehistoric, four-story pueblo with an adjacent museum.

In Search of Carne Seca

Food is important in Tucson. So important that in their survey of the "Best of Tucson," *Tucson Weekly* urged readers to seek out the best food in the city and pay particular attention to regional specialties. "It is your duty," the editors wrote to the public, "to eat green corn *tamales* in every restaurant and report your findings to the green corn tamale hot line." Another dish to watch out for in Tucson is that unusual—but tasty—sun-dried beef.

It's fitting that *carne seca*, one of the hallmark dishes of Sonoran fare, should be prepared in part by sun-drying. Tucson, along with most of southern Arizona, is part of the Sonoran Desert, one of the hottest and most arid regions of North America. *Carne seca* is one of those foods that tastes a lot better than it sounds. Its name translates literally as "dried meat." But this is no jerky. In fact, although it's called *carne seca* south of the Gila River, it's called *machaca* north of the river, and there it's not air dried.

When it's done right in Tucson, *carne seca* is a rare treat: shreds of tender but slightly chewy beef, infused with a complex, smoky savor from its marinade of garlic and citrus juices, and its hours of sun-drying, then sauteed with onions, tomatoes, green chiles, and more garlic. The dish, like much of Sonoran food, differs from other Mexican styles of cuisine in several ways—its emphasis on beef and cheese (a result of the ranching heritage of the region), its more extensive use of flour tortillas, and the more subtle heat of its seasonings. Sonoran cooks usually have a deft but light hand with chiles, but I've made an effort to find some spicier recipes.

Filomeno Chavoya making chile sauce,
El Charro Restaurant, c. 1960.

Photographer unknown

Some of the best *carne seca* in Tucson is served at El Charro, 311 N. Court Avenue. This restaurant has been operated by the same family since 1922, and owners Carlotta and Ray Flores still make *carne seca* using the same method developed by Carlotta's aunt, Monica Flin, the restaurant's founder, nearly ninety years ago. Each day, about fifty pounds of thinly sliced beef is marinated in pureed garlic and lemon or lime juice. Then it's placed in a wire basket and hauled up to the top of El Charro's roof and spread out to dry in the sun. The drying time varies according to the weather, and the beef is usually chewier in summer than in winter.

After several hours, the beef is brought down and shredded. When a customer orders it, the *carne seca* is sauteed with chiles, onions, garlic, and tomatoes, then served in one of a myriad of ways—anything from tucked in a taco to deep-fried inside a *chimichanga*.

There are plenty of Sonoran specialties to try if you visit Tucson's Mexican restaurants, but don't miss your chance to savor *carne seca*—it's a truly unique product of Tucson's sun and climate as well as of the city's cultural heritage.

Beginning with retailers of Arizona foods, the Food Conspiracy Co-op (412 N. 4th Avenue) has been in business since 1971. *Tucson Weekly* staffers picked this "conspiratorial cooperative" as a likely spot for produce, 200 herbs and spices, bulk foods, and the large selection of salsas and hot sauces. Sandwiches and salads are available for carry-out. Rincon Food Market (2513 E. 6th Street) has been around since 1926 and has expanded greatly since 1975, and the market's evolution is evident as you move from the older room to a newer, much larger Eurostyle deli/bottle shop cum cafe on the east end. It is the culinary/social nexus of the affluent Sam Hughes neighborhood—known to locals as "Barrio Volvo." The market has a great selection of deli meats, dried and frozen pastas, local products, plus there's an in-house bakery offering cakes, cookies, pastries, and muffins of considerable local reputation.

Cheri's Desert Harvest (1840 E. Winsett Street) is a combo processing plant and retail location specializes in desert fruit and bread products, including prickly pear jelly, *margarita* marmalade, *jalapeño* corn bread, pecan bread, cactus syrup, pomegranate syrup, and even a Southwestern beer bread. Chile Pepper (22 Tubac Road in Tubac) is a Southwestern shop with a taste of Europe with its cappucino bar. It sells a wide variety of specialty foods, including local jams and jellies, *ristras*, salsas, hot sauces, BBQ sauces, Southwestern mustards and English mustards. All of their foods are available for tastings, and there's a wide selection of cookbooks here, too. The Pecan Store (1625 East Sahuarita Road in Sahuarita, 15 miles south of Tucson, exit 75 of I-19) is a food lover's delight. In addition to fresh pecans and pecan candies, this shop, nestled in the world's largest irrigated pecan orchard (6,000 acres), offers a complete line of Southwestern gourmet foods, including salsas, mustards, jellies, and jams.

They make their own products at the Santa Cruz Chili & Spice Company, 1868 E. Frontage Road, in Tumacacori. Since 1943, this gift shop with the Western Ranch Museum next door has been spicing up the lives of Arizona food lovers. They specialize in chile, including *ristras*, pastes, pods, and powders. Their sauces include locally-produced salsas, green sauces, and barbecue sauces. The Tucson Botanical Gardens Gift Shop (2150 North Alvernon Way) loves chile peppers and features books, tee-shirts, and food products. Additionally, there are nature books, travel guides, and calendars about Arizona and the Sonora Desert.

Perhaps Tucson's most highly-rated brewery is Thunder Canyon Brewery, 7401 N. La Cholla Boulevard, Suite 178. It is a full-service restaurant and brewery, offering contemporary bistro cuisine and a wide variety of hand-crafted beers brewed on-site in their state-of-the-art 15-barrel brewery. Their signature brews are Sandstone Cream Ale, Deep Canyon Amber and Obsidian Porter, plus eight others on tap at any given time. They also brew many seasonal beers.

Recommended Restaurants

The Hacienda del Sol has been around since 1929, but the Grill there (5601 N. Hacienda Del Sol Road) was built in 1997. The Grill is regarded as one of the finest restaurants in the Southwest, serving upscale food like *foie gras*, Muscovy duck, and lobster. That said, the chef at The Grill offers some specialties like buffalo sirloin with chocolate chile sauce. In 2004, 2006 and 2007 readers of *Tucson Weekly* named it the best restaurant for Upscale Dining. On October 31, 1983, chef Janos Wilder opened Janos at 150 North Main Avenue in the El Presidio Historic District downtown. Fifteen years later he moved to the current location (3770 E. Sunrise Drive) on the grounds of the Westin La Paloma Resort. He combines impeccably fresh local ingredients with wit and imagination, and diners can expect to find an astonishing diversity on the menu from *hamachi ceviche* with mangos, candied *jalapenos*, candied orange, mint and basil to lamb from the heart of Mexico with *chipotle recado* to

Original sign for Café Terra Cotta, c. 1991.
Photographer Dave DeWitt

smoked salmon, mushroom, roasted chile and corn bisque.

In 1986, when Donna Nordin opened Café Terra Cotta (3500 Sunrise Drive), she had a vision for the food she would serve: "First, it would be based on the fundamental ingredients native to the American Southwest and northern Mexico—chiles, corn, tomatoes, squash, and beans. And second, it would reach deeper into Mexico, especially to the Yucatan, central Mexico, and Oaxaca, where the sauces are more robust, complex, and balanced." Some of her dishes include red chile beef & avocado *quesadilla*, *chipotle* maple glazed chicken, and braised bison short rib.

El Charro (311 N. Court Avenue, and other locations) open since 1922, claims to be the birthplace of the *chimichanga*, the home of the best *carne seca*,

and the site of the home of the gigantic *USA Today* *chimichanga*, a *chimi* the size of a folded newspaper. It could very well be all those things, but we do know it's located in an historic downtown house, has been run by the same family for decades, and serves great Sonoran-style food. Don't miss the green corn *tamales* in season. El Minuto Café (354 S. Main Avenue) is located in Barrio Viejo and has been a popular late-night spot since 1939 that serves up great cheese crisps, award-winning *carne seca*, plus classic Sonoran cowboy fare. The waiters are attired in *guayaberas*, Tucson's official summer business attire. A favorite with locals, Crossroads Restaurant Drive-In (2602 S. Fourth Avenue) is a lively weekend spot that offers Guaymas shrimp in a variety of preparations (try *al mojo de ajo*) and *cabrilla* sea bass as their specialities, but also serves an assortment of Sonoran-style dishes too.

Chimichanga: Translated at Last?

It has long been written that the word *chimichanga* has no translation into English except as the vague "thingamajig." But recently, word sleuths have been tracking down its meaning. Since the word *changa* means "female monkey" in Spanish, that was the logical place to begin. Idiomatic slang was suspected and Tucson freelance writer Janet Mitchell put the question to Jim Griffith, then director of the University of Arizona Southwest Folklore Center. "No doubt about it," he answered, the word *chimichanga* is a polite version of an unmentionable Mexican expletive that mentions a monkey."

So, a monkey was a part of the translation, but what did it mean? And how was it connected to a deep-fried *burro*? The next step was to look at the first part of the word, *chimi*. The closest Spanish word seemed to be *chimenea*, meaning chimney or hearth—and both words indicated heat.

Investigator Mitchell had heard tales about the first chimichanga being created when a *burro* was accidentally knocked into a deep-fat fryer and the the cook exclaimed, "Chimichanga!" She had also heard that a baked burro cooked in a bar in Nogales in the 'Forties had been called a "toasted monkey."

The logical conclusion, then, was that the idiom *chimichanga* means "toasted monkey," and is an allusion to the golden brown color of the deep-fried burro.

The roots of La Indita (622 N. Fourth Avenue) are Tarascan, from the state of Michoacán, Mexico. Their homemade Indian items run the gamut from Tarascan tacos filled with *carne seca* to Tohono O'odham red chile to Navajo tacos to Sonoran *chiles rellenos*. Dine outside in warm weather here. The universal choice by *Tucson Weekly* readers for best in most categories of Sonoran-style food, Mi Nidito ("My Little Nest") at 1813 S. Fourth Avenue, is always crowded but the wait is worth it. Recommended dishes include their *chiles rellenos*, cheese crisps, and *chimichangas*. The service is brisk, the portions are large, and the prices are reasonable. It's been delighting food lovers here since 1952, and celebrity diners include Linda Ronstadt, Rich Little, William Shatner and Fran Tarkenton.

Lunch is tasty at the Tohono Chul Tea Room (7633 N. Paseo del Norte in Tohono Chul Park) with *enchiladas*, *quesadillas*, and Pepperjack ziti, a pasta dish with grilled chicken, roasted chiles, fresh tomatoes, cilantro and Pepperjack and Cheddar cream sauce. Surrounded by the native flora and fauna of the Sonoran desert, the scenery is as great as the restaurant. The enclosed courtyard, with its fountain and bougainvilla, is delightful.

Li'l Abner's (8501 N. Silverbell Road) began its life in the 19th century as a stop on the Butterfield Stage Line, and its history shows in its scarred adobe walls. There are two rustic dining rooms and a bar inside, but a picnic table on the back patio is the place to eat. They serve a monster porterhouse steak which is grilled over mesquite on the back patio. The trimmings of this classic ranch-style meal include ranch beans, garlic toast, salsa *fresca*, and salad, all washed down with Dos Equis or Negra Modelo beer. Since 1951, Jack's Original Barbeque (5250 E. 22nd Street) has been luring customers into his parking lot with the aroma of wood smoke and sizzling meats. They call this mouth-watering style of BBQ ribs, links, and sliced beef and pork 'cue Kansas City style, but the truth is that it has Tucson written all over it. Jack Banks sold the place a few years ago, but public outrage brought him back.

5. Salsas, Sauces, Chile of the Past, and a Rub

Salsas and sauces are essential to Southwestern cuisine. They are similar in that they utilize chile peppers of one variety or another, and contain fresh vegetables commonly grown in the Southwestern states. The difference between them is simple—salsas are usually uncooked and sauces are usually cooked. I've also included my favorite rub for smoking and grilling meats and poultry.

Tomatillos.

Photographer Aaron Sandoval

Pico de Gallo Salsa

This universal salsa, also known as salsa fria, salsa cruda, salsa fresca, salsa Mexicana, and salsa picante, is served all over the Southwest and often shows up with non-traditional ingredients such as canned tomatoes, bell peppers, or spices like oregano. Here is the most authentic version. Remember that everything in it should be as fresh as possible, and the vegetables must be hand-chopped. Never, never use a blender or food processor. Pico de Gallo is best when the tomatoes come from the garden, not from the supermarket. It can be used as a dip for chips, or for spicing up fajitas and other Southwestern specialties. Note: It requires advance preparation and will keep for only a day or two in the refrigerator.

4 serrano or jalapeño chiles, seeds and stems removed, chopped fine (or more for a hotter salsa)
2 large, ripe tomatoes, finely chopped
1 medium onion, chopped fine
1/4 cup fresh cilantro, minced
2 tablespoons vinegar
2 tablespoons vegetable oil

Combine all ingredients in a large bowl, mix well, and let the salsa sit, covered, for at least an hour to blend the flavors.

Yield: 3 cups   Heat Scale: Medium

Serrano Salsa with Mangos and *Tomatillos*

Not all Southwest salsas are tomato-based; this one utilizes tomatillos, the small "husk tomatoes" that are grown mostly in Mexico, but are available fresh or canned in many U.S. supermarkets. The natural sweetness of the mango blends perfectly with the tartness of the tomatillos. Note: This recipe requires advance preparation.

6 red serrano chiles, stems and seeds removed, minced
1 clove garlic, minced
2 tablespoons green onions, including the greens, chopped
1 mango, pitted and coarsely chopped
6 tomatillos, husks removed, chopped
1/2 cup fresh cilantro, chopped
1 lime, juiced
2 tablespoons olive oil

Combine all ingredients in a bowl and allow to sit for at least three hours—and preferably overnight—to blend the flavors.

Yield: 4 servings   Heat Scale: Medium

Salsa Casera

This diabolically hot sauce from Arizona is also called chiltepín pasta (paste). It is used in soups and stews and to fire up machaca (shredded beef), eggs, tacos, tostadas, and beans. Because it is so hot, the amount of sauce in this recipe could last for years when stored in the refrigerator. Note: This recipe requires advance preparation.

2 cups chiltepíns (yes, 2 cups)
8 to 10 cloves garlic
1 teaspoon salt
1 teaspoon Mexican oregano
1 teaspoon coriander seed
1 cup water
1 cup cider vinegar

Combine all ingredients in a blender and puree on high speed for 3 to 4 minutes. Refrigerate for one day to blend the flavors before using. From then on, it keeps indefinitely in the refrigerator.

Yield: 2 cups   Heat Scale: Extremely hot

Xnipec (Dog's Breath Salsa)

Fresh habanero chiles are sometimes hard to find, so serranos may be substituted, but double the number used. However, the salsa won't have the same marvelous aroma without the "habs". Use as a salsa with grilled fish or grilled chicken, or try it over eggs.

4 habanero chiles, stems and seeds removed, minced
4 limes, juiced
1 red onion, finely chopped
1 tomato, diced

Soak the diced onion in the lime juice in a bowl for at least 30 minutes. Add all the other ingredients and mix, salt to taste, and add a little water if desired.

Yield: 1 1/2 cups   Heat Scale: Extremely hot

Guajillo Sauce

This basic recipe can be used for guajillos, New Mexican reds, pasillas, cascabels, or any other dried chiles. This sauce is rather mild, so you can use a lot of it. Dried chile sauces are traditionally served with pork.

5 dried guajillo chiles, stems and seeds removed and if you wish to make a very mild sauce, deveined
2 tomatoes, diced
2 cloves garlic, minced
1/2 onion, diced
2 tablespoons olive oil
Salt to taste

Toast the chiles 2 minutes in a hot skillet, flipping often (beware of fumes). Soak the toasted chiles in enough water to barely cover them until soft, about ten minutes. Saute the onion and garlic in the olive oil. Add the tomatoes to the softened chiles and puree in a blender. Add the puree to the sauteed onions and peppers and cook for 20 minutes on low. Add salt to taste.

Yield: 1 1/2 cups   Heat Scale: Mild

Roasted *Poblano*-Corn Salsa with Morels

One of the tenets of New Southwestern cooking is innovative combinations of farm-fresh ingredients. This recipe, made with mostly New World foods, is a good example. It's a salsa served like an entrée.

5 ears of corn in husks
7 teaspoons olive oil
5 tablespoons morels (or other wild mushrooms), diced
2 poblano chiles, roasted, peeled, stems and seeds removed, diced
1/4 cup sundried tomatoes, minced
2 tablespoons cilantro, minced
1 tablespoon chipotles in adobo, minced
2 teaspoons fresh marjoram, minced
1 teaspoon lime juice
Salt to taste

Place the corn on a baking sheet and bake at 400 degrees for 30 minutes, turning often, until the corn is blackened on all sides. Allow to cool.

In a small skillet, cook the morels in 2 teaspoons of the olive oil until well browned, about 5 minutes.

Shuck the corn and brush with 2 tablespoons of olive oil. Place on a baking sheet and broil the corn until the kernels brown, about 10 minutes. (You can also do this on the grill.) Cut the kernels from the cob and reserve.

In a bowl, combine the corn and the morels with the remaining ingredients (and the remaining olive oil) and mix well. Serve warm on a bed of greens.

Yield: 4 servings   Heat Scale: Mild

Salsa de Jalapeño o Serrano Asado

(Roasted *Jalapeño* or *Serrano* Salsa)

The simplicity of this salsa, imported from northern Mexico and popular in Texas, is deceiving, for it is one of the best all-around table sauces. The charred tomatoes and chiles have a robust flavor, and you can control the texture.

2 large tomatoes
2 jalapeño or serrano chiles, stems removed
1/4 teaspoon salt, or to taste

Grill the tomatoes and chiles by placing them 3 to 6 inches above the flames. Turn them often; they should be soft and the skins should be charred.

In a blender, pulse the tomatoes and chiles for 30 seconds to the desired consistency. Add salt to taste. The texture is smooth and the sauce is flecked with tiny bits of the charred chile and tomato skins, which add an interesting flavor.

Yield: 2 to 4 servings   Heat Scale: Medium

Christine's Hot Sauce

I confess I've never met Christine. Her recipe was passed on to us by friends in Scottsdale, and it's a good example of an Arizona-style, all-purpose hot sauce that can be used for a chip dip, or can be added to soups and stews.

2 tablespoons chiltepíns
3 New Mexican red chiles, stems and seeds removed, crushed and rehydrated in 1/2 cup water
1 1/2 cloves garlic
1/2 onion, minced
1/4 teaspoon cumin
Pinch of oregano
Pinch of salt
2 tablespoons vegetable oil
2 tablespoons vinegar
8-ounce can tomato sauce

Puree all ingredients, except the tomato sauce, in a blender, then place the mixture in a bowl. Add the tomato sauce and mix well.

Yield: 2 cups   Heat Scale: Hot

Texas Green Sauce

When you order "green sauce" in Texas, this is what you will be served. It differs from New Mexico's green sauce in that the color is derived from tomatillos rather than from green chiles. This sauce can be used as a dipping sauce, with enchiladas, or as a topping for grilled poultry or fish.

3 pounds tomatillos
1 bunch green onions
1 small bunch cilantro
1 tablespoon garlic in oil
2 teaspoons sugar
2 teaspoons lime juice
1 tablespoons chicken base dissolved in 2 tablespoons water
6 serrano chiles, stems removed

Roast the tomatillos in a roasting pan under the broiler until they are brown and squishy. Turn them over with a pair of tongs and repeat the process. Take the roasted tomatillos, including all the liquid from the roasting process, and combine them with the remaining ingredients in a food processor and puree.

In a saucepan, simmer this mixture for ten minutes before serving or incorporating into another recipe.

Yield: 4 cups   Heat Scale: Medium

Classic New Mexico Red Chile Sauce

This basic sauce can be used in any recipe calling for a red sauce, either traditional Mexican or New Southwestern versions of beans, tacos, tamales, and enchiladas.

    10 to 12 dried whole red New Mexican chiles
    1 large onion, chopped
    3 cloves garlic, chopped
    3 cups water

Place the chiles on a baking pan and put in a 250 degree F. oven for about 10 to 15 minutes or until the chiles smell like they are toasted, taking care not to let them burn. Remove the stems and seeds and crumble them into a saucepan.

Add the remaining ingredients, bring to a boil, reduce the heat and simmer for 20 to 30 minutes.

Puree the mixture in a blender until smooth and strain if necessary. If the sauce is too thin, place it back on the stove and simmer until it is reduced to the desired consistency.

Yield: About 3cups   Heat Scale: Medium

Variations: Spices such as cumin, coriander, and Mexican oregano may be added to taste. Some versions of this sauce call for the onion and garlic to be sauteed in lard—or vegetable oil these days—before the chiles and water are added.

Classic New Mexico Green Chile Sauce

This all-purpose sauce recipe is from the southern part of New Mexico, where green chile is the number one food crop and is used more commonly than the red variety. It is used with enchiladas and is often served over scrambled eggs.

    1 small onion, chopped
    2 cloves garlic, minced (optional)
    2 tablespoons vegetable oil
    6 green New Mexican chiles, roasted, peeled,
        seeds and stems removed, chopped
    1/2 teaspoon ground cumin
    2 cups chicken broth or water

In a pan, saute the onion and garlic in 2 tablespoons of oil until soft.

Add the chiles, cumin, and water and simmer for 1/2 hour. The sauce may be pureed in a blender to the desired consistency.

Yield: About 2 cups   Heat Scale: Medium

Variations: To thicken the sauce, make a roux by sauteeing 1 tablespoon flour in 1 tablespoon vegetable oil, taking care not to let it burn. Slowly stir the roux into the sauce and cook to the desired thickness. Coriander and Mexican oregano may be added to taste. For added heat, add more New Mexican chiles or a serrano or two.

¡Ole Mole Sauce!

Here is my Southwestern version of the classic Mexican sauce that originated in Puebla, Mexico. The traditional lard is replaced with vegetable oil. Lard, however, does lend an authentic taste to this sauce. This sauce goes well with any poultry dish, and can be used in place of red or green chile sauce for enchiladas.

4 dried pasilla chiles, stems and seeds removed (or substitute anchos)
4 dried red New Mexican chiles, stems and seeds removed
3 cups water
1 medium onion, chopped
2 cloves garlic, chopped
2 medium tomatoes, peeled and chopped
3 tomatillos, chopped
1 tablespoon sesame seeds
1 tablespoon pumpkin seeds
1/2 cup finely chopped almonds
1 corn tortilla, torn in pieces
1/4 cup raisins
1/2 teaspoon oregano
1/4 teaspoon each ground cloves, cinnamon, and coriander
3 tablespoons vegetable oil
2 cups chicken broth
1 ounce unsweetened chocolate (or more to taste)

In a large pan, simmer the chiles in water for 15 minutes to soften. Remove the chiles and reserve the water.

Combine the chiles, onion, garlic, tomatoes, tomatillos, seeds, almonds, tortilla, raisins and spices in a blender and puree, in small amounts, until smooth.

Heat the oil in a skillet and saute the puree for 10 minutes, stirring frequently. Add the broth, 1 cup of the chile water, and the chocolate and cook over a very low heat for 30 to 45 minutes, or until thick.

Yield: 4 cups   Heat Scale: Medium

Chipotle BBQ Sauce

The smoked red jalapeño, known as the chipotle chile, has gained such popularity that there are even a couple of cookbooks devoted to it! It particularly works well with barbecuing and grilling, both of which have considerable smoke associated with them.

3 dried chipotle chiles
1 cup water
1 1/2 tablespoons vegetable oil
1 medium onion, chopped fine
2 cloves garlic, minced
2 red bell peppers, quartered, seeds removed
2 onions, sliced thickly
3 tomatoes, cut in half
2 cups ketchup
1/4 cup Worcestershire sauce
1/4 cup red wine vinegar
1/4 cup brown sugar

In a bowl, combine the chipotle chiles with very hot water and soak for 30 minutes or more to soften. Chop the chipotles finely. In a medium saucepan, heat the oil and saute the onion. After the onion is translucent, add the garlic and continue to saute for 2 minutes.

To roast the bell peppers, onions, and tomatoes, place them on the grill over a medium fire and grill until they are soft and slightly blackened. Remove, peel, and chop the vegetables.

In a large saucepan, combine all the ingredients and bring the mixture to a low boil over a medium heat. Reduce the heat and simmer for 20 minutes. Let the mixture cool and puree in a blender or food processor until smooth. You can thin the mixture with water if you so desire.

Yield: About 4 cups   Heat Scale: Medium

Deep, Way Deep in the Heart of Texas Barbecue Sauce

Until recently, New Mexican chiles were rarely used in Texas cooking. But as the popularity of chili con carne cookoff contests increased, cooks began experimenting with chiles other than just piquíns and jalapeños. Here is one result of this broadening of the chile pepper experience.

4 dried red New Mexican chiles, stems and seeds removed
4 small dried red chiles such as piquíns or chiltepíns
2 cups water
1 large onion, chopped
4 cloves garlic, chopped
2 tablespoons vegetable oil

1 and 1/2 cups ketchup
12 ounces beer, Shiner Bock preferred
1/4 cup brown sugar
3 tablespoons cider vinegar
2 tablespoons Worcestershire sauce
2 teaspoons dry mustard
1 teaspoon freshly ground black pepper

In a pan, simmer the chiles in the water for 15 minutes or until softened. Puree the chiles in the water to make a smooth sauce. Strain the sauce.

In a saucepan, saute the onions and the garlic in the oil until soft. Add the pureed chiles and the remaining ingredients and bring to a boil. Reduce the heat and simmer for an hour.

In a blender, puree the sauce until smooth. If the sauce is not thick enough, return to the heat and continue to simmer until the desired consistency is obtained.

Yield: 2 cups   Heat Scale: Medium

Chile *Pasado*

Translated as "chile of the past," this is the original recipe for preserving green chile before the advent of canning and freezing. Be forewarned that the result looks awful—nearly black and stringy. However, when rehydrated, it regains its greenish color and makes a fine green chile sauce for casseroles or enchiladas. It can also be used in soups and stews. Since chile pasado costs up to $16 a pound in Southwestern markets (if you can find it), it makes sense to prepare your own. The light weight of the chile pasado is convenient, say, when traveling to Italy to make enchiladas for friends there, as I did once.

    35 to 40 green chile pods

Follow the instructions (p. 215) for roasting and peeling green chile. When finished, cut the pods into wide strips and place them on a Teflon-coated cookie sheet. Cover with cheesecloth to keep insects off and place it in the full sun. Take the chiles in at night to prevent dew from accumulating. The number of drying days depends on the humidity. A food dehydrator can also be used. When dry, the chile should be black and brittle. The best way to preserve *chile pasado* is to put it in Ziplock bag and freeze it, though it can be stored in jars in the pantry. To use it, simply place it in warm water for a half hour and it will rehydrate.

Yield: About 1/2 pound   Heat Scale: Varies

North of the Border Chile Rub

This is my spin on a Southwestern rub that would work on goat, as in cabrito, pit roasted goat. Can't find goat at Winn-Dixie? Use this rub for either grilling or smoking beef, pork, and lamb.

    3 tablespoons ground ancho chile
    2 teaspoons ground chile de arbol
    2 teaspoons ground chipotle chile
    2 teaspoons dried oregano, Mexican preferred
    2 teaspoons onion salt
    1 teaspoon ground cumin
    1 teaspoon powdered garlic

Combine all the ingredients in a bowl and mix well. Store any unused rub in a sealed container in the freezer.

Yield: approximately 2/3 cup   Heat Scale: Hot

6. Aperitivos: Drinks and Appetizers

In other parts of the country they are called "appetizers" or "hors d'oeuvres," but in the Southwest the word is *aperitivo*. It refers to anything served before the main courses—drinks or snacks. Here is a collection of some of my favorite cocktails, drinks and finger foods.

A *margarita* with limes.

Photographer Aaron Sandoval

The Perfect *Margarita*

Contrary to popular belief, the perfect margarita is made not with Triple Sec but with Cointreau. Also necessary for the perfect margarita are a great tequila such as Herradura and Mexican limes (also called Key limes), rather than Persian limes.

1/2 Mexican lime (or more to taste)
Coarse salt
1 1/2 ounces white tequila
3/4 ounce Cointreau

Squeeze the lime into a shaker full of ice cubes. Rub the lime around the lip of an iced cocktail glass and dip the lip into the coarse salt in a saucer. Add the tequila and Cointreau, shake well, and strain into the cocktail glass.

Yield: 1 serving

Variations: The margarita can also be served on the rocks, or blended with ice to make a frozen margarita.

Bloody Maria

Think this drink is just a Bloody Mary with tequila switched for the vodka? Well, almost. ¡Salud!

2 ounces tequila
3 ounces tomato juice
1/4 ounce lime juice
Dash Worcestershire sauce
Dash celery salt
Dash black pepper
Dash salt

1 1/2 teaspoons bottled chipotle hot sauce or habanero hot sauce
Slice of lime for garnish

Combine all ingredients in a large glass, stir well and pour over ice in another glass. Garnish with a slice of lime and serve.

Yield: 1 serving   Heat Scale: Medium

Chiltepín Pepper Vodka

The Russians are the true inventors of pepper vodka and they flavor their vodka most commonly with cayenne. Any type of small fresh or dried chile pepper that will fit in the bottle will work. Be sure to taste it often and strain to remove the chiles when it reaches the desired heat—the longer the chiles are left in, the hotter the vodka will get! Serve over ice or in tomato juice for an "instant" Bloody Mary. Note: This recipe requires advance preparation.

4 to 6 dried chiltepín chiles, left whole
1 quart vodka

Place the chiles in the vodka and let them steep for a week or more. Periodically taste the vodka and remove the chiles when it is hot enough.

Yield: 1 quart   Heat Scale: Medium to Hot

Sangrita with Three Juices

Serve this tasty drink as a chaser to straight tequila in a glass rimmed with salt. Sip the tequila, then the sangrita, then suck on a lime slice. Repeat the procedure as often as you dare! Or, mix the tequila into the sangrita.

3 green New Mexican chiles, roasted, peeled,
    stems and seeds removed, chopped
3 cups tomato juice
1 cup orange juice
1/4 cup lime juice
2 tablespoons onions, chopped
1 teaspoon sugar
Salt to taste

Place all the ingredients in a blender and puree until smooth. Chill before serving.

Yield: 1 quart   Heat Scale: Medium

Agua Fresca de Tamarindo

(Tamarind Drink)

On a really hot summer day in the Southwest, this is the perfect drink. Agua Fresca is thirst quenching, has more nutritional value than tea or water, and you can drink lots of it without worrying about caffeine or alcohol. Kids love it, and it goes great with hot and spicy food, too!

1/2 pound tamarind beans (available in Latin
    markets or by mail order)
3/4 cup of sugar or honey
1 gallon water

Rinse the beans and drain them. Place the beans in a soup pot and add enough water to cover them. Cook at a low boil for ten minutes or so. In the liquid, mash the softened beans vigorously with a potato masher. Strain the coffee-colored liquid into a gallon container discarding the seeds and outer pods as you go. Add the sugar or honey while the liquid is hot. Add water to fill the container. Refrigerate and serve over ice.

Yield: 1 gallon

Variation: Adjust the sugar level to your taste. Use the specified equivalent amount of artificial sweetener for the diet version. Serve over more or less ice to make it as strong or weak as you like it.

Tequila Sunrise

Here is another quintessential Southwestern drink. This one was immortalized in song by the rock group The Eagles.

Crushed ice
2 ounces tequila
1/4 ounce grenadine
3 ounces freshly squeezed orange juice

Fill a tall glass with crushed ice, add the tequila and grenadine, and fill with the orange juice. Stir well.

Yield: 1 serving

Variation: Use 2 ounces of orange juice and 1 ounce of sparkling water

Cantina *Chile con Queso*

Chile con Queso can be served as a dip for tostada chips, as a sauce for topping hamburgers, or even as a thick soup.

4 jalapeño chiles, stems removed, seeded, and chopped
3 medium onions, quartered
2 pounds fresh tomatoes, quartered
1/4 cup vegetable oil
5 pounds American cheese, sliced
1 pound Cheddar cheese, grated
6 medium eggs, beaten
1 tablespoon chicken base

Boil the jalapeños in 2 quarts of water for 5 minutes. Add the tomatoes and onions and boil for 10 minutes. Drain the vegetables and retain 3 cups of water. In a blender, blend the vegetables and the retained water on the lowest speed for 5 to 7 seconds.

In a large pan, saute this puree in the oil over medium heat for 90 seconds. Lower the heat and add the American cheese one slice at a time, allowing it to melt slowly, stirring constantly.

Add the Cheddar cheese and stir until completely melted. Combine the eggs with the chicken base in a bowl, mix, and add to the cheese. Cook for 5 minutes, stirring constantly.

Yield: 12 or more servings as a dip
Heat Scale: Medium

Spicy Lamb *Carnitas*

Serve these "little pieces of meat" with toothpicks and several salsas for dipping from Chapter 5, or guacamole (see recipes, this chapter). Note: This recipe requires advance preparation.

1 tablespoon ground red New Mexican chile
3 cloves garlic, minced
1/4 cup minced onions
2 teaspoons fresh cilantro, finely chopped
1 teaspoon dried oregano
1 teaspoon freshly ground black pepper
1 teaspoon ground cumin
1/2 teaspoon salt
1 pound boneless lamb, cut into 1 inch cubes

Combine all the ingredients, except the lamb, in a bowl and rub the meat cubes with the mixture. Allow the meat to sit, at room temperature, for an hour or more to marinate.

Place the meat on a rack over a pan to catch the drippings. Bake the meat at 250 degrees for an hour or until the meat is crisp on the outside. The meat can also be grilled.

Yield: 6 servings   Heat Scale: Mild

Quesadillas with Goat Cheese

These tortas are excellent when served as an appetizer or they can replace sandwiches for a real Southwestern lunch.

6 green New Mexican chiles, roasted, peeled, stems and seeds removed, cut into strips
6 8-inch flour tortillas
8 ounces goat cheese, crumbled or sliced
1 cup nopales (cactus pads) strips (optional)
1 small avocado, peeled, pitted, and diced
1/2 cup chopped onions, finely chopped
1 tablespoon fresh herbs, such as cilantro, oregano, or basil, chopped
Ground red New Mexican chile

On one half of a tortilla, layer some of the cheese, chiles, nopales, avocado, onions, and herbs. Moisten the edges, fold the tortilla over and press to seal. Repeat with each tortilla.

Toast the tortillas on each side on a hot griddle until the cheese melts. Dust with the ground red chile.

Cut each quesadilla into 4 wedges and serve.

Yield: 24 wedges   Heat Scale: Medium

Variation: 4 ounces Feta and 1/4 cup Ricotta cheese may be substituted for the goat cheese.

El Paso Nachos

This appetizer has become so popular that you don't have to travel to Texas to enjoy it, although nachos you buy outside the Southwest may bear little resemblance to the "real thing."

1 dozen corn tortillas, cut into wedges
Vegetable oil for frying
3/4 cup refried beans (see recipe, chapter 13)
1/2 pound sharp Cheddar cheese, grated
1/2 cup sour cream
4 or more jalapeño chiles, stems and seeds removed, sliced in thin rings

In a large skillet, fry the tortillas in 1 1/2 inches of oil, at 350 degrees, until crispy. Remove and drain on paper towels.

Arrange the tortillas on a pan or oven-proof plate. Place a small amount of beans on each chip and top with the grated cheese. Heat the pan under the broiler until the cheese melts or microwave the plate for 3 to 4 minutes.

Top with the sour cream and jalapeño slices and serve immediately.

Yield: 6 to 8 servings   Heat Scale: Medium

Jicama Slices with a Choice of Ground Chiles

The heat of this appetizer will depend on the type of chile powder selected for dipping. Don't limit yourself to jicama—try slices of other fruits and vegetables as well.

1 tablespoon each ground de arbol, pasilla, and red New Mexican chile
1 to 1 1/2 pounds jicama, peeled
1/3 cup fresh lime juice
1/2 cup salt

Cut the jicama into sticks 1/2 inch wide and 3 to 4 inches long. In a bowl, pour the lime juice over the sticks, making sure that they are well coated.

Divide the salt into thirds and mix each type of chile powder in each part of the salt.

To serve. arrange the sticks on a plate with the three chile salts. Guests dip the sticks into their choice of chile salt.

Yield: 6 to 8 servings
Heat Scale: Mild to Medium

Two Versions of *Guacamole*

The combination of avocados and chile is common throughout the Southwest. Here are my two favorite versions. Serve them as a dip with chips, over greens as a salad dressing, with roasted meats and poultry as a dipping sauce, or as a garnish over enchiladas, tostadas, or tacos.

New Mexico Version

3 green New Mexican chiles, roasted, peeled, stems and seeds removed, finely chopped
1 tomato, finely chopped
3 medium avocados, pitted, peeled, and mashed
1 medium onion, finely chopped
1 teaspoon lemon juice
1/4 teaspoon garlic powder
1/4 teaspoon powdered cumin (optional)
Salt to taste

Combine all the ingredients in a bowl and mix well.

Yield: 2 cups   Heat Scale: Mild

Texas Version

3 jalapeño or serrano chiles, stems and seeds removed, chopped fine
3 medium avocados, pitted, peeled, and mashed
1 medium onion, chopped fine
1/4 teaspoon garlic salt
Juice of 1 lemon
Salt to taste

Combine all the ingredients in a bowl and mix well.

Yield: 2 cups   Heat Scale: Medium

Green Chile Tortilla Pinwheels

This is an all-purpose filling that also goes well on crackers and in finger sandwiches. Thin it with milk or light cream to make a great dip for chips or vegetable crudities.

- 1/2 cup chopped green New Mexican chiles that have been roasted, peeled, seeds and stems removed
- 1 3-oz. package light cream cheese, softened
- 2 tablespoons milk or cream
- 1/4 teaspoon garlic salt
- 2 teaspoons minced cilantro
- 3 to 4 flour tortillas

Combine all the ingredients, except the tortillas, in a bowl and mix well.

Wrap the tortillas in a damp towel and place in a warm oven to soften. Spread the cream cheese mixture on the tortillas and roll each tortilla as you would a jellyroll. Slice each roll into 1/2-inch thick rounds.

Yield: 48 to 60 pinwheels   Heat Scale: Medium

Queso Flameado with Poblano Strips

This appetizer is so quick and easy to prepare that you can wait until your guests arrive before starting it. It is from the northern states of Mexico but is often served in the Southwest.

- 2 poblano chiles, roasted, peeled, stems and seeds removed, cut into strips
- 2 tablespoons butter or olive oil
- 2 cups queso blanco, Monterey Jack, or Cheddar cheese, grated
- Corn tortillas or tostadas for dipping

In a pan, saute the poblano strips in the oil until they are soft. In a small casserole dish, add half the cheese, then half the poblano strips, then the remaining cheese. Cover and bake at 300 degrees for about 5 minutes, until the cheese has melted. Uncover, add the remaining strips, and bake for 2 more minutes.

To serve, remove the dish from the oven and use the tortillas or tostadas to dip out the cheese and strips.

Yield: 6 servings   Heat Scale: Mild

Blue Corn *Flautas*

The word flauta means "flute" in Spanish, an allusion to the rolled shape of the tortillas in this dish.

1 pound ground beef
1/2 cup New Mexican green chiles that have been roasted, peeled, seeds and stems removed and chopped
1 red bell pepper, seeds and stem removed, julienned
1 yellow bell pepper, seeds and stem removed, julienned
1 onion, thinly sliced
1/2 teaspoon salt
1/4 teaspoon cumin
12 blue corn tortillas
Vegetable oil for frying
1 cup of your favorite salsa (see recipes, Chapter 5)
1 cup Cheddar cheese, grated
1 cup lettuce, shredded
1 cup guacamole (see recipes, this Chapter)
1 cup tomatoes, chopped

Brown the beef in a skillet and drain the excess fat. Add the chiles, bell peppers, onions, salt, cumin, and cook until the onions and bell peppers are soft.

In another skillet, fry the tortillas in the oil for a few seconds until soft. Remove and drain on paper towels. Place the beef mixture in the center of the tortillas, roll up the tortillas, and secure with toothpicks. Fry the flautas in oil until crisp.

Place the lettuce on plates, place two flautas on top, and top with the salsa, cheese, guacamole, and tomatoes.

Yield: 6 servings   Heat Scale: Medium

Marinated *Rajas*

Rajas, or strips of green chile, are commonly cooked with other vegetables. But New Mexican chile has such a great flavor that the rajas can stand alone. Serve these tasty appetizers with toothpicks. Note: This recipe requires advance preparation.

5 green New Mexican chiles, roasted, peeled, seeds and stems removed, cut into strips
1/4 cup olive oil
1/4 cup red wine vinegar
1 clove garlic, chopped fine

Combine all ingredients and marinate in the refrigerator overnight.

Yield: 10 servings   Heat Scale: Mild to medium

7. A Spicy Kettle of Soups, Stews, and Chilis

There are probably more variations on soups and stews than any other type of Southwestern dish. In fact, an entire cookbook could be written on the subject—and probably will be some day. Here are my favorite recipes, which range from traditional to creative.

Caldillo Paso del Norte in a pot.

Photographer Aaron Sandoval

Cantina *Sopa de Lima*

The Rio Grande Cantina was a popular watering hole and lunch spot near Old Town in Albuquerque that has since closed, but at least I preserved one of their great recipes. The restaurant's motto was: "Salud Amor y Pesetas y Tiempo Para Disfrutarlas," which translates loosely as: "To Health, Love, and Money and the Time to Enjoy Them." This spirited lime soup was one of their enjoyable signature items.

1 New Mexican green chile, roasted, peeled, seeds and stem removed, chopped
1/3 cup onions, chopped
2 teaspoons vegetable oil
4 cups chicken broth
1 cup skinless, boneless chicken, shredded
Salt to taste
1 tomato, chopped
1 lime, juiced
4 large lime slices for garnish
16 tortilla chips for garnish

In a pan, saute the chile and onion in the oil until the onion is soft but not browned. Add the chicken broth, chicken, and salt to taste, cover, and simmer 20 minutes. Add the tomato and simmer 5 minutes longer. Stir in the lime juice, taste, and add more if needed. Serve in bowls garnished with one lime slice and 4 tortilla chips.

Yield: 4 servings   Heat Scale: Mild

Chile Con Queso Soup

The classic combination of cheese and chile appears here as a soup—rather than as a dip or appetizer.

1 medium onion, chopped
2 tablespoons butter
3 tablespoons flour
3 to 4 cups chicken broth
6 green New Mexican chiles, roasted, peeled, seeds and stems removed, chopped
2 tomatoes, peeled and chopped
1 bell pepper, diced (optional)
1 1/2 cups half and half
8 ounces sharp Cheddar cheese, grated

In a pan, saute the onion in the butter until soft, then remove.

Add the flour to the butter and cook for 3 minutes, stirring constantly, taking care not to let the flour brown.

Stir in the broth, sautéed onion, chiles, tomatoes, bell pepper and simmer for 30 minutes.

Bring to a boil, reduce the heat, add the half and half and the cheese and heat until the cheese melts and the soup is thickened.

Yield: 4 to 6 servings   Heat Scale: Medium

Cream of *Jalapeño* Soup with Shredded Chicken

Here is another innocent-looking soup that is hotter than it appears. The combination of chicken and chiles occurs often in all Southwestern cuisines but the use of jalapeños is more prevalent in Texas.

4 jalapeños, stems and seeds removed, chopped
1 3-pound chicken, cut in pieces
1 large onion, chopped
1 stalk of celery, chopped
2 carrots, peeled and diced
1 clove garlic, chopped
1 teaspoon ground cumin
1 quart water
2 cups half and half
1 or 2 jalapeños, stems and seeds removed, finely chopped for garnish

Combine the jalapeños, chicken, onion, celery, carrots, garlic, cumin, and water in a pot. Bring to a boil, reduce the heat, cover and simmer until the chicken starts to fall off the bones. Remove the chicken and bones and reserve the stock. Remove the skin and fat from the chicken and shred the meat.

Puree the stock and strain the mixture so that it is smooth. Pour 3 cups of the stock into a large saucepan, add the half and half, and heat through.

Add the chicken and continue heating through. Pour into bowls and garnish with the finely chopped jalapenos.

Yield: 6 servings   Heat Scale: Medium-Hot

Hearty *Chorizo* and Bean Soup

The spiciness of the chorizo complements the rich flavor of the kidney beans in this easy-to-prepare soup. One look reveals how these beans got their name.

1 pound chorizo, crumbled (see recipe, p. 159)
1 large onion, chopped
3 carrots, diced
1 cup celery, chopped
1 tablespoon crushed red New Mexican chile, seeds included
2 cups kidney beans, cooked
2 tomatoes, peeled and diced
4 cups chicken stock
1 teaspoon Worcestershire sauce
1 teaspoon distilled white vinegar
1/2 teaspoon epazote (optional)
Sour cream for garnish

In a pot, saute the chorizo to render the fat. Pour off the excess fat, add the onion, carrots, and celery and saute for 5 minutes.

Combine the remaining ingredients, except the sour cream, and simmer for 30 minutes.

To serve, dish up the soup in individual bowls, garnish with a dollop of sour cream and serve.

Yield: 4 to 6 servings Heat Scale: Medium

Winter Squash and Apple Chowder with Chile-Dusted Croutons

This hearty soup combines several of the fall crops from Northern New Mexico, namely squash, apples, and both red and green chile. Add a salad, crusty bread, and a nice New Mexican wine and you have a memorable meal. Note: This recipe requires advance preparation.

Soup:

2 tablespoons butter
1 medium onion, diced
1 1/2 pounds Hubbard or butternut squash, peeled, seeded and cut into 1-inch cubes
3 tart green apples, peeled, cored and chopped
1/4 cup chopped green New Mexico chiles that have been roasted, peeled, and seeds and stems removed
4 cups chicken stock or broth
1 teaspoon lemon peel, grated
2 cups cooked chicken, diced
Freshly ground black pepper
2 tablespoons applejack or Calvados
1 to 2 teaspoons cider vinegar (optional)

Chile-Dusted Croutons:

3 slices of white bread, crusts trimmed, cut in cubes
2 teaspoons ground red New Mexican chile
3 tablespoons butter
1 clove garlic, sliced
1/2 teaspoon ground cumin

To make the croutons, spread the bread cubes on a baking sheet and let them dry out at room temperature for 3 hours.

In a pan, saute the garlic in the butter for a couple of minutes, then remove the garlic and discard. Add the chile and cumin and quickly toss the bread until all the cubes are coated with the mixture.

Place the croutons on a cookie sheet in a 350 degree oven for 10 minutes or until they are golden brown.

To make the soup, saute the onion in the butter in a pot until soft. Add the squash and apples and saute for additional 3 minutes.

Add the chile and stock and bring to boil. Reduce the heat, cover partially and simmer until the squash and apples are very tender, about 30 to 45 minutes.

Add the lemon peel, chicken, black pepper, applejack, salt to taste, and simmer for an additional 15 minutes. Add the vinegar if the soup is too sweet.

Pour the soup into bowls, top with the croutons, and serve.

Yield: 4 to 6 servings   Heat Scale: Medium

Chilled Gazpacho with *Chiles Verdes*

This soup, originally from Spain, has been transformed in the Southwest into a dish that while chilled, is heated with chiles. Note: This recipe requires advance preparation.

1/2 cup chopped green New Mexican chiles, that have been roasted, peeled, stems and seeds removed
1/4 cup diced bell pepper
2 cups beef or chicken stock
1 1/2 cups tomato juice
1 to 2 tablespoons olive oil
4 tablespoons lime juice
1 tablespoon red wine
2 large ripe tomatoes, peeled and chopped
1/4 cup red onion, chopped
2 stalks celery, chopped
1 clove garlic, minced
2 teaspoons chopped fresh cilantro, chopped
Salt to taste
Diced cucumbers for garnish
Ice cubes for garnish

In batches, combine all the ingredients, except the garnishes, in a blender and puree until smooth. Chill for at least 3 hours to blend the flavors.

To serve, ladle the soup into chilled bowls, garnish with the chopped cucumbers, and place an ice cube in the center of each bowl.

Yield: 6 servings   Heat Scale: Medium

Green Chile Stew

This is the beef stew or macaroni and cheese of New Mexico—a basic dish with as many variations as there are cooks. Add a warmed flour tortilla and you have a complete meal.

2 tablespoons vegetable oil
2 pounds lean pork, cubed
1 large onion, chopped
2 cloves garlic, minced
6 to 8 green New Mexican chiles, roasted, peeled, seeds and stems removed, chopped
1 large potato, peeled and diced (optional)
2 tomatoes, peeled and chopped
3 cups water

Heat the oil in a pot and brown the pork. Add the onion and garlic, and saute for a couple of minutes.

Combine all the ingredients in a kettle or crockpot and simmer for 1 1/2 to 2 hours or until the meat is very tender.

Yield: 6 servings   Heat Scale: Medium-Hot

Black Bean Soup

This rich and creamy soup could almost be a meal in itself. Some crusty sourdough bread and slices of fruit are all that are needed to make a filling—and spicy—lunch. Note: This recipes requires advance preparation

1 1/2 cups black beans, sorted and rinsed clean
1 large onion, chopped
2 cloves garlic, minced
4 to 6 jalapeños, stems and seeds removed, chopped
2 tablespoons bacon drippings or vegetable oil
1 large ham hock
1 teaspoon ground cumin
1 teaspoon crushed epazote
1 tablespoon red wine vinegar
7 cups chicken stock
1/2 cup heavy cream or half and half
3 tablespoons tequila
Crushed red chile for garnish
Sour cream for garnish

In a large pot, cover the beans with water and soak overnight.

In a skillet, saute the onion, garlic, and jalapeños in the bacon fat until soft.

In the pot, combine the sauteed ingredients, beans, ham hock, cumin, epazote, wine vinegar, and stock, bring to a boil, reduce the heat and simmer until the beans are soft—about 3 to 3 1/2 hours.

Remove the ham hock, shred the meat and set aside.

Puree one-half the bean mixture until smooth. Strain if necessary to obtain a smooth mixture. Return to the saucepan along with the remaining beans, stir in the cream, and heat. Remove from heat and stir in the tequila.

To serve: Stir in the shredded ham and garnish with the crushed red chile and a dollop of sour cream.

Yield: 6 to 8 servings   Heat Scale: Medium-Hot

Variation: Leave all the beans whole for a more robust soup.

Caldillo Paso del Norte

(El Paso Stew)

This variation on green chile stew is often served in El Paso restaurants. It is considered unique because of the addition of potatoes—imported from South America into the American Southwest.

Bacon fat
3 pounds stew beef, cubed
1 large onion, chopped fine
2 cloves garlic, minced
2 large tomatoes, chopped fine
2 cups New Mexican green chile, chopped
2 cups beef stock
1 teaspoon cumin
2 pounds potatoes, peeled and diced
Salt and pepper to taste

In a pot, saute the beef, onion, and garlic in bacon fat. Add the remaining ingredients except the potatoes and simmer until the meat is tender, about two hours. Add more stock if the stew gets too thick. Add the potatoes during the last 40 minutes and cook until they are tender.

Yield: 8 to 10 servings   Heat Scale: Medium

Posole with Chile Caribe

Here is the classic version of posole as prepared in northern New Mexico. Serving the chile caribe as a side dish instead of mixing it with the posole allows guests to adjust the heat to their own taste.

Posole:

2 dried red New Mexican chiles, stems and seeds removed
8 ounces frozen posole corn or dry posole corn that has been soaked in water overnight
1 pound pork loin, cut in 1/2-inch cubes
1 teaspoon garlic powder
1 medium onion, chopped
6 cups water
Minced cilantro for garnish
Chopped onion for garnish

Chile Caribe:

6 dried red New Mexican chiles, stems and seeds removed
1 teaspoon garlic powder

To make the posole, combine all the ingredients in a pot except the pork and boil at medium heat for about 3 hours or until the posole is tender, adding more water if necessary.

Add the pork and continue cooking for 1/2 hour, or until the pork is tender but not falling apart. The result should resemble a soup more than a stew.

To make the Chile Caribe, boil the chile pods in two quarts of water in a pot for 15 minutes. Remove the pods, combine with the garlic powder, and puree in a blender. Transfer to a serving bowl and allow to cool.

Note: For really hot chile caribe, add dried red chile piquins, cayenne chiles, or chiles de arbol to the New Mexican chiles.

To Serve: The posole should be served in soup bowls accompanied by warm flour tortillas. Three additional bowls of garnishes should be provided: the chile caribe, freshly minced cilantro, and freshly chopped onion. Each guest can then adjust the pungency of the posole according to individual taste.

Yield: 4 servings

Heat Scale: Medium, but varies according to the amount of chile caribe added.

Chili Queen's Chili

According to legend, this is one of the San Antonio's "Chili Queen's" original recipes. Some changes have been made in order to take advantage of modern ingredients. Never cook beans with chiles and meat! Serve them as a separate dish if you must.

2 pounds beef shoulder, cut into 1/2-inch cubes
1 pound pork shoulder, cut into 1/2-inch cubes
Flour for dredging
1/4 cup suet
1/4 cup pork fat
1 quart water
4 ancho chiles, stems and seeds removed, chopped fine
1 serrano chile, stems and seeds removed, chopped fine
6 dried red chiles, stems and seeds removed, chopped fine
3 medium onions, chopped
6 cloves garlic, minced
1 tablespoon cumin seeds, freshly ground
2 tablespoons Mexican oregano
Salt to taste

In a bowl, lightly flour the beef and pork cubes. Quickly cook them in the suet in and pork fat in a pot, stirring often. Add the onions and garlic and saute until they are tender and limp. Add the water to the mixture and simmer for 1 hour.

Grind the chiles in a molcajete or blender. Add to the meat mixture. Add the remaining ingredients and simmer for an additional 2 hours.

Remove the suet casing and skim off the fat.

Yield: 6 to 8 servings   Heat Scale: Medium

Sam Pendergrast's Original Zen Chili

Pendergast, who wrote about chili in an early issue of Chile Pepper *magazine when I was the editor, notes: "I have a theory that real chili is such a basic, functional dish that anyone can make it from the basic ingredients—rough meat, chile peppers, and a few common spices available to hungry individuals." Here is his recipe in his own skewed words.*

1 pound fatty bacon
2 pounds coarse beef, extra large grind
1/2 cup whole cominos (cumin seed—yes, one-half cup!)
1/2 cup pure ground New Mexico red chile
1 teaspoon cayenne powder
Water
Salt, pepper, garlic powder, and paprika to taste

Render the grease from the bacon and eat a bacon sandwich while the chili cooks. (Good chili takes time.)

In a pot, saute the ground beef in bacon grease over medium heat. Add the cominos and then begin adding the red chile until what you are cooking smells like chili. (This is the critical point. If you add all the spices at once, there is no leeway for personal tastes.) Let the mixture cook a bit between additions and don't feel compelled to use all of the red chile.

Add water in small batches to avoid sticking, and more later for a soupier chili. Slowly add the cayenne powder until smoke curls your eyelashes. Palefaces may find that the red chile alone has enough heat.

Simmer the mixture until the cook can't resist ladling a bowlful for sampling. Skim excess fat for dietetic chili, or mix the grease with a small amount of cornmeal for a thicker chili.

Finish with salt, pepper, and garlic powder to individual taste, paprika to darken. Continue simmering until served; continue re-heating until gone. (As with wine, time enobles good chili and exposes bad.)

The result should be something like old time Texas cafe chili: a rich, red, heavily cuminesque concoction with enough liquid to welcome crackers, some chewy chunks of meat thoroughly permeated by the distinctive spices, and an aroma calculated to lure strangers to the kitchen door.

Yield: 6 servings   Heat Scale: Hot

Variation: For cook-off contest chili, drink bad tequila two days before starting the chili; burn the mixture frequently; sprinkle it occasionally with sand and blood; serve it cold to a dozen other drunks and call them "judges"; and keep telling yourself you're having a great time.

Lady Bird Johnson's Pedernales River Chili

This recipe originally contained beef suet, but that ingredient was omitted after LBJ's severe heart attack when he was Senate Majority Leader. Remember to skim the fat off the chili.

4 pounds coarsely ground beef
1 large onion, chopped
2 cloves garlic, chopped
1 teaspoon oregano
1 teaspoon ground cumin
6 teaspoons red chile powder (or more for heat)
2 16-ounce cans tomatoes
2 cups hot water
Salt to taste

Combine the beef, onion, and garlic in a skillet and sear until the meat is lightly browned.

Transfer this mixture to a large pot, add the remaining ingredients, and bring to a boil. Reduce the heat and simmer for an hour.

When done, transfer the chili to a bowl and place it in the refrigerator. When the fat has congealed on top, remove it with a spoon.

Reheat the chili and serve it as LBJ liked it—without beans and accompanied with a glass of milk and saltine crackers.

Yield: 12 servings   Heat Scale: Mild to Medium

Arizona *Chili con Carne*

Arizona chili takes advantage of a couple of chiles from south of the border—the pasilla and chiltepíns. To spice up this version, add more chiltepíns. They add heat without changing the flavor.

4 dried red New Mexican chiles, stems and seeds removed
1 pasilla chile, stem and seeds removed
2 pounds beef sirloin, cut into 1-inch cubes
Flour for dredging
1/4 cup vegetable oil
1 small onion, chopped
3 cloves garlic, minced
2 teaspoons dried oregano
3 cups beef broth
4 chiltepín chiles

In a pot, cover the New Mexican and pasilla chiles with hot water and simmer for 15 minutes or until soft. Place the chiles in a blender along with some of the water in which they were soaking, and puree. Strain the sauce.

In a bowl, dredge the beef cubes with the flour and shake off any excess. In a pot, brown the cubes in the oil. Add the onion and garlic and saute for a couple of minutes.

Add the oregano, chile puree, and broth. Bring to a boil, reduce the heat and simmer for an hour or until the meat is tender. Add more broth if necessary

Crush the chiltepíns over the chili and simmer for an additional 30 minutes before serving.

Yield: 6 servings   Heat Scale: Medium

Short Rib Chili

This chili recipe, one of my favorites, was created by my wife, Mary Jane. It is easy to make, cooks in 2 1/2 hours, and combines the best of both red and green chiles. Serve it with fresh bread or corn bread and a big green salad.

4 pounds beef short ribs
2 tablespoons corn oil
1 onion, chopped
1 green bell pepper, chopped
2 cloves garlic, chopped
2 cups beef stock
2 tablespoons New Mexican red chile powder
1 12 ounce can stewed tomatoes, crushed
1 cup New Mexican green chile that has been roasted, peeled, seeds and stems removed and chopped
3 1/2 cups cooked kidney beans, pinto beans, or black beans, drained
2 cups cooked fresh corn off the cob

Trim the excess fat from the short ribs. Heat the oil in a large Dutch oven and brown the ribs. Add the onion, bell pepper, and the garlic and saute for 1 minute. Add the 2 cups of beef stock.

Add the remaining ingredients—except the beans and corn—and bring to a boil. Reduce the heat to a simmer. Cover and cook for 2 and 1/2 hours, stirring occasionally.

Just before serving, add the drained corn and the drained beans and heat through. For convenience, you may want to cut the meat off the bones while it is in the pot.

Yield: 8 servings   Heat Scale: Medium

8. Southwestern Salads

Compared to other Southwestern dishes, salads are a fairly recent innovation because they depend upon the availability of fresh garden greens and vegetables all year long. The trend these days is to add some ingredients to salads unheard of a few decades ago, like meats and various forms of chile peppers.

Jicama.
Photographer Aaron Sandoval

Santa Fe Greens Dressed with Green Chile Mayonnaise

If piñon nuts are not available, substitute sunflower seeds or chopped walnuts in this spicy tossed green salad. Note: This recipe requires advance preparation.

Dressing:

4 to 6 green New Mexican chiles, roasted, peeled, stems and seeds removed, chopped
1/4 cup mayonnaise
2 tablespoons sour cream
1 tablespoon olive oil
1 tablespoon lime juice
1 clove garlic, minced
1/4 teaspoon sugar
1 teaspoon fresh cilantro, chopped
1/4 teaspoon ground cumin

Salad:

1/2 cup jicama, diced
4 green onions, including the green part, chopped
Mixed salad greens—radicchio, butter, and red leaf lettuce
1/4 cup piñon nuts

To make the dressing, combine all the ingredients in a bowl and allow the dressing to sit a few hours to blend the flavors.

To make the salad, combine the jicama, onions, and salad greens in a bowl. Toss with the dressing, top with the nuts, and serve.

Yield: 4 to 6 servings   Heat Scale: Medium

Tex-Mex Coleslaw for the Barbecue

Texans love their barbecues, as do most people throughout the Southwest. This salad goes well with any outdoor extravaganza and works fine as an accompaniment to more mundane meals, such as a pastrami sandwich. Note: This recipe requires advance preparation.

Dressing:

1/4 teaspoon cayenne powder
1/2 cup mayonnaise
1 tablespoon sugar
1 tablespoon white vinegar
1/2 teaspoon celery seed
1/8 teaspoon white pepper
Salt to taste

Slaw:

4 jalapeño chiles, stems and seeds removed, chopped
1/2 head green cabbage, shredded
1/2 head red cabbage, shredded
1 small onion, chopped
2 tablespoons fresh cilantro, chopped

To make the dressing, combine all the ingredients in a jar, stir and let sit for 2 hours to blend the flavors.

To make the salad, toss all the ingredients in a bowl except the cilantro. To serve, combine the dressing with the salad and garnish with the cilantro.

Yield: 6 to 8 servings   Heat Scale: Medium

Julio's *Salpicón*

It is generally believed that one of El Paso's most popular and unique dishes—the shredded meat salad called salpicón—crossed the border because of Julio Ramirez. Julio opened his first restaurant in 1944 in Juárez on Avenida 16 de Septiembre and a second location in El Paso in 1985. The recipe for salpicón has been imitated and begged for, and local restaurateurs have paid hundreds of dollars to professional recipe testers to see if they could approximate the recipe. Finally, the Ramirez family has released it. Here it is. Note: This recipe requires advance preparation.

1 3-pound beef brisket
Water to cover
2 cloves garlic, minced
Salt to taste
1 cup white Cheddar cheese, diced
1/2 cup cilantro, chopped
1/2 cup tomatoes, diced, seeded
1/2 cup vegetable oil
1/2 cup wine vinegar
4 chipotle chiles in adobo, minced
Diced avocado for garnish

In a pot, ring the brisket to a boil in water to cover, with garlic and salt. Reduce heat and simmer for about 1 and 1/2 hours, uncovered, until the meat is tender and can be shredded. Cool the meat in the broth and then shred finely by hand. Reserve the broth to make a stew or soup.

Toss the shredded brisket with the remaining ingredients (except the avocado). Chill the mixture and allow it to marinate for a couple of hours or preferably overnight.

Line a platter with lettuce leaves, place the salpicón on the leaves, and garnish with the avocado. Serve with hot, buttered flour tortillas.

Yield: 12 servings   Heat Scale: Medium

Grilled Chicken Caesar Salad with Chile-Dusted Croutons

The Caesar salad was invented in Tijuana, Mexico, so it has South of the Border roots. Here I give it a Southwestern twist by taking it outside on the grill for a terrific summer entree. Shaved Parmesan cheese as a garnish is a better presentation than just grated. To shave cheese, use a vegetable peeler to make inch-wide shavings, then refrigerate until ready to serve. Note: This recipe requires advance preparation.

Southwestern Chicken:

2 boneless, skinless chicken breasts
Olive oil
2 tablespoons North of the Border Chile Rub, (page 124)
Chile-Dusted Croutons:
1/3 cup olive oil
3 cloves garlic, minced
1 tablespoon ground red chile
1/2 teaspoon garlic salt
10 slices French or Italian bread, cut in ½-inch cubes

Southwestern Caesar Dressing

2 egg yolks
1/4 cup Parmesan cheese, grated
1 teaspoon anchovy paste
2 teaspoons Dijon-style mustard
1 tablespoon lemon juice
1/2 cup red wine vinegar
1 1/2 cup olive oil
2 tablespoons red New Mexico chile powder
1/4 teaspoon cumin seeds
Freshly ground black pepper

Salad

Inner leaves of a head romaine lettuce, torn in
    2-inch pieces
2 thin slices of red onion, separated into rings
1/3 cup Parmesan cheese, shaved

To make the chicken, brush the chicken with a little olive oil and sprinkle with the rub. Allow the marinate at room temperature for 30 minutes to an hour.

Preheat the oven to 350 degrees F.

To prepare the croutons, mix together the garlic, olive oil, and chile, garlic salt in a small bowl. Toss with the bread cubes until thoroughly coated.

Spread on a baking sheet and toast in the oven for 10 minutes.

To make the dressing, in a bowl whisk together the egg yolks, cheese, anchovy paste, and mustard. Add the lemon juice and blend well. While whisking, slowly add the vinegar and then the olive oil, a little at a time. Whisk in the chile, cumin and black pepper. Refrigerate until ready to serve. Taste and adjust the dressing, adding more vinegar if you like it more tart, or more oil if you prefer it less tart, or more chile for heat, or more anchovies for saltiness.

Grill the chicken over medium-hot fire until cooked through, about 20 minutes or until the internal temperature reaches 160 degrees F. for medium. Remove from the grill and cut the chicken crosswise into thin slices.

To assemble the salad, toss the lettuce with some of the dressing until coated but not saturated. Divide the lettuce on individual chilled plates. Top with the onions, chicken and croutons. Garnish with the shaved Parmesan and serve.

Yield: 4 servings   Heat Scale: Medium

Orange and *Jicama* Salad Sprinkled with Red Chile

This lively salad is not only a salute to the citrus crops of Arizona, it also includes the tasty tuber jicama, which is steadily gaining favor even outside the Southwest.

2 oranges
1 small jicama, peeled and diced into 1/2-inch cubes
3/4 cup celery, sliced
1 small red onion, peeled and thinly sliced for rings
4 raw button mushrooms, sliced
1 fresh lime
4 teaspoons red chile powder

Peel the oranges and slice thinly. Divide the slices up among 4 salad plates and arrange them overlapping. Combine the jicama, celery, and onion rings in a bowl, and equally place the mixture atop the orange slices.

Squeeze fresh lime juice over each salad and sprinkle about a teaspoon of chile powder on top. A mixture of lime juice and olive oil can also me used for the dressing.

Yield: 4 servings   Heat Scale: Medium

Sonoran-Style Taco Salad

This popular salad is often served as an entree in Arizona. It is quite dramatic when presented in a "bowl" fashioned from a deep-fried, oversized flour tortilla—which can be eaten along with the salad! Tortilla bowls can be made by deep frying flour tortillas in a "tortilla fryer," which is a double-cup tool made especially for this purpose.

Salad:

1 pound ground beef
1 medium onion, chopped
1 clove garlic, minced
2 teaspoons cayenne powder
1 tablespoon commercial chili powder
1/2 teaspoon ground cumin
1 teaspoon vegetable oil
1/2 cup tomato sauce
1 cup cooked pinto beans
Tortilla bowl, or tortilla chips
Chopped lettuce
1 medium tomato, chopped
1 cup Cheddar cheese, grated
1/4 cup black olives, sliced
1 small onion, sliced and separated into rings
1 avocado, pitted, peeled and chopped, or 1 cup guacamole (see recipes, page 130)
Sour cream for garnish

Optional Dressing for the Salad:

1/4 cup commercial taco sauce
1/4 cup red wine vinegar
1/4 cup salad oil
2 tablespoons lemon juice

To make the salad, saute the ground beef, onion, garlic, cayenne, chili powder, and cumin in the oil in large skillet until the beef is browned. Add the tomato sauce and the beans and continue to cook until heated. Drain off any excess liquid and cool slightly.

Place the lettuce in the tortilla bowl or on the chips. Top with the beef mixture, arrange the tomatoes around the outside, top with the cheese, olives, onion rings, avocado or guacamole, and garnish with the sour cream.

To make the dressing, mix all the ingredients together and allow to sit for a couple of hours to blend the flavors. Serve the dressing on the side.

Yield: 4 to 6 servings   Heat Scale: Mild

Marinated Vegetable Salad with Sun-Dried Tomatoes

Try substituting cauliflower or broccoli for the mushrooms or add your own combination of veggies. Note: This recipe requires advance preparation.

Vegetables:

1 cup water
1 9-ounce package frozen artichoke heart halves
1/2 cup cider vinegar
1/2 pound fresh mushrooms, stems removed
4 sun-dried tomatoes, packed in oil, drained, cut in thin strips
12 black olives

Dressing:

1 tablespoon crushed red chile
1/3 cup olive oil
1/4 cup balsamic vinegar
1 medium lemon, juiced
3 green onions, including some of the greens, chopped
2 cloves garlic, minced
3 teaspoon dried oregano
1/2 teaspoon dried basil

To make the vegetables, bring 1 cup of water and the cider vinegar to a boil in a pan, add the artichoke hearts, and immediately remove the pan from the heat. Let stand for 5 minutes and the remove artichokes, reserving the liquid. Add the mushrooms and simmer for 5 minutes. Remove and drain. In a bowl, combine the artichoke hearts, mushrooms, and the remaining ingredients for the vegetables. Stir well.

To make the dressing, in a bowl, mix together the dressing ingredients and pour over the vegetables. Marinate them overnight before serving.

Yield: 4 to 6 servings   Heat Scale: Mild

Hot Wilted Spinach Salad

The spinach "wilts" when the dressing is poured over it, so be sure the dressing is hot. For a less hearty salad, omit the cheese and the nuts.

4 slices bacon, chopped
2 tablespoons crushed red New Mexican chile, seeds included
1/2 cup cider vinegar
1 tablespoon soy sauce
4 cups fresh spinach
1 medium red onion, thinly sliced
1 cup cauliflower florets
1 cup diced queso blanco or Mozzarella cheese
1/4 cup slivered almonds

In a skillet, saute the bacon pieces until crisp; remove and drain on paper towels. Add the red chile to the bacon drippings and saute for a couple of minutes.

Mix together the vinegar and soy sauce in a bowl.

Combine the spinach, onion, cauliflower and cheese in another bowl. Toss with the vinegar mixture.

Reheat the bacon fat and chile mixture, pour over the spinach and toss well. Top with the nuts and bacon and serve.

Yield: 6 servings   Heat Scale: Mild

Chile Cactus Salad

This interesting salad features nopalitos, the fleshy pads of the Opunita or prickly pear cactus. Of course, the spines are removed from the cactus pads.

Dressing:

2/3 cup olive oil
1/3 cup red wine vinegar
2 jalapeño chiles, stems and seeds removed, finely minced
1 clove garlic, finely minced
1/4 teaspoon dried oregano
Freshly ground black pepper

Salad:

1 large poblano chile, roasted, peeled, stems and seeds removed, cut in strips
1 15-ounce jar nopalitos, drained and rinsed
4 small tomatoes, chopped
2 tablespoons fresh cilantro, chopped
Red leaf lettuce
1/2 pound goat cheese or substitute Feta cheese, crumbled

To make the dressing, combine a small amount of the oil and vinegar in a bowl. Whisk in the chiles, garlic, oregano, and pepper and beat until smooth. Slowly add a little oil and beat well. Then add a little of the vinegar. Repeat the process until completely blended.

To make the salad, combine all the ingredients for the salad in a bowl and toss with only enough dressing to coat and serve.

Yield: 4 servings   Heat Scale: Medium

Variation: For a more elegant presentation, toss the lettuce with the tomatoes and place on individual plates. Arrange the chile and nopalito strips on the lettuce. Top with the cheese, garnish with the cilantro, and serve with the dressing on the side.

Stir-Fry Pork and Avocado Salad

Meat salads have been gaining in popularity with the introduction of Southeast Asian immigrants in the Southwest.

2 tablespoons chile oil
2 teaspoons ground chile de arbol or substitute any hot chile powder
1/2 teaspoon dried oregano
1/4 teaspoon ground cumin
Pinch garlic powder
1 pound boneless pork, cut in strips 2 inches long by 1/4 inch wide and thick
Mixed lettuce leaves
Mung bean sprouts
1 small onion, sliced thinly and separated into rings
1 avocado, pitted, peeled, and sliced
Sliced cucumber
2 tablespoons sesame seeds

In a skillet, heat the oil and add the chile, oregano, cumin, and garlic. Add the pork and quickly cook for a couple of minutes until the pork is done but still tender. Remove and drain.

Place the lettuce on plates. Top with the bean sprouts, onion, avocado, and cucumber slices.

Arrange the warm pork strips on top, garnish with the sesame seeds, and serve.

Yield: 4 servings   Heat Scale: Medium

Texas Caviar

No collection of dishes from the Southwest would be complete without a recipe for black-eyed peas or "Texas caviar," a major crop in eastern Texas. Black-eyed peas are traditionally served on New Year's Day for good luck both in Texas and throughout the South. Note: This recipe requires advance preparation.

4 jalapeño chiles, stems and seeds removed, minced
1/2 cup vegetable oil, olive preferred
1/4 cup vinegar
2 cloves garlic, minced
1/4 teaspoon dry mustard
Freshly ground black pepper
2 cups cooked black-eyed peas
4 green onions, including the greens, sliced
1 stalk celery, chopped

Combine the chiles, oil, vinegar, garlic, mustard, and black pepper to form a dressing in a bowl. Toss the peas, onions, and celery with the dressing and marinate in the refrigerator overnight.

Yield: 4 to 6 servings   Heat Scale: Hot

9. Meat On and Off the Grill

Before the arrival of the Spanish in the Southwest, Native American cooks utilized deer, rabbit, and peccary in their recipes. Nowadays, the selection of meats is far greater, with beef, pork, and lamb preferred in both traditional and new dishes. However, game has made a comeback because of its availability, and is now frequently prepared.

Ribs on the Grill.

Photographer Mike Stines

Grilled *Piñon* Lamb Chops

Here is a delicious combination of ingredients from the Southwest —pine nuts, chile, and lamb. For an authentic, smoky flavor, grill them over mesquite wood or charcoal covered with mesquite chips soaked in water. Note: This recipe requires advance preparation.

1 tablespoon ground red New Mexican chile
3/4 cup olive oil
5 tablespoons piñons, toasted
1/2 cup tomato paste
1/4 cup vinegar
3 cloves garlic
4 lamb chops, cut 1 to 1 1/2-inches thick

Combine all the ingredients, except the lamb, in a blender and puree until smooth. Paint the chops with the mixture and allow them to marinate for at least an hour.

Grill the chops, turning them occasionally until done, about 7 to 10 minutes a side. For medium-rare, the internal temperature should be 150 degrees F.

Yield: 4 servings   Heat Scale: Mild

Pork Chops *Ranchero*

The addition of cumin and chiles gives these pork chops a wonderful Southwestern flavor. Note: This recipe requires advance preparation.

6 green New Mexican chiles, roasted, peeled, stems and seeds removed, chopped
1/4 cup lime juice
2 tablespoons vegetable oil
1/4 cup onions, chopped
2 cloves garlic, minced
2 teaspoons ground cumin
1 teaspoon dried oregano
1/2 teaspoon ground coriander
1/2 teaspoon salt
4 thick-cut pork chops

Combine all the ingredients, except the pork, in a bowl and mix well. Marinate the pork in the mixture for 4 hours or overnight.

Remove the chops from the marinade and grill until the internal temperature reaches about 150 degrees F.

Serving Suggestions: The remaining marinade can be boiled for a few minutes and served on the side as a sauce.

Yield: 4 servings   Heat Scale: Medium

Grilled Marinated Pork Tenderloin with Roasted Corn and *Poblano* Chile Relish

This recipe is courtesy of La Casa Sena restaurant in Santa Fe. Note: This recipe requires advance preparation.

Roasted Corn and *Poblano* Chile Relish:

Vegetable oil
2 poblano chiles
1 teaspoon vegetable oil
1 red bell pepper
2 ears of corn, roasted and kernels cut off the cobs
3 tablespoons shallots, finely chopped
3 tablespoons garlic, finely chopped
1 bunch cilantro, chopped
1/2 cup olive oil
1/4 cup sherry vinegar
Salt and pepper to taste

Pork Tenderloin:

2 jalapeño chiles, stems removed, seeded, and chopped
1/2 cup sherry vinegar
1 cup olive oil
1 teaspoon garlic, chopped
1 teaspoon shallots, chopped
1 teaspoon cumin
1 teaspoon salt
4 8-ounce pork tenderloins, fat trimmed off

To make the relish, lightly brush the vegetable oil on the bell pepper and the poblanos and roast them over a gas flame or grill until the skin is blackened. Peel the skins off, remove the seeds, and dice the chiles. Combine the chiles with the rest of the ingredients in a bowl, mix well, and allow to sit for at least two hours to blend the flavors.

To make the pork, combine all ingredients except non-pork ingredients in a bowl. Add the pork and allow to marinate for 3 hours at room temperature.

Remove the pork from the marinade and grill until it is just done with the internal temperature reading 150 degrees F. Slice the pork into medallions and fan out on individual serving plates.

Carefully spoon the Roasted Corn and Poblano Chile Relish on the medallions so that they are one-half covered.

Yield: 4 servings   Heat Scale: Medium

Jalapeño-Stuffed Steaks

Grilled steaks no longer have to be just a piece of plain meat. Any type of fresh chile or combinations of chiles can be substituted for the jalapeños in this recipe. The stuffing can be prepared a day in advance and refrigerated. An hour before cooking, slice the steaks and fill with the chile mixture.

    10 jalapeños, stems removed, minced
    1 medium onion, chopped
    4 cloves garlic, chopped
    1 tablespoon vegetable oil
    1/2 cup grated Monterey Jack cheese
    3 pounds trimmed fillet of beef, cut into 6 thick
        steaks
    Freshly ground black pepper

In a skillet, saute the chiles, onion, and garlic in the oil for a couple of minutes, until just soft . Remove to a bowl, cool, and mix in the cheese.

Slice into the steaks from the edge, creating a "pocket" for the stuffing. Stuff with the jalapeño mixture and fasten the opening with a toothpick, if necessary. Season the outside of each steak with the black pepper.

Grill over hot charcoal to the desired doneness. Rare steaks should have an internal temperature of 140 degrees F.

Yield: 6 servings   Heat Scale: Hot

Pork Tenderloin with Sage and *Serrano* Lime Cream

Here is a good illustration of innovation in "New" Southwestern cooking. This recipe combines sage, serrano chiles, and limes for both a marinade and a sauce. Note: This recipe requires advance preparation.

    1 1/2 cups fresh sage leaves
    3 serrano chiles, stems removed
    1/2 bunch green onions
    2 cups chicken stock
    1/2 cup milk
    1/2 cup vegetable oil
    6 8-ounce pork tenderloins
    1 cup cream
    3 tablespoons lime juice
    Flour

In a blender, puree the sage, chiles, green onions, and 1 cup of chicken stock. Marinate the pork in 1/2 of this mixture, milk, and oil for about 3 hours. Grill the pork tenderloins for 3 minutes per side, then bake in a 500 degree oven for 10 minutes.

While the pork is baking, combine the remaining chicken stock and cream and cook over low heat for about 25 minutes. Add flour as needed to thicken the sauce. Add the lime juice, salt to taste, and the remaining puree.

Slice the pork and serve the sauce over it.

Yield: 6 servings   Heat Scale: Mild

Barbecued Brisket

Red Caldwell, who wrote for Chile Pepper magazine in the early days when I was editor, developed this recipe. He notes, "Most barbecue in Texas revolves around beef, and more specifically, brisket. When you select your brisket, choose only 'packer trimmed' briskets in the ten to twelve pound category. The smaller briskets don't have enough fat to tenderize them, and the larger ones could have come off of a tough old range bull that no amount of cooking will ever tenderize. Avoid closely trimmed or 'value-packed' brisket pieces. The fat that was cut off to make 'em pretty is the very stuff that would have made 'em tender! All briskets have a fat cover on one side. Ignore this! Squeeze the thick end with both thumbs. When you've found the brisket with the smallest fat kernel, that's the one for you. Take it home and build your fire. While your fire is getting going—I build mine out of a mixture of mesquite and oak—rub your brisket with a dry 'rub.' Make sure that the meat is thoroughly coated. This helps seal the meat and adds a flavorful crust. Never use salt, as it dries and toughens the meat. Use tongs instead of a fork to turn the meat because piercing allows the juices to flow out, leaving a tougher brisket."

Brisket

1 brisket as described about
Lemon juice (about 1/4-1/2 cup per brisket)

Dry Rub

1 11-ounce can of fine ground, light chili powder
1 tablespoon ground Cayenne powder
2 tablespoons (rounded) black pepper
4 tablespoons (rounded) garlic powder

Red's Basting Sauce

1 pound butter or margarine
2 onions, peeled and thick sliced
5 cloves garlic, peeled and crushed
1 12-ounce bottle of beer (Shiner Bock preferred)
1 bunch parsley tops, chopped
4 lemons, quartered
1 pint cooking oil
2 Tablespoons commercial chili powder
1/2 teaspoon cayenne powder
1/4 cup Worcestershire sauce
2 bay leaves

Thoroughly coat all surfaces of the brisket with lemon juice, and rub in well. Combine all of the dry ingredients in a bowl, and sprinkle generously all over the brisket, rubbing in well. Make sure that the brisket is entirely covered. Store leftover rub in a tightly sealed container in the 'fridge.

When the wood has burned down, move the coals to one side of the pit, place the meat *away* from the direct heat, *fat side up* (let gravity and nature do the basting), and close the pit. Some people add a pan of water near the coals to provide added moisture, but I don't. Now, *don't* touch the meat for about 12 hours. Just drink a few beers, cook a pot of beans, and tend your fire. You'd like to hold the cooking temperature around 210 degrees F. in the brisket cooking area. Since "helpers" usually show up at the first whiff of smoke, you probably ought to put some of your leftover rub on a couple of racks of pork ribs, and toss them on the pit, in the hotter end, and baste and turn 'em for four or five hours, just to keep the animals at bay.

To make the Basting Sauce, melt the butter in a pan, add the onions and garlic, and saute for 4 to 5 minutes to soften. Add the beer, squeeze in the lemon juice, and add the lemon rinds to the pot. When the foam subsides, add all of the remaining ingredients and bring to a boil. Reduce the heat to a medium low and simmer for 20 minutes.

By the way, you'll notice that there are no tomatoes, ketchup, or sugar in this recipe. All of these things caramelize and burn quickly, giving the meat a *nasty* taste.

After the 12 hours are completed, generously slather the brisket with a *basting* sauce (not a barbecue sauce), wrap it tightly in aluminum foil, and return to the pit. Close off all of the air supplies to the fire, and allow the meat to "set" in the pit for three or four hours. This step really tenderizes the meat.

Remove the brisket from the foil and slice it thinly against the grain. Serve your brisket with beans, cole slaw, jalapeños, onions, pickles, and plenty of bread. Cold beer or iced tea are the traditional beverages of choice.

Yield: You'll find that a ten pound brisket will yield about 8 to16 servings, depending on the individual brisket and the size of the appetites of the guests.

Heat Scale: Mild

Venison Steaks with Chile Wine Sauce

Game is very popular in Texas despite the fact that there is no public land open for hunting in the state. To fill this void, hunters pay ranchers and other private landholders for the right to hunt on their property. If venison is not available, beef or lamb can be substituted in this recipe. Note: This recipe requires advance preparation.

8 chilipiquíns or chiltepíns, crushed
1/2 cup dry red wine
1/4 cup vinegar
1/4 cup vegetable oil
2 cloves garlic, minced
1 tablespoon crushed fresh rosemary
Freshly ground black pepper
2 venison steaks, 1 1/2 to 2-inches thick

Combine all the ingredients in a bowl, except the venison, and stir well. Marinate the meat in the mixture for at least 24 hours. Remove the meat and drain, reserving the marinade.

Rub the steaks with vegetable oil and sear quickly to hold in the juices. Grill the steaks, basting frequently with the marinade until just done, internal temperature 150 degrees F.

Yield: 2 servings   Heat Scale: Medium

South Texas *Fajitas*

About the late 1970s, fajitas were "discovered." Since then, an awful lot of good meat has been wrecked, and skirt steak—once a "grinder" item—has risen sharply in price. Because skirt doesn't come from a "tender quadrant" of the carcass, some care is needed to turn it into good food. First, it needs to be marinated to tenderize and flavor it. You'll notice that I haven't said anything about chicken fajitas—that's a contradiction in terms. Note: This recipe requires advance preparation.

2 to 4 jalapeños, canned or fresh, stemmed, seeds
   removed, and minced
3 tablespoons chili powder
1 teaspoon cayenne powder
1 8-ounce bottle of herb and garlic, oil-based
   salad dressing
1 12 ounce can of beer, preferably Lone Star
1 1/2 teaspoons garlic powder
4 small Mexican limes, juiced
2 teaspoons cumin seeds, crushed
1 large onion, minced
2 tablespoons cilantro, minced
1 tablespoon Worcestershire sauce
1 bay leaf
2 to 3 pounds beef skirt steak

In a bowl, mix all of the ingredients except the meat together to make a marinade. Pour over the skirt steak, in a non-reactive container, cover, and turn the meat in the marinade occasionally for six to eight hours.

Fajitas can be cooked in several ways. If you have the space, smoke the fajitas for about 30 minutes with pure mesquite smoke, and then cook for 4 to 7 minutes per side over direct heat—mesquite coals being the heat of choice. Baste with the marinade throughout the cooking process. If you need to cook completely over direct heat, then use a fairly slow fire, about like you should use when grilling chicken, and cook, covered if possible, for about 10 to15 minutes per side, basting with the marinade. For medium-rare, the internal temperature should be 150 degrees F.

Figure about a half-pound of meat and 3 to 4 tortillas per person. When slicing fajitas, you'll notice that the grain of the skirt steak all runs the same way. If you slice the skirt at a forty five degree angle to the grain, and hold your knife on a forty five degree angle as well, you'll find that the fajitas are much more tender! Serve the fajitas with flour tortillas, pico de gallo salsa, guacamole, and cold beer.

Yield: 4 to 6 servings   Heat Scale: Medium

Tournedos *Chipotle*

Here is a Mexican import from Puerto Vallarta that's served in upscale restaurants in Southwest. Serve these steaks with twice baked potatoes and a salad from Chapter 8.

4 beef fillets, 1 to 2 inches thick
Olive oil
1 onion, chopped
3 cloves garlic, minced
2 tablespoons vegetable oil
3 canned chipotle in adobo chiles
1 medium tomato, peeled and seeds removed, chopped
1/2 teaspoon oregano
1/2 teaspoon sugar
1/2 teaspoon freshly ground black pepper
2 cups beef broth
1 cup dry red wine

Brush the steaks with olive oil and let sit while preparing the sauce.

In a pan, saute the onion and garlic in the vegetable oil until browned. Add the chipotle, tomato, oregano, sugar, and pepper. Saute for an additional couple of minutes. Stir in the broth and wine and simmer for 20 to 30 minutes or until reduced by a half.

Remove from the heat and puree in a blender until smooth and then strain. Return to the pan and keep warm until ready for serving.

Grill the steaks to the desired doneness. Medium rare is 150 degrees F.

To serve: place some of the sauce on a plate, place the steak on the sauce and top with additional sauce.

Yield: 4 servings   Heat Scale: Medium

Chorizo

This traditional Mexican sausage is often served with huevos rancheros for breakfast. Unlike other sausages, it is usually not placed in a casing but rather served loose or formed into patties. Note: This recipe requires advance preparation.

1 clove garlic
1/2 cup hot red chile powder
1/2 teaspoon freshly ground black pepper
1/4 teaspoon each: ground cloves, cinnamon, oregano, cumin
1/2 teaspoon salt
1 teaspoon oregano
1/2 cup vinegar
2 pounds ground pork

In a blender, combine the non-pork ingredients and puree. Knead this mixture into the pork until it is thoroughly mixed together. Cover and let sit at room temperature for at least a day, then refrigerate. At this point the chorizo may be frozen.

To cook, crumble it in a skillet and fry. Drain it before serving.

Yield: 8 servings   Heat Scale: Medium

Barbecued Beef Ribs, Texas-Style

The Texas Panhandle is beef country and was once the land of cattle drives through such cities as Amarillo and Abilene. Texans love to barbecue beef, which can take hours or even days, but the results are worth it. The following recipe doesn't take twenty-four hours, but the ribs should be cooked slowly over charcoal while taking care that the sauce doesn't burn.

4 jalapeño chiles, stems and seeds removed, chopped
1 medium onion, chopped
3 cloves garlic, chopped
2 tablespoons vegetable oil
1 cup tomato sauce
2 cups beef broth
1/4 cup cider vinegar
Juice of 1 lemon
1 tablespoon mustard
1 tablespoon brown sugar
1/2 teaspoon dried oregano
1/8 teaspoon ground habanero chile
Freshly ground black pepper
4 pounds beef ribs

In a skillet, saute the jalapeños, onions, and garlic in the oil until soft. Place the mixture in a blender and puree until smooth.

Transfer to a saucepan, add the remaining ingredients, except the ribs, and bring to a boil. Reduce the heat and simmer until the sauce has thickened enough to hold its shape.

Grill the ribs about 6 inches from the heat until browned, about 30 to 45 minutes. Baste the ribs with the sauce and continue to baste every 10 minutes for an additional 30 minutes, being careful that they do not burn. Remove and serve.

Yield: 4 servings   Heat Scale: Hot

New Mexico *Carne Adovada*

This simple but tasty dish evolved from the need to preserve meat without refrigeration since the chile acts as an antioxidant and prevents the meat from spoiling. It is a very common restaurant entree in New Mexico. Note: This recipe requires advance preparation. Serving suggestions: Place the carne adovada in a flour tortilla to make a burrito, use it as a stuffing for sopaipillas, or use it as filling for enchiladas. If quartered potatoes are added during the last hour of baking, the dish becomes a sort of stew.

1 1/2 cups crushed dried red New Mexican chile, seeds included
4 cloves garlic, minced
3 teaspoons dried oregano
3 cups water
2 pounds pork, cut in strips or cubed

In a bowl, combine the chile, garlic, oregano, and the water and mix well to make a "caribe" sauce.

Place the pork in a glass pan and cover with the chile caribe sauce. Marinate the pork overnight in the refrigerator.

Bake the carne adovada in a 300 degree oven for a couple of hours or until the pork is very tender and starts to fall apart.

Yield: 6 servings   Heat Scale: Hot

Arizona Beef Jerky

Preserving meat by drying has always been popular throughout the Southwest where the hot dry weather speeds up the process. Jerky, or carne seca, can be used in burritos and enchiladas, and with scrambled eggs. Or, snack on it while watching football on TV.

2 pounds extra-lean beef sirloin or flank steak
4 cloves garlic, cut in half
2 tablespoons lime juice
4 tablespoons red New Mexican chile powder
1 teaspoon crushed chiltepíns
1 teaspoon ground cumin
Coarse salt
Freshly ground black pepper

Rub the beef with the garlic cloves. Cut the meat across the grain in slices 1/8-inch thick and 1 inch wide. If you are having difficulty, partially freeze the meat before cutting.

Combine the remaining ingredients in a bowl and rub the strips with the mixture.

Place the strips on a rack over a drip pan in the oven.

Bake at 150 degrees, turning a couple of times, for 6 to 8 hours or until the meat is very dry. Leaving the door to the oven slightly ajar, will help speed up the drying process.

Yield: Approximately 1/2 pound
Heat Scale: Medium Hot

Adovado Ribs

Here's a Phoenix version of pork baked with red chile. Increase the spiciness of this dish by adding a few chiltepíns to the sauce. Serve with a rice dish and a bean dish from chapter 13.

10 New Mexican red chile pods
4 cloves garlic
2 cups water
1 teaspoon Mexican oregano
1/2 teaspoon freshly ground black pepper
4 pounds country-style pork ribs
1 cup onions, chopped

Place the chile pods, garlic, water, oregano, and black pepper in a blender and puree. Rub the ribs with fresh garlic and salt and place them in a shallow baking pan. Pour the chile sauce over the ribs and top with the onions.

Cover and bake at 325 degrees for 6 hours.

Yield: 4 to 6 servings   Heat Scale: Medium

Smoked Pork *Mole Enchiladas*

Serve these unusual enchiladas with a chilled citrus salad, rice pilaf, and a seasoned green vegetable dish from Chapter 11.

2 ancho chiles, stems and seeds removed
2 pasilla chiles, stems and seeds removed
3 dried red New Mexican chiles, stems and seeds removed
3 cups water
2 cups chicken broth
1 large onion, chopped
1 4 to 6-pound pork butt
1 dozen corn tortillas
2 tablespoons vegetable oil
8 ounces sour cream
Ole Mole Sauce (see recipe, p. 122)
1/4 cup sesame seeds

In a pot, simmer the chiles in the water for 15 minutes to soften. Remove and drain.

Place the chiles, onion, and the chicken broth in a blender and puree until smooth. Strain the sauce if desired.

Make diagonal slits about 1-inch deep in the pork roast. Rub the chile mixture over the roast, being sure it goes deep into the cuts.

Smoke the roast in a smoker with indirect heat, until the internal temperature reaches 170 degrees F. and the pork pulls apart easily. When the roast is done, after smoking approximately 1 hour per pound, pull it apart with forks.

Soften the tortillas by frying them in oil for a few seconds on each side, then drain them on paper towels. Place the pulled pork in the tortillas, top with sour cream and sesame seeds, and roll up. Place them in a baking dish, cover with the mole sauce, and bake in a 325 degree oven for about 20 minutes. Sprinkle the sesame seeds on top and serve.

Yield: 6 to 8 servings   Heat Scale: Medium

Machaca

Common throughout the Southwest in restaurants but not-so-common in home cooking (who knows why?), this savory shredded meat is a very versatile ingredient for tacos, enchiladas, and burritos. The word is derived from the Spanish machacar, to pound, an apt description of the appearance of the meat.

3-pound arm roast
Water
1 1/2 cups New Mexican green chile that has been roasted, peeled, seeds and stems removed and coarsely chopped
1 tomato, chopped
1/2 onion, diced
1/2 teaspoon garlic powder

Place the roast in a large pan with water to cover and simmer until tender and the meat begins to fall apart, about 3 to 4 hours. Remove the roast from the pan, remove the fat and bone, and shred the meat by hand or with a fork.

Return the meat to the pan, add the remaining ingredients, stir well, and simmer until all the liquid has been absorbed by the meat.

Yield: 6 to 8 servings   Heat Scale: Medium

10. Firebirds of a Feather

Southwestern poultry dishes illustrate the diversity of preparation methods used in the region: roasting, baking, sautéing, smoking, grilling, and prepared in combination with other ingredients—especially corn and chile peppers. Substitutions are encouraged in these recipes—for example, duck for chicken and pheasant for quail.

Gambel's Quail.
Photographer Aaron Sandoval

Pollo en Mole Almendrado

(Chicken in Almond Mole)

This recipe is from Chef Miguel Ravago, formerly of Austin's fine Fonda San Miguel restaurant, which specializes in interior and coastal Mexican cuisine. Serve the mole accompanied by corn tortillas and a vegetable dish of choice from Chapter 11.

10 cups water
2 white onions, peeled and quartered
2 heads garlic, all the cloves peeled
1 cinnamon stick, 4 inches long
8 whole cloves
2 chickens, cut up
3/4 cup vegetable oil
1 and 1/2 white onions, peeled and quartered
8 garlic cloves, peeled
2 cups almonds, blanched
1 cup roasted unsalted peanuts
1 cinnamon stick, 4 inches long
4 whole cloves
16 black peppercorns
1 croissant, torn into pieces
4 large ripe tomatoes, roasted over an open flame
4 ancho chiles, torn into pieces
Salt to taste
1/2 cup vegetable oil
2 slices white onion
Salt to taste

Bring the water to a boil, add the onions, garlic, cinnamon, cloves, and chicken pieces, reduce the heat and simmer 25 minutes until the chicken is partially cooked. Remove the chicken from the broth and remove the skin and bones. Reserve and strain the broth.

Heat the 3/4 cup oil in a large saucepan. Add the onions, garlic, almonds, peanuts, cinnamon, cloves, peppercorns, and croissant saute for 25 minutes, adding more oil if the mixture tends to stick. Place the mixture in a blender, add the tomatoes and chiles, and puree.

Heat the 1/2 cup oil in a saucepan and brown the onion slices. Stir in the pureed mixture and cook for about 10 minutes. Salt it to taste. Add 2 or 3 cups of reserved chicken broth (or as needed to thin the sauce), add the reserved chicken, and simmer an additional 25 minutes.

Yield: 6 servingsHeat Scale: Mild

Grilled Herb-Marinated Chicken Breasts with Roasted *Poblano-Piñon* Salsa

Rosa Rajkovic, who then was executive chef at the Monte Vista Fire Station in Albuquerque, prepared this recipe at the 1992 National Fiery Foods & Barbecue Show at the Albuquerque Convention Center. The foodies who tasted it were delighted with the intriguing blend of fresh and spicy flavors. Note: This recipe requires advance preparation.

8 chicken breasts, boned and skinned

Fresh Herb Marinade:

1 cup canola oil
1/4 cup champagne wine vinegar
3 tablespoons fresh lemon juice
2 tablespoons Dijon mustard
2 tablespoons fresh parsley, chopped
1 tablespoon fresh basil, chopped
1 tablespoon fresh marjoram, chopped
1 tablespoon fresh chives, chopped
1 tablespoon fresh tarragon, chopped
1 tablespoon fresh oregano, chopped
1/4 teaspoon salt
1/8 teaspoon freshly ground black pepper

Roasted *Poblano-Piñon* Salsa:

6 poblano chiles, roasted, peeled, seeds and stems removed, chopped
1 eggplant, peeled, sliced lengthwise, salted and blotted, then baked and chopped
4 tomatoes, peeled, cored, seeded, and chopped
1/2 cup roasted piñon nuts
1/4 cup virgin olive oil
2 tablespoons balsamic vinegar
3 tablespoons fresh lime juice
3 scallions, chopped
3 tablespoons cilantro, chopped
2 cloves garlic, chopped
Salt to taste

To make the herb marinade, combine all ingredients in a bowl and allow to sit at room temperature for at least 1 hour to blend the flavors. Marinate the chicken breasts with the marinade in large bowl for at least 4 hours, preferably longer.

To make the salsa, combine all ingredients in a bowl and mix well.

Grill the breasts with charcoal and aromatic wood chips such as pecan until they reach and internal temperature of 160 degrees and serve them topped with the salsa.

Yield: 8 servingsHeat Scale: Mild

Chicken *Barbacoa*-Style

The word "barbecue" comes from the Spanish barbacoa, but the two words no longer mean the same thing because barbacoa is cooked in a rock-lined pit. It is difficult to duplicate the flavor of wrapping meat or poultry in banana leaves and cooking it in a pit, but we're going to make a noble effort by grilling the chicken while it's covered with a chile paste. Serve with jicama-lime sticks, potatoes with green chile, grilled zucchini and corn, and warm corn or flour tortillas. Note: This recipe requires advance preparation.

Sesame-Chile Paste:

8 guajillo chiles, or substitute dried red New Mexican chiles, stems and seeds removed
4 de Arbol chiles, stems and seeds removed
2 tablespoons sesame seeds
1 1-inch piece cinnamon stick or 1 teaspoon ground
8 whole allspice berries
6 whole cloves
2 teaspoons dried oregano, Mexican preferred
1/2 cup onions, chopped
4 cloves garlic, chopped
2 tablespoons cider vinegar
1 cup chicken broth
1 tablespoon vegetable oil

Chicken:

1 3-pound chicken, cut into serving-size pieces

Toast all the chiles on a hot dry griddle or skillet until they turn slightly dark, taking care that they don't burn. Place in a bowl and cover with very hot water and allow to steep for 20 minutes until softened. Drain the chiles.

Toast the sesame seeds in the hot skillet until browned, taking care that they don't burn. Allow to cool.

Place the sesame seeds, cinnamon stick, allspice, and cloves in a spice grinder or coffee mill and process until there is a fine powder. Put the ground spices, chiles, oregano, onions, garlic, vinegar, and broth in a blender or food processor and puree until smooth. Strain if desired.

Heat the oil in a frying pan, add the sauce, and saute over medium heat, stirring occasionally, for 5 minutes to thicken. Allow to cool.

Spread the paste all over the chicken pieces (even under the skin), place in a plastic bag, and refrigerate overnight.

Be sure the pieces are thickly coated and grill slowly, over a medium or low fire so the paste doesn't burn. Cook about 40 minutes, turning occasionally, or until the internal temperature reaches 160 degrees F.

Yield: 4 servings   Heat Scale: Medium

El Pollo al Carbón

The concept of marinating chicken in a spicy fruit juice and then char-broiling it originated in northern Mexico and became quite popular throughout the Southwest. The chicken is served with warm corn tortillas, fresh salsa, and a side of pinto beans. Customers remove the chicken from the bones, place it in the tortilla, top with salsa, and enjoy. Note: This recipe requires advance preparation.

1 small onion, chopped
2 cloves garlic, minced
2 tablespoons vegetable oil
2 tomatillos, husks removed, chopped
1/2 cup orange juice
2 tablespoons lime juice
1 tablespoon lemon juice
1/4 teaspoon ground cinnamon
1/4 teaspoon ground cloves
1/4 teaspoon ground habanero chile
2 small chickens, cut in half lengthwise
Salsa of choice from Chapter 5
Corn tortillas

In a pan, saute the onion, garlic, and tomatillos in the oil until soft. Add the remaining ingredients, except the chicken, and simmer for 10 minutes. Place in a blender and puree to make a sauce.

Place the sauce and the chicken in a plastic zip bag and marinate the chicken for at least 3 hours.

Grill the chicken, until done to an internal temperature of 160 degrees F., basting frequently with the sauce.

Yield: 4 servingsHeat Scale: Medium

Margarita-Marinated Game Hens

This is the recipe for people who would like to eat their Margarita rather than drink it. The hens can be either baked or split and cooked on a grill with the marinade used as a basting sauce. Note: This recipe requires advance preparation.

4 to 5 serrano chiles, stems and seeds removed
1/2 cup lime juice
1/4 cup vegetable oil
2 tablespoons tequila
2 teaspoons sugar
1 teaspoon fresh cilantro, chopped
4 Cornish game hens

Combine all the ingredients, except the hens, in a blender and puree. Pour the marinade over the hens and marinate for 2 hours at room temperature or overnight in the refrigerator.

Place the hens in a 450 degree oven and immediately reduce the heat to 350. Roast for 30 to 45 minutes or until done, basting often with the marinade.

Yield: 4 servings   Heat Scale: Medium

Stuffed Chicken Breasts with Walnut *Pipián*

The Mayans are credited with creating pipiáns, or sauces that are both flavored and thickened with seeds and/or nuts. In the case of this recipe, the pipián also adds color to the dish.

Chicken:

3 chicken breasts, skinned, bone removed, cut in half
6 green New Mexican chiles, roasted, peeled, stems and seeds removed, left whole
6 thin slices ham
6 slices asadero or Monterey Jack cheese
1 large avocado, peeled and sliced
3 tablespoons fresh cilantro, chopped
1/4 cup melted butter
Chopped walnuts for garnish
Cilantro leaves for garnish

Pipián:

1 medium onion, chopped
1 clove garlic, chopped
1 poblano chile, roasted, peeled, stem and seeds removed, chopped
4 tablespoons butter or vegetable oil
1/2 cup walnuts, chopped
1/4 cup fresh cilantro, chopped
2 cups chicken broth

Pound the chicken breasts until thin. Top each piece of chicken with the chile, ham, cheese, avocado, and the cilantro. Roll each piece tightly, place in a glass baking dish, fold down, and brush with the melted butter. Cover and bake for 45 minutes at 325 degrees. Remove the cover and continue to bake until the top is golden brown.

To make the pipián, in a saucepan, saute the onion, garlic, and chile in the oil until the onion starts to brown. Place the mixture and the walnuts and in a blender and puree until smooth, using a little broth to thin if necessary.

Return the blended mixture to the saucepan, stir in the broth, and simmer for 20 to 30 minutes until thickened.

To serve, place the chicken on a plate, pour the sauce over the top and garnish with a few chopped walnut pieces and cilantro leaves.

Yield: 4 to 6 servings   Heat Scale: Mild

Habanero-Marinated and Pecan-Smoked Quail

The wild quail most commonly eaten are the bob-white and the crested, or Gambel's, quail. The Courternix, a domesticated variety, is raised on farms in South Carolina and Georgia. The taste can be mild to strong depending on the age of the bird. Quail are small and lean, so they must be marinated before cooking. The lengthy marinating time is countered by the short time it takes to smoke these birds. Serve with a wild rice and white rice pilaf and sauteed carrots and pearl onions. Note: This recipe requires advance preparation.

Habanero Marinade:
1/4 cup golden raisins
1/4 cup soy sauce
2 habanero chiles, stems and seeds removed, chopped
4 cloves garlic, chopped
2 tablespoons fresh ginger, minced
2 teaspoons ground coriander
1 teaspoon ground turmeric
1 teaspoon ground cinnamon
1/2 teaspoon ground cloves
2 limes, juiced
1/3 cup vegetable oil

Quail:

6 whole quail

In a bowl, soak the raisins in the soy sauce for 15 minutes to soften. Place the raisins and the soy sauce and all the remaining marinade ingredients, except for the oil, in a blender or food processor and puree until smooth. Add the oil a little at a time. Place the quail in nonreactive pan or in a large plastic bag and marinate for 24 hours, or overnight if you are strapped for time.

In a smoker, build a fire with pecan or fruitwood and bring the smoke to 200 to 220 degrees F. Place the quail on a rack in the smoker and smoke until the leg bones move easily, about 2 hours. Or, smoke-grill the quail over a hot fire for about 20 minutes, turning often. In either case, the internal temperature should be 160 degrees F.

Yield: 6 servings   Heat Scale: Hot

Smoked Turkey Basted with *Cascabel* Oil

This simple dish yields a complex taste. Serve the turkey hot with the chile oil and a salsa on the side, or cold on a bolillo roll. You can substitute anchos or pasillas for the cascabels. Note: This recipe requires advance preparation

1/2 cup vegetable oil
6 cascabel chiles, stems and seeds removed, crushed
4 cloves garlic, chopped
2 teaspoon dried oregano
Salt and freshly ground black pepper
1 10-pound turkey

Heat the oil in a pan and saute the chiles and garlic until softened, about 10 minutes. Remove from the heat and add the oregano, salt, and pepper.

Split the turkey in half by cutting in through the breast and backbone. Brush the chile oil over the turkey, sprinkle with the oregano and salt and pepper and marinate for a couple of hours at room temperature.

Place the turkey sections, breast side up, on a grill in a smoker and smoke with indirect heat over an aromatic wood such as pecan, apple, or hickory. Baste the turkey with the oil every half hour until the turkey sections are done to an internal temperature of 160 degrees F., approximately 4 hours.

Yield: 8 or more servings   Heat Scale: Mild

Grape-Grilled Quail with Goat Cheese Rounds

Although many Southwest barbecues and grilled meats utilize mesquite, it is not the only aromatic wood to use—experiment with pecan, apple, peach, and grape clippings. If you use charcoal for the main fire, be sure to soak the wood for an hour in water before grilling. Note: This recipe requires advance preparation.

12 quail
2 ancho chiles, seeds and stems removed
2/3 cup olive oil
1/4 cup orange juice
2 tablespoons lime juice
1 clove garlic
6 2-ounce goat cheese rounds
2 tablespoons olive oil
1/4 cup dried corn bread crumbs
6 6-inch pieces of thick grape vine clippings,
    soaked in water
Salsa of choice from chapter 5

Cut the wing tips off the quail, then split the birds down the back and remove the backbone. With a knife tip, remove the rib bones from each quail, and then slice open the thigh bones to remove the bones and joint, taking care to keep the skin intact. Open up each quail and press the legs together, securing them with toothpicks.

Simmer the chiles in water for 15 minutes. Place the chiles in a blender along with the olive oil, orange and lime juices, and the garlic and puree. Pour this sauce over the quail and marinate for an hour.

While the quail are marinating, prepare a medium-hot charcoal fire and preheat the oven to 350 degrees. Brush each goat cheese round with olive oil, coat with corn bread crumbs, and bake for 5 minutes. If you start the baking just when the quail are being grilled, both should be done at the same time.

Add the grape clippings to the coals, arrange the quail skin side down on the rack and grill for 2 minutes, taking care not to burn them. Turn the quail and grill for an additional 2 minutes.

If the skin is not yet crisp, turn once more and grill for an additional minute. The internal temperature should be 160 degrees F.

Serve 2 quail on each plate with a goat cheese round and garnished with the salsa.

Yield: 6 servings   Heat Scale: Mild

Tamale-Stuffed Game Hens

Here is an intensely flavored poultry dish that should be served with a rice dish from Chapter 12, a salad from Chapter 8, and a squash dish from Chapter 11. Select the tamales from Chapter 12.

2 tablespoons hot red New Mexican chile powder
1/4 cup onion, chopped
2 tablespoons garlic, minced
3 cups tomato juice
1 tablespoon cumin
1 tablespoon oregano
2 bay leaves
1/2 cup olive oil
3 game hens, rinsed and cleaned
6 tamales
2 cups grated Monterey Jack cheese
1/4 bunch green onions, minced fine
1 teaspoon granulated garlic
1 teaspoon cumin
1 teaspoon oregano
1 teaspoon hot chile powder
2 cups tomatillo or red chile sauce (see recipes, chapter 5)

Combine the chile powder, onion, garlic, tomato juice, cumin, oregano, bay leaves, and olive oil in a bowl and mix well. Transfer to 3 large zip bags and add the hens. Marinate the hens in the mixture for at least 4 hours and preferably overnight

Steam the tamales for 25 minutes, then remove them from the wrappers and crumble them. In a bowl, combine the crumbled tamales, add the remaining ingredients and mix well.

Stuff the hens with this mixture and roast them for an hour at 325 degrees F., or until they are crispy. Remove the hens from the oven and carefully cut them in half lengthwise, taking care to keep the stuffing in the cavity. Serve stuffing-side up and top with a tomatillo or red chile sauce.

Yield: 6 servings   Heat Scale: Medium

Honey-Drenched Smoked Turkey Breast with Rainbow Chile-Mango Salsa

Here is one of my favorite summer dishes. The turkey breast should be smoked with either hickory or pecan wood. Do not use mesquite because the flavor is too intense for smoking.

Turkey:

1 cup honey
1/2 cup soy sauce
1 turkey breast
Fresh cilantro leaves for garnish

Rainbow Salsa:

2 red jalapeño chiles, chopped fine
2 green serrano chiles, chopped fine
2 yellow wax hot chiles, chopped fine
1 red onion, diced
2 tomatoes, cored and diced
1 mango, peeled and pitted
2 tablespoons cooking oil
1 tablespoon vinegar

To make the turkey, combine the honey and the soy sauce to make a basting sauce. Paint the breast with a thin coating of sauce.

Place the breast on a cookie sheet in the smoker, and smoke with indirect smoke for 4 to 5 hours, depending on the size of the breast and the heat of the smoke. Continue basting as the breast smokes. The skin on the breast will turn dark brown, almost black, and should be removed before carving.

To make the salsa, combine the chiles, onion, and tomatoes in a bowl. Puree the mango with the oil and vinegar in a blender, then add it to the bowl. Mix well.

To serve, carve the breast, then place the slices on a plate. Spoon some of the salsa on top and garnish with cilantro leaves.

Serves: 12 or more   Heat Scale: Medium

11. A Harvest of Wholesome Heat

Chile peppers are high in vitamins A and C, low in sodium, high in fiber, and, of course, have no cholesterol. When combined with other vegetables, as in these recipes, they create very healthy hot dishes.

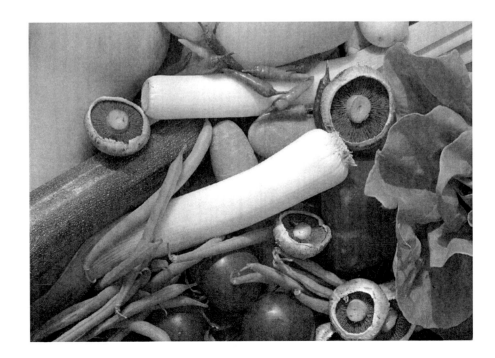

Vegetable harvest.
Photographer Aaron Sandoval

Chile Rellenos Classicos

The Big Jim variety of New Mexican chile makes excellent chiles rellenos ("stuffed chiles") because the pods are large and meaty, but any of the New Mexican varieties work well in this recipe. Top these chiles rellenos with either a Classic Green Chile Sauce or Red Chile Sauce (see recipes, Chapter 5). Serve with shredded lettuce and guacamole (see recipes, Chapter 6), Spanish rice, and refried beans.

> 4 green New Mexican chiles, roasted, peeled, with stems left on
> Cheddar or Monterey Jack cheese, cut in sticks
> Flour for dredging in a large bowl
> 3 eggs, separated
> 3 tablespoons flour
> 1 tablespoon water
> 1/4 teaspoon salt
> Vegetable oil for frying
> Chile sauce for topping

Make a slit in the side of each chile and stuff the chiles with the cheese sticks. Dredge the chiles in the flour.

Beat the egg whites until they form stiff peaks.

Beat the yolks with the water, flour, and salt until thick and creamy. Fold the yolks into the whites.

Dip the chiles in the mixture and fry in 2 to 3-inches of fat until they are a golden brown. Serve topped with the chile sauce.

Yield: 4 servings   Heat Scale: Medium

Pueblo Chile Fritters

I have made some changes to the traditional Native American recipe from New Mexico for a more contemporary flavor. Serve these with a soup or stew from Chapter 7.

> 1/3 cup all purpose white flour
> 1/3 cup water
> 1 egg, slightly beaten
> 1/2 teaspoon baking powder
> 4 green New Mexican chiles, roasted, peeled, stems and seeds removed, chopped
> 1/4 cup whole kernel corn
> 2 tablespoons onion, chopped
> Vegetable oil for frying

In a bowl, slowly add the water to the flour, stirring constantly, to make a thin sauce. Add the remaining ingredients, except the oil, and mix well.

Drop the batter by tablespoons into 360 degree oil and fry until golden brown. Remove and drain on paper towels.

Yield: 12 fritters   Heat Scale: Medium

Chiles Rellenos with Smoked Chicken and *Tomatillo*-Spinach Sauce

Here is a variation on chiles rellenos that utilizes a very non-traditional sauce. Serve the chiles with a Southwestern salad from Chapter 8 and a bean dish from Chapter 13. Note: This recipe requires advance preparation.

Sauce:

2 poblano chiles, stem removed, roasted, peeled, and seeded
16 tomatillos
1/4 bunch fresh cilantro
4 tablespoons lime juice
20 spinach leaves, washed and dried
Salt and pepper to taste

Batter:

1 and 1/4 cups all purpose flour
Pinch baking powder
1/2 teaspoon salt
2 egg yolks
1 bottle of beer
2 egg whites

Chiles:

15 green New Mexican chiles, roasted, peeled, stems left on
Prepared hot sauce to taste
1 whole egg
1 egg yolk
12 ounces Ricotta cheese
10 ounces goat cheese
4 ounces grated Mozzarella or Jack cheese
4 ounces grated Parmesan or Asiago cheese
1/2 cup cilantro, chopped
3 cups smoked chicken
Salt and pepper to taste
Vegetable oil for deep frying

To make the sauce, place all the ingredients in a blender and blend until smooth.

To make the batter, mix together the flour and baking powder in a bowl. Combine the beer and the egg yolks and mix gently with the flour. Whip the whites to a medium peak and fold into the flour mixture. Let sit 1 hour.

To make the chiles, cut a slit in the chiles near the stem and remove the seeds. In a bowl, whisk the hot sauce, egg and the yolk until foamy. Add the Ricotta and mix thoroughly. With a rubber spatula, fold in the goat cheese. Add the rest of the filling ingredients and fold together, mixing thoroughly. Chill until very cold.

Using a pastry bag, stuff the chiles with the filling, coat them with the batter, and deep fry at 350 degrees F. for 4 to 6 minutes.

Warm the sauce, spoon some out on plates, and place the chiles on top. Garnish with sprigs of cilantro.

Yield: 8 to 10 servings   Heat Scale: Medium

Chiles en Nogada

Here is another variation on stuffed chiles, this one courtesy of Zarela Martinez, the famed New York Mexican restaurateur, who says that her version is based on the classic recipe served on national holidays in Mexico. She, however, bakes the chiles instead of deep frying them and eliminates the walnuts that give the dish its name. No matter—Zarela says the dish is "one of our most beloved at Zarela Restaurant."

Salsa de Tomate Asado:

1 and 1/2 cups heavy cream
6 medium garlic cloves, unpeeled
1 medium onion, unpeeled and halved crosswise
3 to 4 large tomatoes (2 and 3/4 pounds)
Salt to taste

Stuffed *Poblanos:*

6 large green poblano chiles, roasted, peeled,
    seeded, stems left on
1 stick unsalted butter
1 medium onion, chopped
2 medium garlic cloves, minced
1/2 cup pimiento-stuffed green olives, sliced
1/2 cup each pitted prunes, dried apricots, and
    dried peaches, diced
1 1/2 teaspoons ground cumin seed
1 1/2 teaspoons ground cinnamon
1/4 teaspoon ground cloves
2 cups cooked chicken, shredded
Salt to taste

To make the salsa, in a small saucepan, simmer the cream until reduced to about 1 cup. In a large skillet or griddle, roast the garlic cloves and the onion over high heat, turning several times, until the garlic is dark on all sides and somewhat softened, and the onion is partly charred. Add the tomatoes and roast until the skins start coming off. Peel the garlic, onions, and tomatoes into a blender. It's okay if a few charred bits get into the mixture. Puree on medium speed until smooth. Add the cream and repeat. Season with salt to taste and keep warm.

Melt the butter in a saucepan and saute the onion and garlic until the onion is soft. Add the olives and the fruits and continue to saute until the fruits are soft. Add the spices and cook 1 more minute. Combine this mixture with the shredded chicken and mix well. Adjust for salt.

Cut a slit in the side of each chile and carefully fill the chiles with the mixture and bake on a greased baking sheet for 7 minutes at 350 degrees F.

To serve, spoon the Salsa de Tomate Asado on individual plates and place one chile on each plate over the salsa.

Yield: 6 servings   Heat Scale: Mild

Calabacitas Caliente

This recipe combines three Native American crops—squash, corn, and chile. It is one of the most popular dishes in New Mexico and is so colorful that it really highlights meat and chicken entrees.

3 yellow squash, peeled and cubed
1/2 cup onion, chopped
1/2 cup green New Mexican chile that has been, roasted, peeled, stems removed and chopped
4 tablespoons butter
2 cups whole kernel corn
1 cup milk
1/2 cup Monterey Jack cheese, grated

In a skillet, saute the squash and onion in the butter until the squash is tender.

Add the chile, corn, and milk. Simmer the mixture for 15 to 20 minutes to blend the flavors. Add the cheese and heat until the cheese is melted.

Yield: 4 to 6 servings   Heat Scale: Medium

Marinated *Chipotle* Zucchini

One of the chiles of choice when preparing Southwestern food, the chipotle imparts a wonderful smoky-hot flavor to the squash. Serve as a side to grilled meats.

3 to 4 tablespoons olive oil
1 medium onion, cut in 1/4-inch slices
4 small zucchini, cut lengthwise in half
1 tablespoon wine vinegar
2 canned chipotles in adobo, minced
Chopped fresh cilantro or parsley

In a pan, heat the oil and saute the onion until soft. Place the zucchini halves, cut sides down, on top of the onion. Reduce the heat, cover the pan and cook for 20 minutes or until tender. Remove the vegetables and keep warm.

Stir the vinegar, chipotle and simmer the mixture for a couple of minutes to blend the flavors.

Place the zucchinis on a plate and top with the onions. Pour the marinade over the top and allow to sit for 15 to 20 minutes before serving.

Top with the chopped cilantro and serve either warm or at room temperature.

Yield: 4 to 6 servings   Heat Scale: Medium

Sauteed Butternut Squash

Slow cooking brings out the butternut's natural sugars and fresh sage adds a wonderful contrasting flavor accent. I thank Renee Shepherd of Shepherd's Garden Seeds for this recipe. Her seed catalog contains varieties that are hard to find anywhere else, including some specialty pumpkins. Feel free to add some red chile powder to spice up the squash.

3 tablespoons vegetable oil
1 1/2 pounds butternut squash, seeded and cut into 1 inch chunks (about 3 1/2 cups)
1 large clove garlic, minced
Salt and pepper to taste
1 tablespoon fresh sage, shopped
1 tablespoon fresh Italian parsley, chopped

In a heavy skillet (preferable non-stick), heat the oil until it is sizzling. Add the squash and garlic and toss to coat well with the oil. Saute the mixture slowly over a low heat, stirring frequently for about 30 minutes, or until the squash is golden and tender (add a tablespoon or two of water if the squash begins to stick). Add the salt and pepper to taste, then sprinkle the sage and parsley over the squash and mix to combine.

Yield: 4 servings

Southwestern Summer Vegetables

This recipe combines a variety of summer vegetables, so use whatever you have available. Serve in a flour tortilla for an unusual meatless burrito.

1/4 cup olive oil
2 tablespoons red wine vinegar
1 tablespoon crushed red New Mexican chile, including the seeds
1 tablespoon fresh cilantro, chopped
1/4 teaspoon crushed cumin seeds
4 ears of corn, cut into 2-inch lengths
1 bell pepper, stem and seeds removed, cut in wedges
2 large onions, cut into 1 1/2 inch pieces
2 zucchini, cut in 1-inch rounds
Cherry tomatoes

In a pan, combine the oil, vinegar, chile, cilantro and cumin. Simmer for a couple of minutes to blend the flavors.

Thread the vegetables on skewers and grill for 7 to 10 minutes or until done, basting frequently with the sauce.

Yield: 4 to 6 servings   Heat Scale: Mild

Grilled Sweet Onions with *Poblano* Cream

Vidalia onions, which hail from Vidalia, Georgia, are large and exceedingly sweet and juicy. They are available in May and June by mail order, but if you can't find them, substitute Texas sweets or Walla Wallas. Note: This recipe requires advance preparation.

Poblano Cream:

2 poblano chiles, stems removed, roasted, peeled, and seeded
1/2 teaspoon salt
1 bunch cilantro, leaves only
1 cup sour cream
1 lime, juiced

Grilled Vidalia Sweet Onions:

4 Vidalia onions, peeled and halved along the equator
Olive oil
Salt and pepper

To make the Poblano Cream, combine all ingredients in a food processor and puree. Chill in the refrigerator.

Make 1/4 inch X-shaped incisions on the flat side of each half onion.

Grill the onion halves over a hot fire and partially caramelize them. Puddle some Poblano Cream on small plates and serve the onion halves in it, flat side up. Drizzle olive oil and sprinkle salt and pepper over the X-shaped incisions.

Yield: 8 servings   Heat Scale: Mild

Spicy Grilled Green Onions

These onions go well with a variety of foods such as steaks, fajitas, and hamburgers. Marinate the onions overnight and throw them on the grill while cooking the entree. Note: This recipe requires advance preparation.

1 tablespoon ground red New Mexican chile
1 cup olive oil
3 cloves garlic, minced
18 to 24 large green onions, including 3 to 4 inches of the green

Combine all the ingredients and marinate the onions for at least 4 hours and preferably overnight.

Grill the onions over hot coals until all sides are browned.

Yield: 6 servings   Heat Scale: Mild

Texas *Jalapeño* Onion Rings

These fiery onion rings go with any barbecue or serve in place of french fries to spice up a hamburger plate.

3 jalapeño chiles, stems and seeds removed, chopped
12 ounces beer, at room temperature
1 1/3 cups flour
1 egg beaten
3 large onions, sliced in rings 1/4 thick, separated
Vegetable oil for frying

Place the chiles in a blender with a little of the beer and puree. Combine all the ingredients in a bowl, except the oil.

Pour about 1-inch to 1 1/2-inches of oil in a skillet and heat to 350 degrees.

Dip the rings in the batter and drain the excess. Fry in the oil until golden brown, remove and drain.

Yield: 6 servings   Heat Scale: Medium

Potatoes Colorado

Although the word "colorado" here refers to the red color of the chile rather than the state of the same name, this dish is commonly prepared there—and all over the Southwest. Serve these red chile potatoes in place of hash browned potatoes for a terrific Southwestern breakfast.

2 tablespoons butter
1/2 cup onions, chopped
1 clove garlic minced
2 tablespoons crushed red New Mexican chile, including the seeds
2 large potatoes, peeled and diced
1 tablespoon grated Parmesan cheese

In a pan, heat the butter and saute the onions and garlic until soft, then add the chile. Toss the potatoes in the mixture.

Place the potatoes on a shallow pan with a little water and bake in a 350 degree F. oven until the potatoes are done, about 45 minutes.

Sprinkle the cheese over the top of the potatoes and serve.

Yield: 4 servings   Heat Scale: Medium

Potato-Stuffed Chiles

Here is an unusual twist on stuffed potatoes, which are often baked, removed from their skins, mixed with green chile and other ingredients, stuffed back into their skins and baked some more.

1 egg yolk
1 tablespoon sour cream
1/2 teaspoon crushed New Mexican red chile
1 large baked potato
1 large green New Mexican chile, split
    lengthwise, stem and seeds removed
Salt to taste
Minced fresh chives for garnish

In a bowl, whisk together the egg yolk, sour cream and red chile. Scoop the potato out of its skin, add to the mixture, and whisk until smooth. Fill a pastry bag with this mixture and, using a star tip, pipe it into each chile pepper half.

Bake the chile halves in a 400 degree F. oven until golden brown, about 15 minutes. Sprinkle with the chives and serve.

Yield: 2 servings   Heat Scale: Mild

Double-Baked Potato Baptized in Salsa

Cut calories by using salsa in place of butter in this tasty, interesting side dish that goes well with any grilled or barbecued meats.

1 potato
Salt and pepper to taste
1 tablespoon black olives, sliced
1 tablespoon salsa of choice from chapter 5, or
    bottled salsa
1/3 cup extra sharp Cheddar cheese, grated
1 1/2 tablespoons sour cream

Bake the potato at 375 degrees for 1 hour or until tender when pierced with a fork. Let the potato cool slightly and cut in half lengthwise. Scrape out the pulp and place it in a bowl (do not tear the skin).

Salt and pepper the skin and reserve. In a bowl, mash the potato pulp and stir in the chopped olives, salsa, cheese, and sour cream. Fill the potato skins with the mixture and top with extra cheese. Bake for another 15 minutes and serve.

Yield: 2 servings   Heat Scale: Mild

12. Los Huevos, Los Quesos y Los Otros

The eggs, the cheeses, and the others are the famous Southwest combination dishes. I have included the various incarnations of enchiladas and tamales here; but first, let's have breakfast.

Tamales ready for the sauce.
Photographer Chel Beeson

Huevos Rancheros

These ranch-style eggs are ubiquitous throughout the Southwest and appear in many variations. This is the one served in New Mexico.

  2 cups Classic New Mexico Red Chile Sauce (see
      recipe, Chapter 5)
  2 medium tomatoes, chopped
  8 eggs
  4 corn tortillas
  Oil for frying
  1/2 cup Cheddar cheese, grated

Heat the chile sauce and the tomatoes in a large saucepan over medium heat for 5 minutes.

In a small skillet, fry each tortilla in the hot oil for a few seconds until soft, turning once, then drain on paper towels.

Crack the eggs into the sauce and poach them.

To serve, place a tortilla on each plate, then slip two eggs and sauce on top of each one. Garnish with the shredded cheese and serve.

Yield: 4 servings   Heat Scale: Medium

Chilaquiles

This extremely simple breakfast dish takes only a few minutes to prepare. It is rarely found in restaurants for some unknown reason.

  1 dozen corn tortillas
  Vegetable oil for frying
  2 cups salsa, either bottled or homemade (see
      recipes, Chapter 5)
  2 cups grated Monterey Jack cheese

Cut the tortillas in quarters and fry them in the oil in a skillet until they are slightly crisp.

Place a layer of 16 wedges on the bottom of a casserole dish. Add 1/3 of the salsa and sprinkle 1/3 of the cheese on top. Repeat this process 2 more times.

Bake the casserole for 20 minutes at 350 degrees.

Yield: 4 servings
Heat Scale: Mild to medium, depending on the salsa

Blue Corn *Tamales* with Spiced Goat Cheese

Tamales are very versatile and are no longer made with just traditional ingredients. For example, here is a recipe that uses goat cheese, which is made everywhere in the Southwest.

Masa:

1 package dried corn husks
2 cups blue corn masa
1 teaspoon salt
2 cups chicken broth
1/3 cup shortening

Filling:

6 serrano chiles, stems removed, minced
4 ounces goat cheese or substitute Feta cheese
1/4 cup onion, finely chopped
1/3 cup heavy cream
1/4 cup fresh cilantro, chopped
1/4 cup piñon nuts

To make the masa, soak the corn husks in hot water in a large bowl for 15 to 30 minutes, or until they are soft and pliable. In another bowl, mix together the masa and salt. Slowly add the broth until the mixture holds together. In another bowl, whip or beat the shortening until fluffy. Add the masa to the shortening and continue beating to make a dough. Drop a teaspoonful of the dough into a glass of cold water and if it floats, it is ready. If it sinks, continue to beat and test the mixture until it floats.

To make the filling, combine all the ingredients together in a bowl and mix well.

To assemble, overlap a couple of the corn husks so that they measure about 5 by 8 inches. Place 2 tablespoons of the masa in the center of the husk, and pat or spread the dough thinly and evenly into a 2 by 3 rectangle.

Place about 2 teaspoons of the filling down the center of the masa and fold the husk around the masa and filling and firmly tie each end of the tamale, being careful not to squeeze it.

Place a rack in the bottom of a steamer or large pot over a couple of inches of boiling water. Place the tamales on the rack. Cover the tamales with additional husks or towel to absorb the moisture. Bring the water to a boil and steam for 2 hours or until done.

Yield: 12 to 18 tamales   Heat Scale: Medium

Blue Corn *Tamales* with Corn Kernels

Blue corn, native to the southwest, gives these tamales a distinctive, nutty taste. Make them smaller than an entree tamale and serve as a side dish, instead of a vegetable. You will need four bowls to prepare this recipe.

Corn husks as needed
6 green New Mexico chiles, roasted, peeled,
    stems and seeds removed, chopped
2 cups whole kernel corn
3/4 cup grated Cheddar cheese, plus 1/4 cup for
    topping
2 cups coarse blue corn masa
1 teaspoon salt
2 cups chicken broth
1/3 cup lard or shortening

In a bowl, combine the chiles, corn, and cheese together for the filling and mix well.

In another bowl, soak the corn husks in water to soften.

In a third bowl, mix together the masa and salt. Slowly add the broth, stirring with a fork until the mixture holds together. In a fourth bowl, whip the lard or shortening until fluffy. Add the masa to the shortening and continue to beat. Drop a teaspoon full of the dough into a glass of cold water. If the dough floats, it is ready. If it sinks, continue to beat it until it floats.

To assemble. select corn husks that measure about 5 x 8 inches or overlap smaller ones together. Place 2 tablespoons of the masa in the center of the husk, and pat or spread the dough evenly into a 2-by 3-inch rectangle. Place about 2 to 3 tablespoons of the filling down the center and top with some cheese. Fold the husk around the masa and filling, being careful not to squeeze the tamale.

There are two basic ways of folding the husks. The first is to take two strips of the corn husks and firmly tie each end of the tamale. This method works well with smaller corn husks.

The second method is to fold the tapered end over the filled husk, and then fold the remaining end over it. Tie the tamale around the middle with a strip of the corn husk to keep the ends folded down.

Place a rack in the bottom of a steamer or large pot. Make sure that the rack is high enough to keep the tamales above the water. Place the tamales on the rack, folded side down, or if the pot is large enough, stand them up. Do not pack them tightly as they need to expand as they cook. Cover with addition husks or a towel to absorb the moisture. Bring the water to a boil, reduce to a gentle boil, and steam for an hour for each dozen tamales or until done. To test for doneness, open one end of the husk and if the masa pulls away from the wrapper, it is done.

Yield: 24 tamales   Heat Scale: Mild

Green Corn *Tamales*

The "green" in this favorite Arizona tamale refers both to the green chiles and the fresh, or "green" corn used in the filling. They are usually a seasonal dish prepared in the summer and early fall, when fresh corn is available. This recipe is from Poncho's on South Central in Phoenix and is delicious as a side dish.

3 cups corn masa
3/4 cup lard or shortening
1/2 teaspoon baking powder
Pinch of salt
1 1/2 cups green chile cut into thin strips
1 1/2 cups Longhorn cheese, grated
3 cups freshly cooked white corn, pureed in a
 blender
20 or more corn husks, rinsed

In a bowl, combine the masa, lard, baking powder, and salt and thoroughly mix until the dough is very fluffy. Add the remaining ingredients except the corn husks and mix again, taking care not to crush the chile strips. Let the mixture sit for at least ten minutes.

Place a large spoonful of the mixture on a corn husk, roll up, and tie each end in a bow with a thin sliver of corn husk.

Place the tamales in a steamer and steam over medium heat for about an hour.

To serve, place the tamales on a plate and allow the guests to unwrap their own.

Yield: 20 or more tamales   Heat Scale: Mild

El Paso Green Chile Casserole

No other dish says "party" in El Paso like the green chile casserole, which is served at luncheons, cocktail parties, and even bar mitzvahs. This is the dish that's the cheater's chiles rellenos and avoids the tedious stuffing of all the chiles. It is assumed that you will use fresh green chiles, roasted and peeled by hand. If you must, you may sneak in canned chiles.

10 to 12 whole fresh green chiles, roasted,
 peeled, stems removed, seeded
8 ounces Monterey Jack cheese, grated
8 ounces Longhorn or Cheddar cheese, grated
4 eggs, separated
2/3 cup evaporated milk
1 tablespoon flour
Salt and pepper to taste

Butter the bottom of an ovenproof casserole dish. Place the chiles in the bottom of the dish and sprinkle with the Jack cheese, then the Longhorn or Cheddar.

In a bowl, beat the egg yolks with the evaporated milk, flour, salt and pepper until thick and light-colored. In another bowl, beat the whites until stiff peaks form. Fold the whites into the yolks and spread the egg mixture over the casserole. Run a spatula through the eggs to fill the air pockets.

Bake at 350 degrees for one hour or until a toothpick comes out clean.

Yield: 8 servings   Heat Scale: Mild

Tamale Pie with Cheese and Chicken

This recipe is a delicious alternative to traditional tamales. A salad from Chapter 8 is all that is needed to complete a meal.

    1 4-pound chicken, cut in pieces
    2 large onions, chopped
    2 cloves garlic, minced
    4 green New Mexican chiles, roasted, peeled,
        stems and seeds removed, chopped
    3 jalapeño chiles, stems removed, chopped
    1 teaspoon New Mexican red chile powder
    1 cup ripe olives, chopped
    1 cup whole kernel corn
    2 cups sour cream
    2 cups chicken broth
    1 cup masa harina
    2 eggs, separated
    2 cups Monterey Jack cheese, grated

In a large pot, simmer the chicken, 1/2 of the onions, and the garlic in water to cover until the chicken is done and starts to fall away from the bones. Remove the chicken. Strain the broth and reserve.

Remove the meat from the bones and chop the chicken along with the remaining onion. In a bowl, combine the chicken with the chiles, chile powder, olives, corn, and sour cream. Place the mixture in a casserole dish.

In a pan, bring the broth to a boil and gradually add the masa while stirring constantly. Reduce the heat and cook until the mixture thickens, about 10 minutes. Remove from the heat and stir in the egg yolks. Whip the egg whites until stiff and fold them into the masa mixture. Spread this batter over the casserole and top with the grated cheese.

Bake for 35 minutes at 375 degrees.

Yield: 6 servings   Heat Scale: Medium

Tex-Mex *Enchiladas*

I'm going to attempt to establish the various styles of Southwestern "Mexican" cooking. To that end, I have included four totally different recipes for "red" enchiladas—one from Texas, one from New Mexico, and two from Arizona. Cooks can decide for themselves which one is best, but I already know the answer. Here is the first recipe, as prepared in Southwestern Texas.

2 tablespoons shortening
3 tablespoons flour
2 tablespoons red chile powder (or more for heat)
3 cups warm water
2 tablespoons vegetable oil
12 corn tortillas
2 onions, chopped
4 cups Longhorn cheese, grated

Melt the shortening in a skillet, stir in the flour, and make a roux. Add the chile powder and water, stir, and cook until this "chile gravy" is thick. Keep this gravy warm on the stove.

Lightly grease a glass, ovenproof casserole dish and preheat the oven to 450 degrees.

Heat the oil in a skillet and using tongs, lightly fry each tortilla for about 5 seconds on each side. Do not overcook or they will get rubbery. Drain them on paper towels.

Dip each tortilla in the gravy, then place it in the casserole dish. Place some of the onion and cheese on the tortilla and roll it up, then place it in the

dish with the seam on the bottom. Continue until all the rolled tortillas fill the dish.

Pour the chile gravy over the tortillas, top with more cheese, and bake in the oven for 10 minutes.

Yield: 4 servings   Heat Scale: Mild

Stacked Red Chile *Enchiladas*

Here is my second "red" enchilada recipe. This is the classic enchilada dish served at the early 1960s Albuquerque restaurant, Videz, owned by Pete Benavidez. The restaurant was torn down to make way for Interstate 40, but the recipe lives on.

6 to 8 dried red New Mexican chiles, stems and seeds removed
1 clove garlic
1 teaspoon ground Mexican oregano
1/2 pound pork, cubed from a roast or chops
1 to 1 and 1/2 pounds very lean ground beef
12 corn tortillas
Vegetable oil for frying
2 cups Cheddar or Monterey Jack cheese, grated
1 medium onion, chopped

Cover the chiles with very hot water and soak for 20 to 30 minutes or until limp and partially rehydrated. Place the chiles in the blender (they should loosely fill 3/4 of the container, if more, make two small batches.) Fill the container up near the top with water. Drop in the clove of garlic and sprinkle the top with the oregano. Add a little salt at this stage if you wish. Blend for 2 to 3 minutes on high or until a homogeneous or orange-red mixture is obtained.

Pour the mixture into a saucepan and add the pork. Cook, covered over a very low heat or uncovered at a slight bubble, for 2 to 3 hours. If cooked uncovered, periodically add water back to original level to maintain proper consistency, which I can only describe as medium soupy.

Remove the pork pieces and save for another meal such as carne adovada. Place the chile sauce in the refrigerator and cool. Remove any fat that congeals on the top.

Season the beef with a little salt and pepper and saute in a skillet until the meat is no longer pink. Combine the sauce and beef and simmer, covered, for an additional 30 to 45 minutes.

Fry three tortillas per person in a couple of inches of oil until they are slightly harder than taco shells. As they are removed from the oil with tongs, dip each into the red chile pot until they are fully submerged. Remove, place on a plate and top with some cheese and onion.

Continue the process until the tortillas are stacked three high on each plate.

Ladle red chile, including a small amount of the meat, over the tortilla stack until it is puddled up as deep as it will stand around the base of the stack. Cover the enchilada lightly with grated cheese and place in a 250 degree oven for 20 minutes.

Yield: 4 servings   Heat Scale: Medium

Red Chile Pasta with Green Chile Pesto

Several manufacturers produce red chile pastas. If you can't find them, simply add red chile powder to pasta recipes and make your own! Serve with a Southwestern salad from Chapter 8.

5 green New Mexican chiles, roasted, peeled, stems and seeds removed, minced
1/2 red bell pepper, roasted, peeled, stems and seeds removed, minced
3 cloves garlic, minced
1 cup cilantro or substitute Italian parsley
1/2 cup piñon nuts, toasted
1 teaspoon lime juice
2 tablespoons olive oil
1 package red chile pasta, cooked al dente in salted water
1 cup grated Romano cheese

In a molcajete or mortar, crush the chiles, bell pepper, garlic, cilantro, nuts, lime juice, and olive oil into a rough pesto.

Toss the pasta with the pesto and sprinkle liberally with the Romano cheese.

Yield: 4 servings   Heat Scale: Medium

Sonoran-Style *Enchiladas*, Arizona Version

For generations, American cooks of Mexican heritage have lived in Arizona and have developed their own interpretations of such classic dishes as enchiladas. Here is my third Southwestern enchilada recipe, as prepared in Phoenix and other parts of southern Arizona. Note the similarity of the sauce to the Tex-Mex chile gravy.

3 tablespoons vegetable oil
3 tablespoons flour
3 cups water
6 tablespoons red chile powder
1/2 teaspoon garlic, crushed
4 tablespoons vegetable oil
6 corn tortillas
2 cups cooked ground beef, drained
1/2 cup black olives, chopped
1 cup Cheddar cheese, grated
1 cup onion, finely chopped

Heat the oil in a skillet and add the flour. Stirring constantly, brown the flour into a roux. In a bowl, combine the chile powder and the water, mix well, and add this mixture to the roux. Add the crushed garlic and bring the sauce to a boil. Reduce heat and simmer until thickened, about 15 minutes.

Heat the cooking oil in a skillet, and using tongs, lightly fry each tortilla for about 5 seconds per side to soften them. Do not overcook. Place three tortillas on a plate, spread a row of ground beef over each end, add a little sauce, and roll up each tortilla. Repeat with the other plate. Pour the rest of the sauce over the rolled tortillas on each plate, sprinkle the olives, cheese, and onions over the sauce, and serve immediately. An option is to keep the plates warm in a 250 degree oven until the cheese melts slightly.

Yield: 2 servings   Heat Scale: Mild

Sonoran-Style *Enchiladas*, Mexican Version

My fourth and final enchilada recipe differs greatly from the Arizona version above. The main differences are the use of freshly made, thick corn tortillas and the inclusion of chiltepíns in the sauce. I dined on these enchiladas one night in Tucson, and as Cindy Castillo was preparing them, I wrote down her recipe exactly.

Sauce:

15 to 20 chiltepíns, crushed
15 dried red New Mexican chiles, seeds and
    stems removed
3 cloves garlic
1 teaspoon salt
1 teaspoon vegetable oil
1 teaspoon flour

Tortillas:

2 cups masa harina
1 egg
1 teaspoon baking powder
1 teaspoon salt
Water
Vegetable oil for deep frying

Garnish:

3 to 4 scallions, minced (white part only)
2 cups queso blanco or Monterey Jack cheese, grated
Shredded lettuce

To make the sauce, combine the chiles, salt, and enough water to cover in a saucepan. Boil for ten or fifteen minutes or until the chiles are quite soft.

Allow the chiles to cool and then puree them in a blender along with the garlic. Strain the mixture, mash the pulp through the strainer, and discard the skins. Heat the oil in a saucepan, add the flour, and brown, taking care that it does not burn. Add the chile puree and boil for five or ten minutes until the sauce has thickened slightly. Set aside and keep warm.

To make the tortillas, mix the masa, egg, baking powder, and salt together thoroughly in a bowl, adding enough water to make a dough. Using a tortilla press, make the tortillas. Deep fry each tortilla until it puffs up and turns slightly brown. Remove and drain on paper towels and keep warm.

To assemble and serve, place a tortilla on each plate and spoon a generous amount of sauce over it. Top with the cheese, lettuce, and onions.

Yield: 4 to 6 servings   Heat Scale: Hot

Tomatillo-Chicken *Enchiladas* with Two Kinds of Green Chile

Southwestern cooks are forever improvising on traditional recipes. This interesting variation on green chile and chicken enchiladas has been tested so many times in our kitchens that I now consider it a New Southwest classic.

4 chicken breasts
8 ounces cream cheese
1 cup onions, finely chopped
1 cup cream or half and half
3 green serrano chiles, stems and seeds removed, chopped fine
5 green New Mexican chiles, roasted, peeled, seeds and stems removed, chopped
1 cup tomatillos, husks removed, washed, and chopped fine
1/4 cup fresh cilantro, chopped
1/2 teaspoon freshly ground black pepper
1 egg
Vegetable oil for frying tortillas
12 corn tortillas

In a pot, cover the chicken with water, bring to a boil, reduce the heat, and simmer for 30 minutes. Remove the chicken and reserve the stock. When the chicken has cooled, remove the skin and meat. Shred the meat using two forks.

In another bowl, combine the cream cheese, onions, and 1/4 cup of the cream. Add the chicken and mix well.

Place the serranos, green chile, tomatillos, cilantro, pepper, egg, remainder of the cream, and 1/3 cup of the chicken stock in a blender and puree to make a smooth sauce.

Heat a couple inches of oil in a pan until hot. Fry each tortilla for a few seconds on each side until soft, taking care that they do not become crisp. Remove and drain.

To assemble the enchiladas, dip a tortilla into the green sauce and place it in a shallow casserole dish. Spread about 1/4 cup of the chicken mixture in the center of the tortilla, roll it up and place it at the end of the dish with the end side down. Repeat the process until the enchiladas form a single layer in the dish. Pour the remaining sauce over the enchiladas.

Bake the enchiladas, uncovered, in a 350 degree oven for 20 minutes and serve immediately.

Yield: 5 servings ` Heat Scale: Medium

Chicken, Chile, and Cheese *Chimichangas*

These sweet chicken chimichangas with fruit are lighter than the more traditional beef and bean recipe popular in Arizona.

1 medium onion, chopped fine
1 tablespoon vegetable oil
4 green New Mexican chiles, roasted, peeled, stems and seeds removed, chopped

3 cups cooked chicken, diced
1/2 teaspoon ground cinnamon
1/4 teaspoon ground cloves
1 small orange, peeled, seeded, and chopped
6 flour tortillas
1 cup Monterey Jack cheese, grated
Vegetable oil for deep-fat frying
Chopped lettuce and tomatoes for garnish

In a skillet, saute the onion in the oil until soft. Add the chiles, chicken, and spices and saute for an additional 5 minutes. Add the chopped orange and mix well.

Wrap the tortillas in a moist towel and place them in a warm oven to soften for 10 minutes. Place approximately 1/2 cup of the chicken mixture in the center of each tortilla and top with cheese. Fold the tortilla like an envelope and secure with a toothpick.

Deep-fry the chimichangas, one at a time, in 375 degree oil until well browned. Drain on paper towels and remove the toothpick.

Serve topped with shredded lettuce, chopped tomatoes, and a salsa selected from Chapter 5.

Yield: 6 servings Heat Scale: Mild

13. The Legumes, the Grains, and the Flours

Or, as I sometimes say, the beans, the rice, and the breads. All are staple foods spiced up with Southwestern touches, and believe it or not, some of them *do not* contain chile peppers!

Black beans.

Photographer Aaron Sandoval

Beans Dobie-Style

This recipe for J. Frank Dobie's Texas beans originally appeared in 1949. Note: This recipe requires advance preparation.

1 pound dried pinto beans, picked clean and washed thoroughly
1 1/2 inch salt pork, cubed
12 chilipiquíns (chiltepíns)
4 teaspoons raw onion, grated
Vinegar

Soak the beans overnight, then drain and rinse. Place them in a pot with the salt pork and enough water to cover and cook them over medium heat until they are tender. Drain the beans and keep them warm.

Divide the beans onto four plates, mash three chilipiquíns into the beans with a teaspoon of raw onion, and sprinkle vinegar on top.

Yield: 4 servings   Heat Scale: Hot

Scholey Beans

From the famous Scholey and Stephans Saloon in historic Tombstone, Arizona comes the "best darned beans in the state." They were part of the saloon's free lunch. Note: This recipe requires advance preparation.

1 quart dried red beans, picked clean and washed thoroughly
1/2 pound salt pork or bacon
1 onion, chopped
1 cup lard or substitute vegetable oil
5 red chile pods, seeds and stems removed
1/2 pound round steak
1 cup green New Mexican chiles, chopped
1 clove garlic, minced
Salt to taste

Cover beans with water and soak overnight. In a kettle, combine the beans, salt pork, onion, and lard and cook until the beans are tender. Boil the chile pods in a little water until they soften. Work them through a colander and reserve the pulp.

Fry the round steak in its own suet until it is well done and then run it through a meat grinder. Add the ground steak, chile pulp, green chiles, and garlic to the beans and cook for at least a half hour to blend the flavors. Adjust the salt before serving.

Yield: 12 servings   Heat Scale: Medium

Frijoles Borrachos

Not only do these "drunken beans" contain fine Mexican beer, they are usually consumed with the same. Serve as an accompaniment to any barbecued meat or poultry dishes. Use as a filling for burritos or sopaipillas, or serve by itself with a flour tortilla. Note: This recipe requires advance preparation.

2 cups pinto beans, picked clean and washed thoroughly
Water
1/4 cup chopped jalapeño chiles, stems removed
12 ounces dark Mexican beer, such as Negra Modelo
1 small onion, chopped
1 large tomato, peeled and chopped
1 teaspoon Worcestershire sauce

In a pot, cover the beans with water and soak overnight. Drain the beans.

Cover the beans with fresh water, bring to a boil, reduce the heat and simmer until the beans are done, about 2 to 2 1/2 hours. Remove and drain, reserving 1 to 2 cups of the bean water.

Combine the remaining ingredients, the beans, and the reserved bean liquid in a pot. Simmer the beans for 30 minutes to blend the flavors or until the liquid has been reduced to the desired amount.

Serves: 6 to 8   Heat Scale: Medium

Border Beans

Beans are so ubiquitous in the Southwest cuisines that there are literally hundreds—if not thousands—of recipes for them. This version originated in El Paso.

3 cups cooked pinto beans (either canned or simmered for hours until tender)
1 onion, minced
2 tablespoons lard, or substitute vegetable oil
5 slices bacon, minced
3/4 cup chorizo sausage (see recipe, chapter 9)
1 pound tomatoes, peeled, seeded, and chopped
6 serrano chiles, seeds and stems removed, minced
1/2 teaspoon cumin

In a skillet, saute the beans and onion in the lard or oil for about five minutes, stirring constantly. In another skillet, saute the bacon and chorizo together. Drain.

Combine the beans and onion with the drained bacon and chorizo in a pot, add the remaining ingredients, and simmer for 30 minutes.

Yield: 4 servings   Heat Scale: Medium

Southwestern *Chipotle* Baked Beans

Pinto beans are not the only variety served in the Southwest. Try these interesting Great Northern beans as a spicy side dish.

3 canned chipotle chiles in adobo, stems removed, chopped
1 large onion, chopped
2 cloves garlic, chopped
1 tablespoon vegetable oil
2 teaspoons ground New Mexican red chile
2 tablespoons adobo sauce (from the canned chiles)
1/4 pound slab bacon, cut in 1/2 inch pieces
1/2 cup catsup
1/2 cup beer
1/4 cup dark brown sugar
1 teaspoon dry mustard
3 cups cooked Great Northern beans

In a skillet, saute the chipotle chiles, onions, and garlic in the oil until the onions are soft. Combine this mixture with the remaining ingredients in a baking dish.

Cover and bake the beans in a 325 degree oven for 2 hours or until the beans are tender and coated with the sauce. Add water if the mixture gets too dry.

Yield: 6 servings   Heat Scale: Medium

Sopa Seca with Garbanzos

Translated as "dry soup," this dish is actually a variant of Spanish rice, which was transferred to Mexico by early Spanish settlers and eventually made its way northward. More modern versions substitute coiled vermicelli, which is broken into small, rice-sized pieces.

1/2 cup New Mexican green chiles, chopped
1 onion, chopped
2 cloves garlic, minced
3 tablespoons bacon fat
1 cup long grain rice
2 cups chicken broth
1 cup tomatoes, finely chopped
1 cup canned garbanzo beans, drained
Salt and pepper to taste

In a large skillet, saute the chiles, onion, and garlic in the bacon fat until the onion is soft. Add the rice and cook over low heat until the rice is browned. Add the broth and the tomatoes and bring to a boil.

Transfer the mixture to a oven-proof casserole dish and bake at 350 degrees for about 45 minutes, covered. Remove the cover during the last ten minutes for a crispier rice. Add the garbanzos and stir during the last 5 minutes of cooking.

Yield: 4 servings   Heat Scale: Mild

Refried Black Beans with Goat Cheese

This is a variation on the traditional refritos, or refried pinto beans so commonly served in the Southwest. Serve these with any of the enchilada dishes in Chapter 12.

1 pound dried black beans, cleaned
2 small white onions, one quartered and one diced
2 cloves garlic, minced
2 cups chicken stock
1/2 pound bacon, minced
3 jalapeños, stems removed, seeded, and chopped
3 tablespoons safflower oil
Salt and pepper to taste
3/4 pound goat cheese, grated

Place the beans in a stockpot and add water until the beans are covered by 3 inches. Cover the pot and bring to a boil, skimming off any foam. Reduce the heat to a simmer and cook for about 1 hour.

Add the jalapenos, quartered onion, garlic, and the chicken stock. Simmer for another hour, skimming off the foam, until the beans are very tender and are splitting apart at the seams. Drain the beans, reserve the liquid, and let the beans cool to room temperature.

In a large skillet, saute the bacon until crisp and almost burned. Pour off the fat, reserving about 3 or 4 tablespoons, and drain the bacon on paper towels and reserve it. Saute the diced onion and the jalapeños in the bacon fat until the onions are soft.

Place the beans in a blender along with 3 to 4 cups of the reserved liquid. Add the bacon, onion, and jalapeños, and any remaining bacon fat. Puree to a thick but still chunky consistency. Depending on the size of the blender, this process may have to be done in several batches.

Oil a saute pan with the safflower oil and cook the beans, stirring constantly, until most of the liquid is evaporated, about 5 to 10 minutes. Remember that cooked black beans burn easily, so don't rush this process.

Serve with goat cheese sprinkled on top.

Yield: 6 servings   Heat Scale: Medium

New Mexican Green Chile Rice

This is not a traditional Southwestern recipe, but rather a striking vegetarian rice dish that is loaded with vegetables. It would make a good accompaniment to any of the poultry dishes in Chapter 10.

1 small potato, peeled and diced
1 carrot, peeled and diced
2 large tomatoes, chopped
1 small onion, chopped
1 cup tomato juice
1 cup peas
1/2 cup New Mexican green chile, chopped
1 cup rice, rinsed
2 tablespoons vegetable oil
1 cup chicken broth

Cook the potatoes and carrots in water until tender.

Place the tomatoes, onions, and tomato juice in a blender or food processor and puree until smooth. Remove this juice mixture and reserve. In a bowl, combine the peas, chile, potatoes, and carrots and reserve.

Saute the rice in the oil until brown, being careful that it does not burn. Add the juice mixture and the broth. Bring to a boil, reduce the heat and cook until done, about 25 minutes. Toss the peas, chiles, potatoes, and carrots with the rice. Return to the oven for 10 minutes, then serve.

Yield: 6 servings   Heat Scale: Medium

Rice, Green and Hot

Somehow, this pilaf dish of Middle Eastern origin emigrated to the Southwest, where it seduced the serrano and lived happily ever after in the gullets of gourmands.

2 cups long-grain white rice
2 tablespoons butter or vegetable oil
1 small onion, chopped fine
6 green serrano chiles, stems and seeds removed
2 cloves garlic, minced
4 cups chicken stock

Saute the rice in the butter for 2 minutes. Add the onions and continue to saute until the onions are soft and the rice is golden brown, taking care not to let it burn.

In a blender, puree the chiles, garlic, and a little stock until smooth. Add this to the rice and continue cooking over a low heat for 5 minutes.

Stir in the remaining stock and transfer this mixture to a baking dish. Cover and bake at 350 degrees for 45 minutes. Fluff with a fork before serving. Removing the cover for the final 15 minutes of baking will produce a crispier pilaf.

Yield: 6 servings   Heat Scale: Medium

Indian Fry Bread

Fry bread is very similar to sopaipillas, which are smaller and more "puffed." These large round pieces of bread are used as a basis for Navajo tacos and can also be folded over a stuffing and eaten as a sandwich. At fairs, festivals, and rodeos throughout New Mexico, they are cooked by Native Americans in large round frying pans over open fires and are easily found due to the wonderful aromas.

3 cups flour
1 1/2 teaspoons baking powder
1/2 teaspoon salt
1 1/3 cups warm water
Vegetable oil for frying

In a large bowl, mix the flour, baking powder, and salt together.

Add the water and knead the dough until soft. Roll out the dough until it is 1/4 inch thick. Cut out 8-inch diameter rounds.

Fry the bread in 2 to 3 inches of hot oil until puffed and browned on both sides.

Yield: 4 pieces of fry bread

Traditional New Mexican *Sopaipillas*

In the early days these "little pillows" were usually served as a bread with New Mexican meals and garnished with honey. Nowadays they are all that and more, as home chefs stuff them with meat, or beans, or cheese, or chile or all of the above. Serve with honey, dusted with cinnamon and sugar as a dessert.

4 cups all-purpose flour
2 teaspoons baking powder
1 teaspoon salt
4 tablespoons shortening
1 1/2 cups warm water
Vegetable oil for frying

In a large bowl, combine all the dry ingredients and cut in the shortening.

Add the water to form a dough. Knead the dough until smooth. Cover and let sit for 30 minutes.

Roll the dough to 1/8-inch thick and cut into 4-inch squares. Fry the sopaipillas in 375 degree oil until puffed and browned on both sides, about 15 minutes. Drain on paper towels and serve.

Yield: 4 dozen

Pueblo Blue Corn-Chile Bread

The addition of green chile to corn bread is an ancient pueblo tradition. Blue corn has made a comeback in products such as chips and cornmeal.

1 1/2 cups blue cornmeal
2 tablespoons sugar
2 teaspoons baking powder
1/2 cup green chile, chopped
3/4 cup milk
1 egg
2 tablespoons bacon fat or substitute cooking oil

In a bowl, combine the cornmeal, sugar, and baking powder and mix well. In a separate bowl, combine the chile, milk, egg, and bacon fat and mix well. Add the liquid ingredients to the dry ingredients and mix well.

Pour the mixture into a greased baking dish and bake at 350 degrees for 30 minutes.

Yield: 4 to 6 servings   Heat Scale: Mild

Toasted Baguettes with *Chipotle* Chile Butter

Use this smoky butter as a topping for hamburgers and steaks, as well as a spread for breads. You can also scramble eggs in it.

1 chipotle chile, soaked in water to soften it (or more to heat it up)
1 pound sweet butter
2 tablespoons chives, minced
3 tablespoons cilantro, minced
2 scallions, minced
1 lime, juiced
Toasted baguettes

Cut the butter into eighths to soften and place it with the other ingredients (except the baguettes) in a food processor. Blend until smooth. Spread over as many baguettes as needed.

Yield: 1 pound   Heat Scale: Mild

Southwestern Green Chile Corn Bread with Prickly Pear Butter

This intriguing combination of recipes is courtesy of chef Lenard Rubin, who was at one time responsible for the Southwestern dishes at the Windows on the Green restaurant at the exclusive Phoenician Resort in Scottsdale.

Corn Bread:

1 cup butter
3/4 cup sugar
4 eggs
1/2 cup green chile, chopped
1 1/2 cups cream-style corn
1/2 cup Cheddar cheese, grated
1/2 cup Jack cheese, grated
1 cup flour
1 cup yellow corn meal
2 tablespoons baking powder
1 teaspoon salt

Prickly Pear Butter:

1 pound unsalted butter
2 ripe prickly pear fruits (*tunas*), or substitute
    1/2 cup strawberries or raspberries (or, use 1
    cup commercial prickly pear syrup and
    eliminate the honey)
1 bunch cilantro, stems removed and chopped fine
1/2 cup honey

To make the Corn Bread, cream the butter and sugar together in a bowl and add the eggs slowly, one at a time, stirring constantly. Add the remaining ingredients and mix well. Pour the mixture into a 9-inch, buttered square pan. Bake at 325 degrees for approximately 1 hour.

To make the Prickly Pear Butter, let the butter soften slightly at room temperature. Peel the cactus fruits, puree them in a blender, and strain the juice through a fine sieve. Combine the juice or the cup of syrup and the remaining ingredients in a blender or food processor and blend until smooth.

Put the mixture in a bowl in the refrigerator until it begins to harden. Lay out a sheet of waxed paper and spread the butter out in a wide strip. Roll up the paper as you would a cigar to make a cylinder of butter. Freeze this cylinder solid and return it to the refrigerator to soften slightly for easy slicing.

Serve the Corn Bread topped with slices of the butter.

Yield: 6 to 8 servings

Guacamole Bread

This unusual bread has all the makings for the famous appetizer baked right in it. Serve it plain or make chicken and chile sandwiches for a unique Southwestern flavor.

    2 tablespoons onion, chopped
    1 tablespoon butter
    2 cups flour
    1 1/2 teaspoons baking powder
    1/2 teaspoon salt
    1/4 teaspoon ground cumin
    1/2 cup butter, softened
    1 cup sugar
    1 cup mashed avocado
    2 eggs, beaten
    3 green New Mexican chiles, roasted, peeled,
        stems and seeds removed, chopped

In a skillet, saute the onion in 1 tablespoon of butter until softened.

Sift together all the dry ingredients in a bowl.

In another bowl, cream together the butter and sugar. Add the avocado, eggs, onions, and chiles. Add the flour to the batter and mix well.

Pour the batter into a buttered 9 by 5-inch loaf pan and bake for 15 minutes at 375 degrees. Reduce heat to 350 degrees and continue to cook for 55 minutes or until done.

Yield: 1 Loaf   Heat Scale: Mild

Chile-Dusted Cheese *Bolillos*

I first tasted the heavenly bolillo rolls in Juárez, where they are stuffed with ham and avocados for tortas, Mexican sandwiches. Here is my spiced up version. Note: This recipe requires advance preparation

2 cups very warm water
1 package dry yeast
1 tablespoon sugar
2 teaspoons salt
5 1/2 cups flour, sifted
1 cup Cheddar cheese, grated
1/2 tablespoon cumin seeds
1 tablespoon red chile powder
1 egg white, unbeaten

In a bowl, pour the yeast over the water and stir until dissolved. Allow to sit for 5 minutes.

Add the sugar, salt, and three cups of flour and beat until smooth and shiny. Add the cheese and cumin seeds. Stir in 2 cups more flour. Sprinkle the remaining flour on a board and knead the bread, adding more flour if necessary, until it is smooth and shiny, about 5 to 7 minutes. Shape into a ball.

Rub a bowl lightly with shortening and press the top of the ball of dough into the bowl, then turn the dough over. Cover with a warm, damp towel. Place in a draft-free area and allow to rise until doubled in size, about 2 hours.

Punch down the dough and let rest for 5 minutes. Rub a little shortening on your hands and divide the dough into 6 equal portions. To form the roll, shape each portion into an oblong and place on a lightly greased sheet pan. Make two horizontal indentations on each roll and bake in a 375 degree oven for 30 minutes or until lightly browned.

Sprinkle the chile powder on the egg white and brush each roll with the egg and return to the oven for 2 minutes. Remove and cool.

Yield: *6 bolillos*   Heat Scale: Mild

14. Desert Desserts

The finest complement to heat is sweet. For dousing the danger of fiery foods, the combination of sugar, dairy products, and fruits just can't be beat. Here are my favorite Southwestern cool-down desserts, plus one at the end that *does* have chiles in it!

Shelled *piñon* nuts.

Photographer Aaron Sandoval

New Mexican Hot Chocolate with Cinnamon

This chocolate drink is not only a great way to start the day, it's also a fine way to end a meal or to warm the body and soul on a cold winter night.

1 quart whole or low-fat milk
1-inch stick of cinnamon
2 tablespoons instant coffee
2 squares sweet chocolate
1/2 cup boiling water
1/2 teaspoon vanilla
1/2 teaspoon ground nutmeg

In a pan, heat the milk, cinnamon, and coffee to the boiling point, then remove from heat. In a bowl, combine the chocolate and boiling water. Strain the milk and add it to chocolate water. Return to the pan and heat to the boiling point and then remove from the heat again.

Add the vanilla and nutmeg and beat with a molinillo, a low-tech but efficient Mexican chocolate beater, until foamy and serve immediately. You can also use a whisk.

Yield: 1 quart

Prickly Pear Jam

A Navajo legend holds that in order not to offend the spirit of the plant when the tunas (fruits of the cactus) are being picked, the gatherer must pluck a hair from his or her head. This is a sacrifice indeed for balding men! The prickly pear fruits are often available in border markets such as the Centro Mercado in Ciudad Juárez, or you can pick your own as the Opuntia cacti are easily grown in well-drained xeriscape gardens in most temperate parts of the country, and usually produce plenty of fruits.

14 to 20 ripe prickly pear fruits
1 cup water
3 tablespoons lime juice
2 cups Mesquite honey (or more or less to taste)

If the fruits have spines, remove them by holding the fruits with tongs over an open flame until the spines burn off. Peel the fruits, remove as many seeds as possible, chop them fine, and place this fruit in a pan with water. Simmer the fruit until it is soft and pulpy.

Add the lime juice, honey, and more water if needed and simmer until the jam is thick, about 30 minutes, taking care not to burn the mixture.

Remove from heat, cool, and place in sterilized jars.

Yield: 2 cups or more, depending on the size of the fruits

Hill Country Peach Crisp

Some of the best peaches I've ever eaten are grown in the Hill Country outside of Austin and San Antonio. Here's how to use them in a wonderful dessert.

    10 cups sliced fresh peaches
    2 teaspoons lemon juice
    1/2 teaspoon almond extract
    1 cup brown sugar
    3/4 cup whole wheat flour
    3 cups quick oats
    1 1/2 cups pecans, chopped
    3/4 cup coconut, grated
    1 cup butter, melted
    1 teaspoon almond extract
    1 teaspoon nutmeg

In a bowl, toss the peaches with the lemon juice and almond extract and then place them in a 9 by 13 inch baking dish.

In another bowl, combine the sugar, flour, oats, pecans, and coconut and then stir in the butter and almond extract. Spread this mixture over the peaches and sprinkle it with nutmeg.

Bake in a 350 degree oven for 45 to 60 minutes, or until the top is golden brown.

Yield: 12 servings

Mesilla Pecan Tarts

Here's a simple but delicious dessert that captures the flavor of New Mexico's largest nut crop. In 2006, New Mexico became the second largest pecan producer in the country, after Texas, but look for Georgia to bounce back. Note: This recipe requires advance preparation.

    3 ounces cream cheese, softened
    1/2 cup butter, softened
    1 cup sifted flour
    1 egg, slightly beaten
    3/4 cup brown sugar
    1 teaspoon vanilla
    1 tablespoon butter, softened
    3/4 cup pecans, chopped

In a bowl, blend the cream cheese with the butter with a fork until smooth. Add the flour and mix well, then chill the dough in the refrigerator for at least 2 hours. Shape the dough into 2 dozen 1-inch balls. Press the dough into 1 3/4-inch muffin or tart pans.

In a bowl, blend the remaining ingredients until they are thoroughly mixed. Top each section of the tart pan with a portion of the mixture. Bake for 20 minutes at 375 degrees and cool the tarts on wire racks before removing them from the pans.

Yield: 24 tarts

Biscochitos

These traditional cookies were created by the descendants of the earliest Spanish settlers of New Mexico based on earlier Mexican recipes transferred from Spain. Now they are staples gracing holiday tables, usually served following midnight church services and the lighting of hundreds of luminarias or farolitos. They are the official New Mexico State Cookie. Note: This recipe requires advance preparation.

1/2 pound lard
1 cup sugar
1 teaspoon anise seeds
1 egg
2 tablespoons brandy or sherry
3 cups flour
1 1/2 teaspoons baking powder
1/2 teaspoon salt
1 1/2 teaspoons ground cinnamon
2 tablespoons sugar

In a bowl, whip the lard using a mixer at high speed to create a very light, airy texture, much like whipped cream. (This is the secret to feather-light cookies.)

Add the sugar very slowly and continue beating until all is well mixed, then add the anise seeds, eggs, and brandy. Continue to beat until fluffy and somewhat frothy. Add all the remaining dry ingredients at once and stir on the lowest speed until they are well mixed and a smooth dough results.

Chill the dough in the freezer until it firms. Allow at least 2 hours in the freezer for the most tender cookies.

To roll, place a ball of dough about 3 or 4 inches in diameter on a lightly floured marble or wood surface. Roll out, using a very light stroke with a rolling pin. The dough should resemble pie pastry more than cookie dough.

Using a sharp knife or cookie cutter, cut the dough into the shapes desired—often a fleur de lis is preferred. Combine the cinnamon and sugar in a bowl and dust the shapes with it. Bake in a 350 degree oven until just done. Traditionally they are served white—never browned or even golden.

Yield: 18

Natillas

This pudding is a wonderful end to a traditional New Mexican meal. The consistency should be that of a soft custard, and it can be served either warm or cold.

3/4 cup sugar
2 tablespoons flour
1/2 teaspoon salt
2 eggs, separated
2 cups milk
1/2 teaspoon vanilla
Ground cinnamon

In a bowl, combine the sugar, flour, and salt and mix well.

In another bowl, beat together the egg yolks and 2 tablespoons of the milk. Add this to the sugar mixture and beat until well combined.

In a saucepan, bring the remaining milk to just below boiling, or scald the milk. Add the egg yolk and sugar mixture, stirring constantly. Reduce the heat and simmer for 10 minutes, being sure to stir constantly until it is the constancy of a thick custard sauce.

Remove from the heat, allow to cool, and stir in the vanilla.

In a bowl, beat the egg whites until they are stiff. Fold the custard mixture into the beaten egg whites. Sprinkle with the ground cinnamon and let sit for 30 minutes.

Refrigerate or serve warm.

Yield: 4 to 6 servings

Piñon Flan with Caramel Sauce

Flan *is a traditional Mexican custard dessert that has been adopted by all parts of the Southwest. This version is flavored with another favorite Southwestern ingredient, piñon nuts.*

2 cups sugar
3 1/2 cups whole milk
1 vanilla bean
6 eggs
1 teaspoon each ground cinnamon, nutmeg, and ginger
1 tablespoon dark rum (optional)
1 cup whole shelled piñon nuts

Place 1 cup sugar and 2/3 cups water in a heavy saucepan and, over a low heat, stir until the sugar is dissolved. Increase the heat and boil until the mix is a light brown. Reduce the heat and simmer until the syrup is an amber color, swirling the pan occasionally to push any crystals back in the syrup. Allow to cool slightly and pour evenly into six warmed custard cups so that this caramel sauce coats them.

In a saucepan, scald the milk and vanilla bean together. Remove from heat and allow to cool. Remove the vanilla bean.

In a bowl, eat the eggs, spices, and rum together until foamy. Whisk in the remaining sugar and the piñons. Gradually add the milk, stirring until the sugar is dissolved.

Pour the mixture into the custard cups. Place the cups in a pan with enough hot water to come half-way up the sides of the cups.

Bake in a 350 degree F. oven for 60 to 70 minutes or until a thin knife inserted halfway between the center and the edge of the custard comes out clean.

To serve, run a thin knife around the outside of the cup and invert the custard onto a dish. The piñons should be on top. Let the custard sit at room temperature for 10 minutes to set before serving.

Yield: 6 servings

Mango Sorbet with Raspberry Sauce

Mexico is one of the top mango-growing countries, so it's no surprise that the fruit is very popular in the Southwest. I have two dwarf mango trees in pots that winter in my greenhouse, and together they produced about 10 fruits in 2007. Here's what I made with two of the fruits.

Mango Sorbet:

2 large mangos, pitted and chopped
2 tablespoons lime juice
1/4 cup sugar syrup

Raspberry Sauce:

2 cups raspberries, fresh preferred
2 tablespoons sugar (or more to taste)
1 lime, juiced

To make the mango sorbet, combine all ingredients in a food processor and puree until smooth. Freeze until solid.

To make the raspberry sauce, combine all the ingredients in a blender and puree until smooth. Transfer to a pan and bring to a boil, then reduce heat and simmer until thickened. Add a little arrowroot to thicken or a little rum to thin the sauce. Allow to cool and serve the sauce over the sorbet.

Yield: 4 to 6 servings

Southwestern Bread Pudding with Tequila Sauce

In 1944, World War II was still raging, I was born, and Rosalea Murphy opened The Pink Adobe in Santa Fe. The restaurant seated only thirty, and the menu was brief, but customers loved Rosalea's eclectic creations and the restaurant flourished. More than a half-century later, it's still one of the top five restaurants in "The City Different." Here is their popular bread pudding

Tequila Sauce:

1 cup sugar
1 egg
1 stick butter, melted
1/3 cup good-quality tequila
1 teaspoon fresh lime juice

Bread Pudding:

1/2 pound stale French bread
1 cup milk
1 stick butter, melted
1/2 cup golden raisins
1/4 cup piñons or pine nuts
3 eggs, beaten
1 and 1/4 cups sugar
1 4-ounce can evaporated milk

1 8 and 1/4-ounce can crushed pineapple with juice

1 tablespoon fresh lemon juice
1 tablespoon vanilla

To make the tequila sauce, cream the sugar and egg together in a bowl. Add the butter and pour into a medium saucepan. Over low heat, stir the mixture until the sugar is dissolved. Remove from the heat and stir in the tequila and lime juice.

To make the bread pudding, preheat the oven to 350 degrees F. Break the bread into bite-sized chunks and soak them in the milk in a bowl for a few minutes. Squeeze the bread to eliminate excess liquid and discard the milk. Place the bread in a large bowl and add the remaining ingredients. Mix thoroughly but gently. Pour the mixture into an 8 by 12 inch buttered baking pan and bake for 1 hour or until a knife inserted in the center comes out clean. Pour the sauce over the individual servings of the bread pudding.

Yield: 8 to 10 servings

Kahlúa Mousse

Kahlúa is the second most popular liqueur in the world and has been made since before World War II. This tasty mousse is easy to make.

> 2 cups whipped non-dairy topping
> 1/2 cup heavy whipping cream
> 1 tablespoon instant coffee
> 2 tablespoons unsweetened cocoa powder
> 3 tablespoons granulated sugar
> 6 tablespoons Kahlúa brand liqueur

In a bowl, whip the non-dairy topping with the whipping cream until stiff. Add the coffee, cocoa,

and sugar and blend well. Add the Kahlúa and stir the mixture with a rubber spatula. Chill the mousse.

When ready to serve, the mousse can be topped with whipped cream, chocolate sprinkles, and a wafer cookie.

Yield: 8 servings

Chiltepín Ice Cream

This novelty was first served in 1988 for the symposium on wild chiles at the Desert Botanical Garden in Phoenix and at the Fiesta de Los Chiles at the Tucson Botanical Gardens. It is very hot in the proportions given (despite the tendency of ice cream to cut the heat), so cooks may wish to reduce the quantity of chiltepíns.

> 1/2 cup fresh green chiltepíns, thoroughly pulverized; or substitute *chiltepínes en escabeche* or dried red chiltepíns that have been rehydrated and pulverized
> 1 gallon vanilla ice cream

Combine all ingredients in a large bowl and mix thoroughly until green (or red) flecks appear throughout the ice cream. Serve in small portions and warn people about what they're eating.

Yield: 20 or more servings   Heat Scale: Hot

Prickly Pear *Sabayon* in a Sweet Cinnamon *Chalupa* Shell

When Farn Boggie (a real name!) was chef at the Piñon Grill at the Inn at McCormick Ranch in Scottsdale, Arizona, he often combined the flavors of the Southwest with cooking techniques from France and Italy. Chapula is Spanish for "boat" and describes the shell in which the filling is placed. Chalupa shell baskets for deep frying are available from mail order kitchen shops.

3 prickly pear pads (*nopales*), peeled and diced
1/2 cup sugar
1/2 cup water
1/2 pint warm, heavy cream
4 eggs, separated
4 6-inch flour tortillas
Cinnamon
Sugar
4 fresh raspberries for garnish
Whipped cream for garnish

Place the pads in a small saucepan with the sugar and water and boil until the sugar dissolves. Puree the mixture in a blender until smooth and set aside.

Add the prickly pear puree to the egg yolks in a bowl. Place the bowl in boiling water and whip the yolks until the mixture is firm and keeps its shape. Slowly add in the heavy cream, mix, and taste for sugar. Add more if necessary. Remove from heat and set aside.

Whip the egg whites into stiff peaks and then fold them into the sabayon sauce. Set aside.

Deep fry the tortillas into the shape of a basket by using a ladle to hold the tortillas under the oil. When crisp, remove from oil. Dust the shells with cinnamon and sugar.

Place the chalupa on a salad plate, fill with the prickly pear sabayon, and garnish with raspberries and whipped cream.

Yield: 4 servings

Tamales Dulce

Sweet tamales are usually served for dessert. Different fruits can be used and they can also be unwrapped before serving and topped with a sweet sauce.

1 cup apricots, chopped
1/2 cup raisins
1/2 cup pecans (or other nuts), chopped
Corn husks
1/3 cup lard or vegetable shortening
1/2 cup sugar
2 cups masa harina
1/2 teaspoon salt
1 teaspoon cinnamon
1 cup water
1 teaspoon baking powder

Combine the apricots, raisins, and pecans in a bowl.

Soak the corn husks in water to soften.

Cream the shortening and sugar together in a bowl. In another bowl, mix together the masa, salt, and cinnamon. Slowly add the water, stirring with a fork until the mixture holds together. In another bowl, whip the lard or shortening until fluffy. Add the masa mixture to the shortening and continue to beat. Drop a teaspoon full of the dough into a glass of cold water. If the dough floats, it is ready. If it sinks, continue to beat it until it floats.

To assemble: Select corn husks that measure about 5 x 8 inches or overlap smaller ones together. Place 2 tablespoons of the masa in the center of the husk, and pat or spread the dough evenly into a 2-by 3-inch rectangle. Place about 2 teaspoons of the filling down the center and fold the husk around the masa and filling, being careful not to squeeze the tamale.

There are two basic ways of folding the husks. The first is to take two strips of the corn husks and firmly tie each end of the tamale. This method works well with smaller corn husks.

The second method is to fold the tapered end over the filled husk, and then fold the remaining end over it. Tie the tamale around the middle with a strip of the corn husk to keep the ends folded down.

Place a rack in the bottom of a steamer or large pot. Make sure that the rack is high enough to keep the tamales above the water. Place the tamales on the rack, folded side down, or if the pot is large enough, stand them up. Do not pack them tightly as they need to expand as they cook. Cover with addition husks or a towel to absorb the moisture. Bring the water to a boil, reduce to a gentle boil, and steam for an hour for each dozen tamales or until done. To test for doneness, open one end of the husk and if the masa pulls away from the wrapper, it is done.

Yield: 2 dozen tamale

Wild Blackberry *Empanaditas*

Curiously, empanada means both "pie" and "swindle" in Spanish, so I suppose that these little stuffed pies are so good that people will steal for them. Dessert empanaditas can be filled with almost any type of fruit; traditionally they are made with a mixture of meat, fruit, and nuts. Note: This recipe requires advance preparation.

Filling:

2 cups fresh blackberries or other fruits such as raspberries, strawberries, apricots, apples, or peaches
1 cup water
1/2 cup raisins
1 1/2 cups water
1/2 cup sugar
1 teaspoon lemon peel, grated
1/2 teaspoon cinnamon
1/4 teaspoon cloves

Pastry:

2 cups flour
2 teaspoons baking powder
1/2 teaspoon salt
1/3 cup shortening
1/3 cup cold water
1 egg, beaten
Sugar

To make the filling, combine the fruit and water in a saucepan and heat over a low heat until the mixture mounds on a spoon, adding more water if needed. Add the remaining ingredients and stir until the sugar dissolves. Allow to cool.

To make the pastry, sift the dry ingredients together into a bowl. With a pastry blender, cut in the shortening until the flour resembles fine crumbs. Add just enough water so that the dough will hold together. Chill for an hour.

Roll the dough out 1/8 inch thick and cut into circles 3 inches in diameter. Place 1 tablespoon of the filling on one half of each circle. Moisten the edges with water and fold over and crimp with a fork to seal.

Brush the top of each empanadita with the egg, sprinkle sugar over them and bake in a 400 degree oven for 15 minutes or until golden brown. Or, omit the egg and sugar, and deep fry in 375 degree oil until golden brown. Remove and drain on paper towels.

Yield: 20 to 24 pastries

Blue Cornmeal Crepes Filled with Two Cheeses

Here is the Southwestern version of dessert crepes, complete with blue corn for that wonderfully exotic color. Again, if blue corn flour is not available, substitute the yellow variety.

Filling:

1/4 cup cream cheese
1/4 cup Ricotta cheese
1/4 cup heavy cream
2 tablespoons sugar
1 tablespoon Amaretto liqueur
1/4 teaspoon almond extract

Crepes:

1 egg, beaten
3/4 cup milk
1 tablespoon butter or margarine, melted
3 tablespoons Amaretto liqueur
1/2 cup blue corn flour
Powdered sugar

To make the filling, allow all the ingredients to come to room temperature and mix together in a bowl.

To make the crepes, slowly whisk the liquid ingredients into the flour in a bowl. Cover and let stand, at room temperature, for an hour.

Lightly oil a crepe or non-stick pan and heat until almost smoking. Pour 2 tablespoons of the batter onto the pan and gently tilt the pan so that the crepe is very thin. Cook until the crepe is turning lightly brown on the edges, about 1 minute. Flip and cook the crepe on the other side. Repeat 3 times.

To serve, place about 2 tablespoons of the filling in each crepe. Roll up, dust with powdered sugar and serve.

Yield: 4 servings

A Pepper Primer

A Pepper Harvest.
Photographer Harald Zoschke

There are literally hundreds of varieties of peppers grown in the world, but only a dozen and a half are used for cooking in the United States and Canada. The following survey is not intended to be exhaustive, but rather a general description of the most popular peppers used in this country.

Fresh Peppers

Available from the garden or market, fresh peppers are becoming increasingly popular as they become more commonly available. The most ubiquitous peppers, are, of course, the familiar bells, which have no heat unless they are a variety called Mexi-Bell, which has a mild bite. The most interesting of the bell peppers are the brightly colored ones, which come in a variety of shades from yellow to orange to red to purple. They are most often used to brighten up salsas and salads. The *poblano*, similar in size to a bell, is a Mexican pepper with moderate to mild heat which is often stuffed with cheese and baked.

The most readily available hot peppers in the produce sections of supermarkets are *jalapeños* and yellow wax peppers. The yellow wax peppers are usually mild and are stuffed or chopped for use in salsas and salads. *Jalapeños*—either green or fresh red—are used in a similar manner, and are often floated whole in soups or stews to provide a little extra bite and are removed before serving. Another variety that sometimes appears fresh is the cherry pepper. This mild pepper is often pickled.

There are several varieties of the long, green New Mexican chiles available fresh in the Southwest and occasionally other locations. The No. 6-4 variety is the most commonly grown and is available from August through early November. It's hotter cousin, Sandia, is usually not seen in the green, or immature form. The mildest New Mexican variety is the Anaheim, a California variety that is available most of the year. Occasionally, New Mexican chiles are identified by their grower (such as "Barker") or by a regional appelation ("Chimayo" or "Hatch" or "Luna County"), which further confuses the issue.

All of these long green chiles must be roasted and peeled before using them in a recipe. Blistering or roasting the chile is the process of heating the chile to the point that the tough transparent skin is separated from the meat of the chile so it can be removed. The method is quite simple.

While processing the chiles be sure to wear rubber gloves to protect yourself from the capsaicin that can burn your hands and any other part of your body that you touch. Before roasting, cut a small slit in the chiles close to the top so that the steam can escape. The chiles can then be placed on a baking sheet and put directly under the broiler or on a screen on the top of the stove.

My favorite method, which involves meditation and a bottle of *Negro Modelo*, is to place the pods on a charcoal grill about 5 to 6 inches from the coals. Blisters will soon indicate that the skin is separating, but be sure that the chiles are blistered all over or they will not peel properly. Immediately wrap the chiles in damp towels or place in a plastic bag for ten to fifteen minutes—this "steams" them and loosens the skins. For crisper, less cooked chile, plunge them into ice-water to stop the cooking process.

Green chile is a low-acid fruit and for that reason I do not recommend the home canning of it. It can be done, however, but only by using a pressure canner and by carefully following all the manufacturer's specific instructions. I find freezing to be a much easier and more flavorful method of preservation.

If they are to be frozen whole (rather than chopped), the pods do not have to be peeled first. In fact, they are easier to peel after they have been frozen. After roasting the chiles, freeze them in the form that you plan to use them—whole, in strips, or chopped. If you are storing in strips or chopped, peel the pods first. A handy way to put up chopped or diced chiles is to freeze them in ice cube trays with sections. When frozen, they can be "popped" out of the trays and stored in a bag in the freezer. When making a soup or a stew, just drop in a cube! This eliminates the problems inherent in hacking apart a large slab of frozen chiles when you just need a couple of ounces.

New Mexican chiles are available fresh in season by overnight delivery (see Resources, p. 223). They are found canned in most U.S. markets and frozen in some parts of the Southwest.

Other fresh chiles that are sometimes found in markets (especially farmer's markets) are *serranos*

and *habaneros*. The *serranos*—smaller, thinner, and hotter than jalapeños—are the classic chiles of the Mexican *pico de gallo* fresh salsas. *Habaneros*, the world's hottest peppers, are lantern-shaped orange or red devils that have a unique, fruity aroma in addition to their powerful punch. Use them with caution. Generally speaking, any of the small fresh peppers may be substituted for each other; however, they are not a substitute for *poblanos* or the New Mexican varieties in recipes. The smaller chiles—*habaneros*, *serranos*, and *jalapeños*—can be frozen without processing. Wash the chiles, dry them, and put them one layer deep on a cookie sheet and freeze. After they are frozen solid, store them in a bag. Frozen chiles will keep for nine months to a year at zero degrees F. All of the small peppers can be frozen whole with no further processing needed, and their texture holds up surprisingly well in the freezer.

Dried Peppers

As is true with fresh peppers, the larger they are, the milder. The large dried peppers, such as *ancho* (a dried *poblano*) and the New Mexican varieties, are mild enough to be the principal ingredients of sauces. The smaller varieties, such as *piquin*, are too hot for this purpose and are generally used as condiments or in stir-frying. All dried peppers can be ground into powders (see below).

There are four main large peppers used as the base for sauces: *ancho*, *pasilla*, New Mexican, and *guajillo*. The *ancho* is a wide, dark pepper with a "raisiny" aroma. It is the only pepper that is commonly stuffed in its dried form (the pod is softened in water first). The *pasilla* is a long, thin, dark pepper that also has a "raisiny" or nutty aroma. Along with the *ancho*, it commonly appears in Mexican *mole* sauces.

The most common use of the red New Mexican chiles is to hang them in long strings, or *ristras*, until they are ready to be used in cooking. Then, they are commonly rehydrated and combined with onions, garlic, oil, spices, and water to make the classic New Mexican red chile sauce, a common topping for enchiladas in the Southwest. The *guajillos*, a shortened and hotter version of the New Mexican chiles, are commonly used in sauces in northern Mexico.

Another favorite dried chile pepper is the *chipotle,* a smoke-dried red *jalapeño* that has a fiery, smoky flavor. It is available loose in the dried form, or canned in *adobo* sauce. The latter is easier to use, because it's already rehydrated. To rehydrate the dried *chipotles*, simply soak them in hot water for an hour or more.

There are a bewildering number of small, hot pods ranging in size from that of a little fingernail (the *chiltepín*) to the six-inch, skinny *cayenne*. Some varieties include *piquin*, Thai, *santaka*, *de arbol*, *mirasol*, and *tabasco*. These chiles appear in stir-fry dishes, are floated in soups or stews, or are used to add heat to sauces that are too mild.

Powders

All chiles can be dried and ground into powder—and most are, including the *habanero*. Crushed chiles, or those coarsely ground with some of the seeds are called *quebrado*. Coarse powders are referred to as *caribe*, while the finer powders are termed *molido*. The milder powders, such as New Mexican, can also be used as the base for sauces, but the hotter powders such as *cayenne* and *piquin* are used when heat is needed more than flavor. In my home, I actually have more powders available than the whole pods because the powders are concentrated and take up less storage space. I store them in small, airtight bottles. The fresher the powders, the better they taste, so don't grind up too many pods. Use an electric spice mill and be sure to wear a painter's mask to protect the nose and throat from the pungent powder. The colors of the powders vary from a bright, electric red-orange (*chiltepíns*), to light green (dried *jalapeños*), to a dark brown that verges on black (*ancho*). I love to experiment by changing the powders called for in recipes.

Other Chile Products

A vast number of foods and condiments now contain chile peppers. Quite a few of these products are handy for cooks who love all things hot and spicy and meatless. Look for chile-infused vinegars, oils, mustards, ketchup, cheeses, pickles, hot sauces, salad dressings, jams and jellies, soups, pastas, potato and corn chips, curry powders and pastes, nuts, and even candies.

Glossary

Southwestern Cooking Terms and Ingredients

achiote: the orange-colored seeds of the annatto tree; used as a coloring agent and seasoning.

adobado or **adovada**: In Texas, a sour marinade paste made with herbs, chiles, and vinegar. In New Mexico and El Paso, a marinade for pork made with New Mexican red chiles, garlic, and oregano.

adobo: a thick cooking sauce comprised of tomatoes, vinegar, and spices.

aguas frescas: fresh fruit drinks.

ajo: garlic.

albóndigas: meatballs.

al carbón: charcoal grilled.

al pastór: cooked on a spit over a fire.

Anaheim chiles: misnomer for New Mexican chiles; now the term for a very mild New Mexican cultivar grown only in California.

ancho chiles: the dried from of poblano chiles. Substitute: pasilla chiles.

antojito: literally, "little whim"; an appetizer.

arbol chiles: hot dried red chiles from Mexico. Substitute dried red New Mexican chiles or pequins.

arroz: rice.

asada or **asado**: roasted or broiled.

asadero: a type of rubbery white cheese at first made only in the Mexican states of Chihuahua and Michoacan but now produced in the U.S. as well. Substitute Monterey Jack.

azafran: saffron.

barbacoa: in Texas, pit-barbecued meat; in Mexico, the barbecued flesh of a cow's head.

biscochitos: (sometimes *bizcochitos*) in New Mexico, anise-flavored cookies.

bolillo: Mexican hard roll; similar to French bread.

borracho: literally, "drunken"; foods containing beer or liquor.

burros (AZ) and **burritos** (NM and TX): flour tortillas stuffed with meats, cheeses, beans, and chile sauces, or a combination thereof.

cabrito: roasted kid (young goat, that is).

calabacita: squash, usually zucchini-types.

calamari: squid.

caldillo: ("little soup"), a thick stew with beef and chiles, commonly served in El Paso and Juarez.

caldo: a broth, stock, or clear soup

canela: cinnamon.

capriotada: a bread pudding dessert

carne: meat.

carnitas: literally, "little pieces of meat"; small chunks of pork fried to a crisp texture.

cascabel chiles: literally, "jingle bells"; small, round, hot chiles that rattle when shaken. Substitute: arbol chiles.

ceviche: raw seafood combined with lime juice, which "cooks" the fish by combining with its protein and turning it opaque.

chalupas: literally, "little boats"; in New Mexico a fried corn tortilla in the shape of a boat containing shredded chicken or beans topped with salsa, guacamole, or cheese.

chicharrón: crisp-fried pork skin.

chicos: corn kernels which are roasted, then dried.

chilaquiles: a casserole made of tortilla wedges, salsa, and cheese.

chile: referring to the plants or pods of the Capsicum genus.

chile caribe: a red chile paste made from crushed or ground red chiles of any type, garlic, and water.

chile con queso: a cheese and chile dip.

chile pasado: literally, "chile of the past," it is roasted, peeled, and sun-dried green chile.

chile pequin or **chilipiquín**: also called "chiltepíns," or "chili tepíns," these small dried red chiles are quite hot. Substitute: cayenne powder or hot red chile powder.

chili: chile sauce with meat; chili con carne.

chiltepíns: small, round, wild chiles that grow in Arizona. Another wild variety is called "chilipiquín" in Texas.

chimichanga: a deep-fat fried, stuffed burro which is topped with cheese and chile sauce.

chipotle chiles: smoked and dried jalapeños. Substitute moritas, smoked serranos.

chorizo: a spicy sausage made with pork, garlic, and red chile powder.

cilantro: an annual herb (*Coriandrum sativum*) with seeds which are known as coriander. Substitute: Italian parsley, or *culantro* (Eryngium foetidum). Commonly used in salsas and soups.

comal: griddle.

comino or **cumin**: an annual herb (*Cuminum cyminum*) whose seeds have distinctive odor—in fact, the dominant flavor in Tex-Mex dishes such as chili con carne.

desayuno: breakfast.

empanada: a pastry turnover.

enchiladas: rolled or stacked corn tortillas filled with meat or cheese and covered with chile sauce.

epazote: known as "Ambrosia" in English, this perennial herb (*Chenopodium ambrosioides*), is strong and bitter and is used primarily to flavor beans.

escabeche: vegetables, especially chiles, marinated or pickled in vinegar.

fajitas: literally, "little belts"; marinated and grilled skirt steak.

flan: a baked caramel custard dessert.

flautas: literally, "flutes"; tightly rolled, deep-fried enchiladas.

frijoles: beans.

gorditas: stuffed corn cakes; literally, "little fat ones."

guacamole: literally, "mixture of vegetables"—in this case, a blend of avocados, tomatoes, garlic, and chiles.

Habanero chiles: literally, "from Havana"; small orange or red chiles from the Caribbean and Yucatan that resemble a tam or bonnet; the hottest in the world. Substitute: jalapeños or serranos.

hongos: mushrooms.

huevos rancheros: literally, "ranch-style eggs."

jamaica: a Mexican flower that flavors drinks and teas.

jamón: ham.

jalapeño chiles: small, fat chiles which are pickled, stuffed, or used in fresh salsas. Substitute: serranos.

jícama: a white tuber (*Pachyrhizus erosus*) used in salads which tastes like a cross between an apple and a potato.

lengua: tongue.

lima: lemon.

limón: lime.

machaca: meat which is stewed, roasted, or broiled and then shredded.

maíz: corn.

manteca: lard.

masa: corn dough.

masa harina: corn dough flour.

menudo: tripe soup, often with chiles.

metate: a stone for grinding corn.

mescal: a liquor distilled from the agave plant.

migas: in Texas, eggs scrambled with chorizo, tortilla chips, onions, tomatoes, cheese, and serrano chiles.

molcajete: a mortar made out of volcanic stone.

mole: literally, "mixture"; usually refers to a thick chile sauce made with many spices and chocolate.

nachos: tostados topped with cheese and sliced jalapeños.

natilla: custard dessert.

New Mexican chiles: "long green" chiles grown in New Mexico; varieties include Big Jim, No. 6-4, Sandia, Española, Chimayo, etc. Substitute: Poblanos.

nopales or **nopalitos:** prickly pear cactus pads, spines removed.

olla: a round, earthenware pot.

pan: bread. *Pan dulce* is sweet bread.

papas: potatoes.

parrilla: grill or broiler.

pasilla chiles: literally, "little raisin," an illusion to the aroma and dark brown color of this long, thin, Mexican chile. Substitute: ancho chiles.

pepitas: roasted pumpkin seeds.

pescado: fish.

picadillo: shredded beef, spices, and other ingredients usually used as a stuffing.

picante: hot and spicy.

pico de gallo: literally, "beak of the rooster"; a salsa with tomatoes, onions, cilantro, and serrano chiles.

piloncillo: brown, unrefined cane sugar.

piñones: the nuts of the piñon tree (*Pinus edulis*).

pipián: a sauce containing ground nuts or seeds and spices.

pollo: chicken.

posole: a thick stew made with pork, chiles, and hominy corn.

poblano chiles: literally, "peppers of the people," these dark green fat chiles are commonly used in Mexico and the Southwest. The dried form is called *ancho*, "wide."

puerco: pork.

quelites: spinach and bean dish seasoned with chile and bacon.

quesadilla: a flour tortilla turnover which is usually stuffed with cheese, then toasted, fried, or baked.

queso: cheese.

rajas: strips; usually refers to strips of chiles

refrito: refried; used mainly to describe beans which are mashed and fried in lard.

relleno: stuffed.

res: beef.

ristra: a string of red chile pods.

salpicón: a Mexican shredded meat salad.

salsa: literally, "sauce," but usually used to describe uncooked sauces (*salsa cruda*).

saguaro: tall cactus found in Arizona; its fruits are made into jams and jellies.

serrano chiles: a small, hot Mexican chile which is usually pickled or used green or red in fresh salsas. Substitute: jalapeños.

sopa: soup.

sopapilla: from *sopaipa*, a fritter soaked in honey; in New Mexico, a puffed, fried bread, served with honey or filled with various stuffings.

taco: a stuffed corn tortilla, either soft or a crisp, fried shell.

taquito: a rolled, deep-fried taco.

tamal: (plural, tamales), any filling enclosed in masa, wrapped in a corn shuck, and steamed.

tamarindo: tamarind.

tequila: a type of mescal produced near Tequila in the state of Jalisco, Mexico.

tomatillo: a small, green husk tomato (*Physalis ixocarpa*); substitute small regular tomatoes.

torta: a sandwich, often made with a bolillo.

tostados: tortilla chips.

tunas: prickly pear cactus fruits.

yerba buena: mint.

Further Reading

Arnold, Samuel P. *Eating Up the Santa Fe Trail*. Golden, Colorado: Fulcrum Publishing, 1990.

Caldwell, Red. *Pit, Pot & Skillet*. San Antonio: Corona Publishing, 1990..

Cox, Berverly and Jacobs, Martin. *Spirit of the Harvest: North American Indian Cooking*. New York: Stewart, Tabori & Chang, 1991.

DeWald, Louise. *Arizona Highways Heritage Cookbook*. Phoenix: Arizona. Department of Transportation, 1988.

DeWitt, Dave. *Texas Monthly Guide to New Mexico*. Houston: Gulf Publishing, 1989.

_____. *The Chile Pepper Encyclopedia*. New York: William Morrow & Co., 1999.

DeWitt, Dave and Gerlach, Nancy. *The Whole Chile Pepper Book*. Boston: Little, Brown, 1990.

Dunmire, William W. *Gardens of New Spain: How Mediterranean Plants and Foods Changed America*. Austin: University of Texas Press, 2004.

Eckhardt, Linda West. *The Only Texas Cookbook*. New York: Gramercy, 1985.

Frank, Lois Ellen. *Native American Cooking: Foods of the Southwest Indian Nations*. New York: Clarkson Potter Inc., 1991.

Hesse, Zora Getmansky. *Southwestern Indian Recipe Book, Vol. 1*. Palmer Lake, CO: The Filter Press, 1973.

Miller, Mark. *Coyote Cafe*. Berkeley, CA: Ten Speed Press, 1989.

Miller, Richard. *The Official Fajita Cookbook*. Austin: Texas Monthly Press, 1988.

Nabhan, Gary. *Gathering the Desert*. Tucson: University of Arizona Press, 1985.

_____. *Enduring Seeds*. San Francisco: North Point Press, 1989.

Neely, Martina and William. *The International Chili Society Official Chili Cookbook*. New York: St. Martin's Press, 1981.

Niethammer, Carolyn. *American Indian Food and Lore*. New York: Macmillan, 1974.

Pascal, Celine-Marie. *The Blue Corn Cookbook*. Albuquerque: Out West Publishing, 1991.

Super, John C. *Food, Conquest, and Colonization in Sixteenth Century Spanish America*. Albuquerque: UNM Press, 1988.

Tate, Joyce L. *Cactus Cookbook*. Cactus and Succulent Society of America, 1971.

Thorne, John. *Just Another Bowl of Texas Red*. Boston: The Jackdaw Press, 1985.

Tolbert, Frank X. *A Bowl of Red: A Natural History of Chili con Carne*. New York: Doubleday, 1966.

Visser, Margaret. *Much Depends on Dinner*. New York: Grove Press, 1986.

Walsh, Robb. *Legends of Texas Barbecue*. San Francisco: Chronicle Books, 2002.

_____. *The Tex-Mex Cookbook*. New York: Broadway Books, 2004.

_____. *The Texas Cowboy Cookbook*. New York: Broadway Books, 2007.

Weiner, Melissa Ruffner. *Arizona Territorial Cookbook*. Norfolk, VA: Donning Co., 1982.

Weir, Bill. *Arizona Traveler's Handbook*. Chico, CA: Moon Publications, 1990.

Resources

Information on Chiles and Fiery Foods:

www.Fiery-foods.com

Chiles, Southwestern Ingredients, and Prepared Foods

www.Nativeseeds.org
www.Melissas.com
www.Chiletraditions.com
www.Friedas.com
www.Buenofoods.com
www.Mexgrocer.com
www.thechileshop.com

Game

www.Exoticmeats.com

Spices

www.Thespicehouse.com
www.Penzeys.com
www.Penderys.com

Wine

Texas Wine: www.texaswines.org
New Mexico Wine: www.nmwine.com
Arizona Wine: www.arizonawine.org

Photo Credits

Introduction:

pg. 1 Geographical confusion. Aaron Sandoval

1. The Native Southwest:

pg. 7 Zuñi "waffle" gardens, 1925. Edward S. Curtis. Courtesy Palace of the Governors, MNM/DCA, #144664.

pg. 9 The *tunas,* or fruits, of the prickly pear cactus. Dave DeWitt.

pg. 11 A *piñon* tree in the snow. Dave DeWitt

pg. 13 The mother of all chiles, the chiltepín. Dave DeWitt

pg. 15 A *metate* for grinding corn. Dave DeWitt

pg. 19 Grinding mesquite pods. Dave DeWitt

2. Lone Star Cuisine

pg. 21 Chuck Wagon—The Cowboy's Kitchen, c. 1920, Beaumont, Texas. Thomas K. Todsen. Rio Grande Historical Collections, NMSU, 02230169

pg. 22 Longhorn Steers, 1909. Thomas K. Todsen. Rio Grande Historical Collections, NMSU, 02230548.

pg. 26 *Fajitas.* Aaron Sandoval.

pg. 29 Ormly Gumfudgin, historian of the International Chili Society, stirs a large pot of chili. Chel Beeson.

pg. 31 A little Texas food humor. Feeding Time, Texas Brag, 1909. Photographer unknown. UTSA's Institute of Texas Cultures, No. 070-0412.

pg. 33 Tiled bullfighting illustration in an Austin restaurant. Dave DeWitt.

pg. 39 Game was very popular in the Hill Country, as we can tell from this photo. Interior of the Buckhorn Saloon, D'Hanis, c.1914. Photographer: Congdon. UTSA's Institute of Texas Cultures, No. 096-0574, Courtesy of Mary Ann Laughlin Abbott.

pg. 41 San Antonio Riverwalk, location of many fine restaurants. Dave DeWitt.

pg. 45 Chile *ristras* for sale in El Paso. Dave DeWitt.

pg. 47 Sign for Sauza *Tequila.* Dave DeWitt.

pg. 49 More Texas food humor. Dave DeWitt.

pg. 50 Original sign for Julio's. Dave DeWitt

3. An Enchanted Feast.

pg. 53 Peppers drying in the backyard of a grocery store, San Juan, New Mexico, 1928. Irving Galloway. Courtesy Palace of the Governors (MNM/DCA), 005143.

pg. 54 Herding sheep north of Santa Fe, c. 1979. Dave DeWitt

pg. 55 Chile pods on the plant. Dave DeWitt

pg. 59 Fabian Garcia in cornfield, c. 1914. Photographer unknown. Rio Grande Historical Collections, NMSU, 00710006.

pg. 60 Central Patio, The Fred Harvey Alvarado Hotel, c. 1920. Rio Grande Historical Collections, NMSU, 02231364.

pg. 63 Seven men sacking chile peppers, Mesilla Valley c.1925. Photographer unknown. Rio Grande Historical Collections, NMSU, 00710241.

pg. 66 Drawings of variations of chile pods, New Mexico Experimental Station, 1914. Fabian Garcia. Rio Grande Historical Collections, NMSU, 00710228.

pg. 67 Chile Sign in the Mesilla Valley. Dave DeWitt.

pg. 68 Historic La Posta Restaurant in Mesilla. Dave DeWitt.

pg. 70 Second Street looking South from Central Avenue, c. 1910. Thomas K. Todsen. Rio Grande Historical Collections, NMSU, 02230747.

pg. 71 Dining Room, Alvarado Hotel, 1904. Louis Charles McClure. Denver Public Library, MCC-3491.

pg. 74 Swayze's Dinner Bell, on U.S, 66, Albuquerque, c. 1940. Thomas K. Todsen. Rio Grande Historical Collections, NMSU, 02230346.

pg. 75 Patio at El Pinto. Josh Costanza

pg. 78 Chile wreath. Harald Zoschke.

pg. 80 Wagon trains, San Francisco Street at the Plaza, Santa Fe, c. 1879. Nicholas Brown. Courtesy Palace of the Governors (MNM/DCA), 070437.

pg. 81 La Bajada Hill c. 1910. Photographer unknown. Courtesy Palace of the Governors (MNM/DCA, 008231.

pg. 82 La Fonda Hotel, c. 1928. T. Harmon Parkhurst. Courtesy Palace of the Governors (MNM/DCA), 010690.

pg. 87 Original sign for the Coyote Café, c. 1988. Dave DeWitt

4. Desert Dining

pg. 92 Interior of American Grocery, Tucson, 1880. Photographer unknown. Courtesy of the Arizona Historical Society, Tucson, photo number 1785.

pg. 93 Covered wagons, c.1890. Photographer unknown. Courtesy of the Arizona State Library, photo number 93-9955.

pg. 95 Red meat drying at Ah Tso Lige, Red Lake, Arizona. Photographer unknown. Courtesy Palace of the Governors (MNM/DCA), 188516.

pg. 96 Tohono O'odham woman grinding corn, c. 1960. Photographer unknown. Courtesy of the Arizona Historical Society, Tucson, photo number 52166.

pg. 98 Arizona grapefruits. Dave DeWitt.

pg. 100 Indian corn with Navajo blanket, c. 1955. Photographer unknown. Courtesy of the Arizona State Library, photo number PhD341.

pg. 104 Sign on a South Phoenix restaurant. Dave DeWitt.

pg. 108 The giant saguaro has tasty fruits. Aaron Sandoval.

pg. 111 Filomeno Chavoya making chile sauce, El Charro Restaurant, c. 1950. Photographer unknown. Courtesy of the Arizona Historical Society, Tucson. Photo number 64845.

pg. 113 Original sign for Café Terra Cotta, c. 1991. Dave DeWitt

5. Salsas, Sauces

pg. 116 *Tomatillos.* Aaron Sandoval

6. Aperitivos

pg. 125 *Margarita* with limes. Aaron Sandoval

7. A Spicy Kettle

pg. 133 *Caldillo Paso del Norte* in a pot. Aaron Sandoval.

8. Southwestern Salads

pg. 144 *Jicama.* Aaron Sandoval

Index